T0214917

SAP S/4HANA Embedded Analytics

Experiences in the Field

Freek Keijzer

Apress®

SAP S/4HANA Embedded Analytics

Freek Keijzer
Almelo, The Netherlands

ISBN-13 (pbk): 978-1-4842-7016-5   ISBN-13 (electronic): 978-1-4842-7017-2
https://doi.org/10.1007/978-1-4842-7017-2

Managing Director, Apress Media LLC: Welmoed Spahr
Acquisitions Editor: Divya Modi
Development Editor: Laura Berendson
Coordinating Editor: Divya Modi

Cover designed by eStudioCalamar

Cover image designed by Freepik (www.freepik.com)

Distributed to the book trade worldwide by Springer Science+Business Media New York, 1 New York Plaza, Suite 4600, New York, NY 10004-1562, USA. Phone 1-800-SPRINGER, fax (201) 348-4505, e-mail orders-ny@springer-sbm.com, or visit www.springeronline.com. Apress Media, LLC is a California LLC and the sole member (owner) is Springer Science + Business Media Finance Inc (SSBM Finance Inc). SSBM Finance Inc is a **Delaware** corporation.

For information on translations, please e-mail booktranslations@springernature.com; for reprint, paperback, or audio rights, please e-mail bookpermissions@springernature.com.

Apress titles may be purchased in bulk for academic, corporate, or promotional use. eBook versions and licenses are also available for most titles. For more information, reference our Print and eBook Bulk Sales web page at www.apress.com/bulk-sales.

Any source code or other supplementary material referenced by the author in this book is available to readers on GitHub via the book's product page, located at www.apress.com/978-1-4842-7016-5. For more detailed information, please visit www.apress.com/source-code.

Printed on acid-free paper

Table of Contents

About the Author

Dr. Freek Keijzer has a background in science (physics), industry (manufacturing, process industry), and ICT (SAP system integration), holding various project management, people management, and specialist positions. He has degrees in natural sciences (PhD) and information management (MIM). In 1996, he became involved in an SAP implementation, initially as an R/3 key user and later as an internal project leader, interim manager of the support organization, and (international) information manager. Since 2001, he has focused on SAP BI consultancy, working for three consultancy firms and more than 50 clients. His responsibilities as a consultant include product development, team competence development, sales support, and resourcing. Freek's technical specialties include SAP business intelligence, HANA, NetWeaver, and ERP integration. His roles include project leader, lead consultant, business consultant (interim) manager, and Scrum master. Since 2015, Freek has been a brewer/owner of the Rubelijn craft beer brand.

About the Technical Reviewers

Attaphon Predaboon is a certified SAP consultant and data and analytics manager at EY. He is passionate about finding innovative ways to use BI and analytics solutions to create business success.

He has led his team in business development and proof of concept as well as in the deployment of SAP and many other data analytics technologies for various local and global firms.

Pascal van Miltenburg is an SAP solution architect with 20+ years of experience in ERP, integrated business processes, and holistic solution design in a variety of industries, companies, projects, and programs.

In 1998, Pascal completed his MBA at the University of Tel Aviv, majoring in international business management and with a minor in information systems. Subsequently Pascal started working as an SAP consultant specializing in finance and controlling, quickly expanding to several other ERP components that SAP supports. Because of this broad experience and interest, he has fulfilled the roles of integration manager and solution architect in many projects.

For the last few years, he has been responsible for the overall solution design in one of the largest recent S/4HANA greenfield implementations in the Netherlands. In this program, Pascal gave special attention to the implementation methodology, utilization of standard SAP, and, after careful consideration, extending functionality in the least disruptive method. S/4HANA Embedded Analytics constituted a large part of the solution scope.

Jeroen Keijzer is an SAP analytics consultant for myBrand in the Netherlands, specializing in SAP BW, SAP HANA, SAP BusinessObjects, and SAP Analytics Cloud. After completing his studies in business informatics (Saxion, 2003) and applied communication sciences (University of Twente, 2005), he joined KLM Royal Dutch Airlines to start his career in SAP consultancy. Specializing in SAP solution management and authorizations at first, he eventually chose to switch to analytics as a working field as this has always been his favorite area of interest. In 2014, Jeroen joined myBrand and started specializing in HANA database modeling and development. Since then, he worked on various projects to implement analytics solutions for a variety of customer fields including retail, financial lease, manufacturing, and real estate.

Acknowledgments

I am grateful to the following people:

- Attaphon Predaboon, Pascal van Miltenburg, and Jeroen Keijzer, for doing an excellent job as technical reviewers.

- Stan Keijsers, for creating the demo presented in Chapter 3. Thanks, Stan! Please notify me when you have a garden. I will mow your lawn for at least a year.

- Yge Pars, for delivering specifications of the "Return List" case in Chapter 5.

- Danny Linders, for being my travel companion during the journey into the world of ABAP CDS views in Eclipse.

- SAP, for allowing me the use of some of its figures. Note that SAP is in no way responsible for the context in which these figures are presented.

- Employers Atos, Ciber, and myBrand, and more than 50 clients, for allowing me to build up SAP business intelligence expertise in numerous diverse and interesting projects over a period of 21 years.

- Clients Ciber (internal project), Pon, and Dutch Railways, for giving me the opportunity to work on various forms of S/4HANA Embedded Analytics in their projects.

- MyBrand and Nederlandse Spoorwegen (Dutch Railways), for allowing me to take screenshots from their systems. Thanks to Stan Jilesen of Dutch Railways for checking the screenshots for sensitive information.

- My family, Jacqueline, Annebel, and Rutger, and our daughter Karlijn, who inspired us from the day she was born and still continues to do so.

Introduction

This is not the first book to be written on the topic of SAP S/4HANA embedded analytics, and it will probably not be the last. The difference from other books on the topic is captured in the subtitle: *Experiences in the Field*. The book was written from a practical implementation perspective, and it focuses on functions that have proven themselves useful in the field.

The target audience of the book is broad—business users, consultants, developers—but that does not mean every chapter is equally interesting to every member of the target audience. Chapters 1 and 7 cover miscellaneous topics of interest to all readers. Chapters 2 to 6 are characterized by an increasing amount of work to obtain the presented analytics functions and also require an increasing level of technical expertise from the reader. Chapter 6 may well be the highlight of the book for developers, while at the same time can be skipped by business users.

As mentioned, Chapter 1, "Before the Work Starts," covers miscellaneous introductory topics, preparing readers for the details of SAP S/4HANA embedded analytics. The chapter also introduces data modeling, different forms of cloud deployment, the Fiori user interface, SAP's business intelligence product portfolio, and of course CDS views, which are the building blocks of SAP S/4HANA embedded analytics.

Chapter 2, "No Work: Use What Is Delivered," does a deep-dive into the standard analytical content delivered with the SAP S/4HANA software. It starts off with an explanation of a certain aspect of Fiori: which tiles are shown to a user and how they are grouped. After that, the chapter focuses on finding, activating, and using SAP-delivered analytical apps. The chapter ends with my contribution to the never-ending battle against the "Excelification" of analytics.

Chapter 3, "Some Work: Smart Business Service," presents a demo of SAP Smart Business Service, which is a KPI-based framework for the development of analytical apps. It has a codeless, menu-driven user interface, and it is targeted at business users and functional consultants.

The real thing in S/4HANA Embedded Analytics are objects named *analytical queries*. Chapter 4, "More Work: Building Analytical Queries Using Tiles," describes how to build these objects in a software-as-a-service environment. The starting point for this type of development is creating SAP-delivered CDS views that can be explored using the Query Browser and View Browser tiles. For the development, you can apply the Custom CDS Views and Custom Analytical Queries tiles.

Chapter 5, "Most Work (Basic): Building Analytical Queries in an IDE," and Chapter 6, "Most Work (Advanced): Building Analytical Queries in an IDE," are an even deeper dive into the creation of analytical queries, but this time in an integrated development environment (IDE) connected to an on-premise S/4HANA system. Chapter 5 covers the basics such as connectivity between S/4HANA and the IDE, naming conventions, documentation including data lineage, and ABAP CDS. It also includes a real-life case study, where requirements and the data model are discussed, and all required layers of the data model are built from the bottom to the top including basic views, data integration, cube view, and query view. Chapter 6 covers diverse, more advanced topics such as custom master data views, complex logic, use of parameters and session variables, compatibility views, how to make data "less real time," multilingual descriptions of field names, "jump to" functionality, how to create a dedicated tile for a query, data authorization, query performance, issues with transporting CDS-views, and Analysis for Office.

Finally, in Chapter 7, "Extensibility, OData, and Beyond," other types of S/4HANA extensibility are addressed in case Embedded Analytics is not sufficient. The chapter also covers OData services, as well as Agile Development and DevOps in the context of analytics. The final section of the book outlines the ideal skillset for an embedded analytics expert.

Please note that I alone am responsible for the content of this book. Software vendor SAP and client Dutch Railways cooperated by providing graphs and allowing me to take system screenshots, but this much appreciated cooperation does not mean these companies are in any way responsible for what I have written.

CHAPTER 1

Before the Work Starts

Let me start by saying that I am a big fan of SAP software. It all started in 1996 when I was a production manager not particularly interested in ICT matters. I became involved in an SAP enterprise resource planning (ERP) implementation as "process owner" of the Production Planning module. I liked the SAP software straightaway. Unlike some opinions that SAP ERP is a top-down system that gives the power to the top level of an organization, I noticed that in our organization it gave "power to the people." More precisely, it gave power to those with knowledge of the system, irrespective of whether they belonged to the top, bottom, or middle part of the organization. In 2001, I became a consultant, soon focusing on business intelligence (BI).

Let me also say that I am not an SAP employee. This has some benefits for you as a reader. SAP employees are more or less obliged to say that all newly developed parts of the SAP software are equally great. I am at liberty to inform you that some parts of the SAP software are definitely greater than others. I will focus on the great parts and will skip the parts that mean well but have little value in practice. This book was not written from the perspective of a software developer, but from the perspective of an implementation consultant who has implemented SAP business intelligence for almost 20 years and in more than 50 organizations. The focus is on what works in practice. That's why the subtitle of this book is *Experiences in the Field*.

© Freek Keijzer 2021
F. Keijzer, *SAP S/4HANA Embedded Analytics*, https://doi.org/10.1007/978-1-4842-7017-2_1

Note that I am a native speaker of the beautiful Dutch language. Despite common belief among English-speaking people, Dutch is not a random collection of throat sounds; it is an international language spoken in the Netherlands, in Belgium, by very old people in Dunkirk, and in remote places such as South Africa, Suriname, the Dutch Antilles, and Indonesia. However, to reach an even larger audience, I have written this book in English, relying on my editor to take out any "Dunglish" that I might leave in. However, I will not hesitate to confront you with the Dutch language in examples and case studies. A person can, for instance, be called *brechtje*, a perfectly normal name for a woman in the Netherlands, which does, I must admit, require some throat sounds.

If by chance you do not know what SAP S/4HANA is, I have a question for you: why on Earth did you buy this book? Just kidding. SAP S/4HANA, from now on often called S/4, is of course the new kid on the block in SAP ERP software. It is optimized for the HANA database, the code was completely rewritten, aggregated tables were removed or replaced with views, and it enables transaction input and analytics output simultaneously in one system. Wow.

S/4 comes with built-in options for operational reporting, including analytics supporting day-to-day decision-making at all levels of an organization. Data is read directly from S/4 tables during query runtime and thereby inevitably in "real time." You'll learn a lot about this throughout the book.

As mentioned in the introduction of the book, Chapters 1 and 7 contain miscellaneous information such as an overview and wrap-up. The other chapters increase in labor-intensiveness sequentially. Chapter 2 covers what analytics are available in SAP S/4HANA with no work at all. Chapter 3 describes how to build analytical apps using Smart Business Service. This requires some work to be done, but the service has a relatively low technical threshold. In Chapter 4, we are going to build analytical queries within the limitations of the software-as-a-service (SaaS) version of S/4HANA, known as S/4HANA Cloud Essential Edition. This means using tiles. This involves more work, but the work consists of mouse clicks. When you have chosen the SaaS solution of S/4HANA for your organization, this is the only way to go for analytical queries. However, if you have chosen the on-premise version of S/4HANA, a choice I would currently encourage for organizations with even the slightest level of complexity, you have the option to build analytical queries with CDS views in a development environment. Then quite a lot more is possible. This work, consisting of die-hard coding, is described in Chapters 5 and 6.

SAP has the tendency to either overestimate the ability of its user groups or underestimate the user-friendliness of its software; I'm not sure which. This became clear to me during a partner training in Waldorf (Europe's Silicon Valley) for an at-the-time-new product named Visual Composer. The accompanying marketing material made it clear that the target group of this product was end users. It had a graphical user interface enabling the development of apps by inserting and connecting certain components. One of the components was a BEx query, an object all too familiar to me as a BI professional. But even I had great difficulty figuring out how to connect things around the query to make it work properly. Having a graphical user interface does not mean that anyone can do it. I am not saying that the SAP software components are bad—I am a fan, remember—but in practice a component is often used by a user group one level higher than the target audience intended by SAP, with "higher" meaning more specialized.

This is also true for the software components described in Chapters 2 to 6. Standard analytical apps are of course used by end users, but activating them is mostly done by a Fiori consultant. Smart Business Service is meant for end users, but in my opinion it will be mostly key users and functional consultants who use this service. Building analytical queries with tiles can also be done by key users and functional consultants, but they definitely need to have some basic understanding of data modeling. For this reason, a BI specialist would probably do a better job. This is definitely true for building analytical queries with CDS views in a development environment. The best person for this job is a "unicorn" professional combining data modeling with programming skills. In Chapter 7, a special section is dedicated to the best skillset for this type of work.

By the way, there's no need to worry about Visual Composer. It was escorted to the software burial ground a long time ago.

In the remaining sections of this chapter, we will be visiting various topics related to analytics in S/4:

- *Business intelligence*: The chapter will cover what it is all about (and why people who are good at this should be paid more).

- *Data modeling*: We'll also cover data modeling.

- *HANA database*: What makes SAP's HANA database so special, and how did it solve the old controversy between online transactional processing (OLTP) and online analytical processing (OLAP)? This chapter will answer this question.

- *The two dominant cloud deployment options for S/4*: We'll explore SaaS and infrastructure-as-a-service (IaaS). I have had the opportunity to work with both deployment options and would like to share some "experiences in the field."

- *Front-end technology*: We'll explore Fiori and UI5. In general, users will access the S/4 system through the Fiori user interface (UI). UI5 is the underlying technology of most S/4 apps. The end result of building an analytical app or query in the upcoming chapters will be a Fiori tile. Some general understanding of Fiori and UI5 is therefore quite useful.

- *SAP's BI product portfolio*: S/4HANA Embedded Analytics is only one of many options that allows you to gain insight into SAP data. Other options are presented, along with some guidelines of when to apply what.

- *CDS views*: We'll introduce CDS views, the technology SAP uses for its analytical queries and underlying views. We will be using this technology to build analytical queries in Chapters 5 and 6.

- *S/4HANA Embedded Analytics*: Learning about this tool will be the final step in preparing for the upcoming chapters.

Business Intelligence: The Art of Enriching Data

A business representative once described my job as "showing the data as it is stored in the SAP tables." If this were true, I would have left this field of work a long time ago. Instead, I have hung in for almost 20 years now. My job as a business intelligence specialist is to add value to data by transforming it, to combine data from various sources, to optimize it for reporting, and to "enrich" it. In other words, business intelligence is the art of enriching data.

Any ERP system will have reporting capabilities as a standard offering. The reports will usually be restricted to data within a certain module such as Finance, Materials Management, or Human Resources. Reports on data covering multiple modules, often labeled *cross-application*, are rarely delivered as standard offerings. The first time I noticed this was when I was still a naïve key user for the PP module and the Spice Girls were very popular. I requested three reports with similar complexity, as far as I could see. The first one was a standard report. The consultant pointed

5

out where to find it. I blushed, apologized for the fact I had not found it myself, and we all went about our business. The second report required some modifications of the logistics information system, a predecessor of a predecessor of…you get the picture. Two days of work, no big deal, we did it. The third report apparently required the integration of data pieces that were far away from each other in the system. All of a sudden we were talking about weeks of programming and development costs far outweighing the benefits. On top of that, higher maintenance costs were expected in case of incidents, changes, and support package upgrades.

This is where business intelligence comes in. A fourth report, slightly different but based on the same data, would again take weeks of programming, as programmed reports have little reusability. In the BI field, we aim to build not only a report but also a platform for future reports by maximizing the reusability of intermediate objects. The "layered approach" described in the next section of this chapter is crucial in achieving this.

Data Modeling for Dummies

Data modeling is hard to do well, and keeping it simple is the key to success. Over the years I have had to do data modeling with widely different tools, but there clearly are tool-independent common denominators in how to approach data modeling. In this section, I will share these generic insights.

Some high-level understanding of data modeling is required to do the work described in Chapters 3 and 4. In Chapter 5, you will need to do your own data modeling from scratch, and for this more detailed knowledge is required.

Where Are the Numbers?

One way in which reporting specifications are delivered is as a list of SAP table name/field name combinations, usually in a spreadsheet. This is great because it is concrete, but it is also rare. Please realize that specifications can be as vague as "I want information on sales, and you as a developer need to guess which information." Sure. So, lists of SAP table name/ field name combinations are more than welcome. But then, where do we start? Start with the key question: where are the numbers? By numbers, I mean, for instance, numbers with currencies or quantities with units or counters, which are dimensionless. These types of numbers can be added up in ways that make sense. A numerical object like a document number is not a number as meant in the question, because why would anyone want to add up two document numbers?

Figure 1-1 illustrates the key question. A person, let's call her Brechtje, bought three bags of Douwe Egberts coffee in the local Albert Heijn store on August 7, 2020.

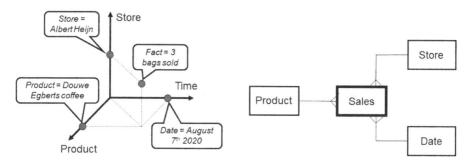

Figure 1-1. *Facts and dimensions*

The number, or fact, is 3, and the unit is *bags*. The three objects along the axes are *dimensions*. The illustration as a whole is a *multidimensional* representation of a sales transaction. The multidimensional characteristic of the situation leads to it usually being drawn as a *cube*, because three is the highest number of dimensions the human brain can still grasp, unless you are a theoretical physicist specialized in string theory. Analyzing facts against certain dimensions, e.g., sales per month against product, is called *slicing and dicing.*

Different words are used to describe objects relevant for data modeling, even within SAP's product portfolio. As you'll see in upcoming sections, SAP S/4HANA Embedded Analytics and SAP Analytics Cloud use *measure* and *dimension*; BW and BEx use *key figure, characteristic,* and *attribute*; HANA calculation views use *measure* and *attribute*; and WebIntelligence uses *measure, dimension,* and *detail.* I will use *key figure, characteristic,* and *attribute,* as this makes it possible to discriminate between detailed objects directly coupled to the fact (characteristics such as product, store, or date, and properties of these characteristics such as the Product Group, Retail Group, and Month attributes). Here, attributes have a one-to-many relation to characteristics. And, of course, these words are also what I am used to using as a BW/BEx veteran.

If the numbers or key figures are all in the same SAP table, the data model can be quite simple. For example, if users are interested only in Actual Amount, then the key figure can be Amount in Global Currency (KSL) in table Universal Journal Entry Line Items (ACDOCA), or in a technical annotation field called `acdoca.ksl`. Table ACDOCA also contains a lot of characteristics, so this can be quite a simple data model based primarily on one table. Adding key figures from another table does not need to add much complexity, as long as this second table is similarly structured to the first one and has many shared characteristics. For example, say you have Planned Amount, which is once again a key figure with the technical name Amount in Global Currency (KSL), but this time in the table Plan Data Line Items (ACDOCP), or in the technical annotation field `acdocp.ksl`. If key figures are added from a table that is only indirectly related to the first table, the data model can become complex, and data integration can be quite cumbersome. For example, this is true for adding Committed Amount, in my case the key figure Total Value in Controlling Area Currency (WKGBTR) in table Commitments Management: Line Items (COOI), or in technical annotation cooi.wkgbtr, to the data model. It's cumbersome, but not impossible. This example will be worked out in Chapter 6.

If the key figures are scattered all over the SAP database, then you are in trouble. But there's no need to panic; stay cool, and take it one step at a time.

Layered Approach

As mentioned at the beginning of this section, I had the opportunity to do data modeling with a wide variety of SAP tools. A clear common denominator in working with these tools is the "layered approach." Querying is not carried out directly on the source data, but there are multiple layers between the source data and the query. In the old days, layers always were *persistent*, containing data. The trend is toward "virtual" layers, not containing data. But still, there are layers.

SAP was late in adopting a layered architecture for its BI tools. The earliest versions of SAP BW standard content had no intermediate objects between source data and cubes. Implementation consultants like me then added layers to improve the flexibility and maintainability of the data model. At some stage, SAP jumped on the bandwagon and presented the Layered Scalable Architecture (LSA) for the BW data warehouse. With the first HANA version of BW, this was enhanced to LSA++, with the main difference being that LSA has less persistency and more virtualization of data.[1] Figure 1-2 shows a graphical overview of SAP's LSA++.

---

[1] "SAP HANA as Driver of EDW Evolution: LSA++ (Layered Scalable Architecture) for BW on SAP HANA," Juergen Haupt, SAP AG, August 2012; https://www.sap.com/documents/2012/08/3273bcde-517c-0010-82c7-eda71af511fa.html

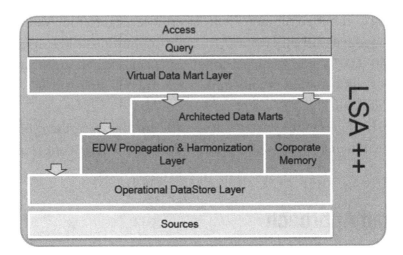

Figure 1-2. *SAP's layered architecture for Business Warehouse LSA++ (source: SAP Helpfiles[2])*

Not all aspects of this architecture turned out to be equally useful in practice. The added value of the corporate memory, for instance, remained unclear to many people including me, even after implementing it in practice, whereas the downside, additional storage costs, is clear.

Figure 1-3 shows my own generalized, simplified, tool-independent, layered approach toward data modeling.

---

[2]SAP help files on LSA++ architecture: https://help.sap.com/viewer/
dd104a87ab9249968e6279e61378ff66/11.0.7/en-US/0062afefa6db41eaa9460
afef1894beb.html

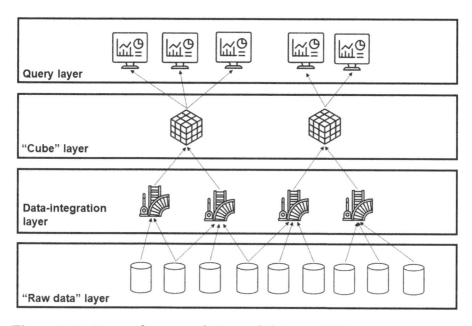

Figure 1-3. *Layered approach toward data modeling*

It consists of four layers: raw data, data-integration, cube and query layer. In the raw data layer, data is stored in its original format without any transformations. If data is coming from another, say non-SAP, system, the field names of the original system are used; therefore, there are no field mappings, at least not yet. The purpose of this layer is twofold: first, have the source data close to the query to improve performance, and, second, provide the flexibility to restart from the original data in case there are second thoughts about the data transformations in higher layers. I said data is stored, but the trend is of course toward virtualization. The current practice is to have a virtual raw data layer for SAP data and a persistent raw data layer for non-SAP data. As will be described in the "SAP's BI Portfolio" section, Smart Data Access also makes it possible to have virtual access to non-SAP data, but usually the benefits of storing non-SAP data are high enough to do it.

The data-integration layer is where the real magic happens. This is where the intelligent part of business intelligence takes place through transforming field names and formats and table structures (e.g., transposing from rows to columns or vice versa). It combines data from different SAP modules, SAP systems, and SAP plus non-SAP systems. Complex selections and aggregations are carried out. Anything is done that brings added value to the data. The choice of the icon for this layer was inspired by one of my current customer projects, Dutch Railways.

In the cube layer, data is transformed into a format optimized for multidimensional reporting. In the old OLAP world, this used to be quite a hassle to connect separate fact tables to dimension tables, but in the HANA era, the structures within this layer are quite flat. But for nostalgic reasons, the community still likes to call them *cubes*.

In a sense, the query layer is the most important layer, as this is the interface to the users. They see lists, tables, graphs, and dashboards, all in an interactive mode. They can filter, navigate, slice and dice, and jump.

These layers and their purpose are also important for developments within S/4HANA Embedded Analytics, the topic of this book, and will be dealt with extensively in upcoming chapters.

Operators for Data Integration

Data transformations of great complexity can be carried out with only a few operators. In this section, I will use the well-known SQL terms for these operators. In the "SAP's BI Portfolio" section, we will see that HANA calculation views are not the most future-proof tooling within the SAP BI portfolio, but they do give good insight into these operators and how they work. See Figure 1-4 for an example.

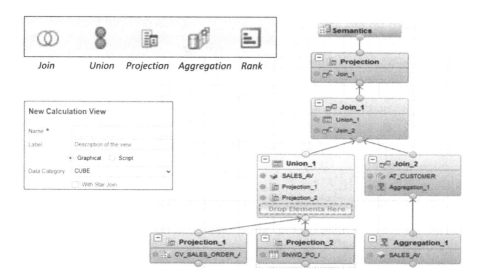

Figure 1-4. *Joins, unions, and aggregations (source: openSAP training Analytics with SAP Cloud Platform[3] ©SAP AG, 2018)*

The most relevant items in the toolset for the HANA calculation views are these operations: left outer join, inner join, union, and aggregation. These are also all you need to survive your first SAP S/4 Embedded Analytics implementation. Joins are easy to understand. You connect datasets on the left and right sides by stating that values of certain fields should be equal on both sides. For example, I have a table with taxpayers, cities, and amounts. In a separate table, I have cities and provinces. By joining these tables by the city, I can report on taxes paid per province. The question is, which type of join do I use: left outer or inner? In most situations, including this one, left outer joins are preferred as numbers on the left side are not influenced by data on the right side being incomplete. See Figure 1-5. Were we to use an inner join, then we would lose an amount of €145, just because the system does not know that Almelo lies in the province of Overijssel. As a result, there is no record for Almelo on the right side.

---

[3]OpenSAP course "Analytics with SAP Cloud Platform," June 2018: `https://open.sap.com/courses/cp6`

Data on left side

Person	City	Tax
Brechtje	Almelo	€ 145.00
Douwe	Amsterdam	€ 231.00
Gien	Rotterdam	€ 28.00
		€ 404.00

Data on right side

City	Province
Amsterdam	Noord-Holland
Rotterdam	Zuid-Holland
Utrecht	Utrecht

Result with left outer join

Person	City	Province	Tax
Brechtje	Almelo		€ 145.00
Douwe	Amsterdam	Noord-Holland	€ 231.00
Gien	Rotterdam	Zuid-Holland	€ 28.00
			€ 404.00

Result with inner join

Person	City	Province	Tax
Douwe	Amsterdam	Noord-Holland	€ 231.00
Gien	Rotterdam	Zuid-Holland	€ 28.00
			€ 259.00

Figure 1-5. *When to use the left outer join operator*

But when is an inner join used? It's used mainly in situations in which you do not want to include certain records from the left dataset, because they are not relevant for some reason. See the example in Figure 1-6. There are many tricks for complex data integration, as will be described in Chapters 5 and 6.

Data on left side

Person	City	Tax
Brechtje	Almelo	€ 145.00
Douwe	Amsterdam	€ 231.00
Gien	Rotterdam	€ 28.00
		€ 404.00

Data on right side

Person	Relevant
Brechtje	X
Douwe	X
Gien	

Result with inner join

Person	City	Relevant	Tax
Brechtje	Almelo	X	€ 145.00
Douwe	Amsterdam	X	€ 231.00
			€ 376.00

Figure 1-6. *When to use the inner join operator*

The union operator is more difficult to comprehend. It is also crucial in situations when key figures are coming from different tables. Figure 1-7 shows a simple example with two types of actual amounts and a planned amount on the company code and year. Actual amounts usually have some kind of document number, and so they do in this case. Planned amounts do not.

cocode	year	docnr	act1	act2
1000	2015	1001	€ 100.00	€ 50.00
1000	2015	1002	€ 20.00	€ 20.00
1000	2016	1003	€ 60.00	€ 50.00
1000	2016	1004	€ 50.00	€ 40.00
1000	2016	1005	€ 10.00	€ 5.00
1000	2017	1006	€ 100.00	€ 60.00
1000	2017	1007	€ 25.00	€ 30.00
1000	2018	1008	€ 5.00	€ 5.00
1000	2018	1009	€ 120.00	€ 90.00
2000	2015	1010	€ 110.00	€ 35.00
2000	2015	1011	€ 110.00	€ 35.00
2000	2016	1012	€ 120.00	€ 55.00
2000	2016	1013	€ 50.00	€ 20.00
2000	2016	1014	€ 50.00	€ 20.00
2000	2017	1015	€ 125.00	€ 50.00
2000	2017	1016	€ 100.00	€ 40.00
2000	2018	1017	€ 125.00	€ 65.00
2000	2018	1018	€ 100.00	€ 30.00
			€ 1,380.00	€ 700.00

cocode	year	plan
1000	2015	€ 300.00
1000	2016	€ 310.00
1000	2017	€ 315.00
1000	2018	€ 315.00
2000	2015	€ 310.00
2000	2016	€ 320.00
2000	2017	€ 330.00
2000	2018	€ 340.00
		€ 2,540.00

Figure 1-7. *Union operator: datasets*

Figure 1-8 uses a graphical HANA calculation view to demonstrate how the union operator works. Fields from the two data sources are not shown side by side, but below each other, making it clear that this is not a join. The output dataset is the combination of all fields from both data sources. Connections are made wherever possible. The characteristics cocode and year are connected to both data sources, and docnr is connected only to the Actuals data source.

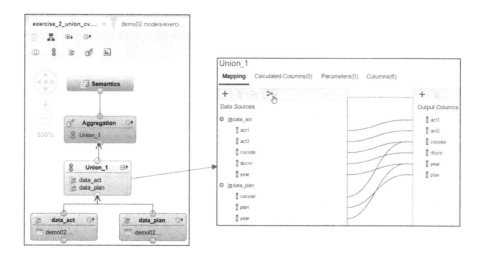

Figure 1-8. *Union operator: graphical explanation of how it works*

The result of the union in data preview mode looks like Figure 1-9.

cocode	year	docnr	act1	act2	plan
1000	2015	1001	€ 100.00	€ 50.00	
1000	2015	1002	€ 20.00	€ 20.00	
1000	2015				€ 300.00
1000	2016	1003	€ 60.00	€ 50.00	
1000	2016	1004	€ 50.00	€ 40.00	
1000	2016	1005	€ 10.00	€ 5.00	
1000	2016				€ 310.00
1000	2017	1006	€ 100.00	€ 60.00	
1000	2017	1007	€ 25.00	€ 30.00	
1000	2017				€ 315.00
1000	2018	1008	€ 5.00	€ 5.00	
1000	2018	1009	€ 120.00	€ 90.00	
1000	2018				€ 315.00
2000	2015	1010	€ 110.00	€ 35.00	
2000	2015	1011	€ 110.00	€ 35.00	
2000	2015				€ 310.00
2000	2016	1012	€ 120.00	€ 55.00	
2000	2016	1013	€ 50.00	€ 20.00	
2000	2016	1014	€ 50.00	€ 20.00	
2000	2016				€ 320.00
2000	2017	1015	€ 125.00	€ 50.00	
2000	2017	1016	€ 100.00	€ 40.00	
2000	2017				€ 330.00
2000	2018	1017	€ 125.00	€ 65.00	
2000	2018	1018	€ 100.00	€ 30.00	
2000	2018				€ 340.00
			€ 1,380.00	€ 700.00	€ 2,540.00

Figure 1-9. *Union operator: result*

At first sight, this may not look too nice, but if you look at it a bit longer, you will realize it is exactly what you want. Looking back at facts and dimensions as described earlier, you'll realize that the union connects each fact precisely to the dimensions that are relevant for that fact. It also starts looking better if you aggregate the data on cocode and year, leaving out docnr. Then the dataset looks like Figure 1-10.

cocode	year	act1	act2	plan
1000	2015	€ 120.00	€ 70.00	€ 300.00
1000	2016	€ 120.00	€ 95.00	€ 310.00
1000	2017	€ 125.00	€ 90.00	€ 315.00
1000	2018	€ 125.00	€ 95.00	€ 315.00
2000	2015	€ 220.00	€ 70.00	€ 310.00
2000	2016	€ 220.00	€ 95.00	€ 320.00
2000	2017	€ 225.00	€ 90.00	€ 330.00
2000	2018	€ 225.00	€ 95.00	€ 340.00
		€ 1,380.00	€ 700.00	€ 2,540.00

Figure 1-10. *Union operator: result after aggregation*

I also just made a "bruggetje" to the final operator to be discussed: aggregation. The best thing about aggregation is that you usually do not need to do anything. The OLAP engine of any BI tool will do it for you on the fly. I have coached a lot of BI colleagues during their first projects, and the ones with a programming background had a tendency to do too much aggregation. If you have a programming background, note that the dataset does not need to look nice in preview mode! The OLAP engine will make it look nice anyway. In exceptional cases, e.g., to optimize performance, we will, however, be using the aggregation operator.

Here's a short and sloppy translation for readers with a BW background: master data = left outer join, infoset = (left outer or inner) join, multiprovider = union, loading to a DSO = a combination of joining and aggregating, and a composite provider can do it all, so they say.

In Chapters 4 and 5, we will see that in the CDS world, a left outer join is called an *association* (or just *left outer join*); an inner join is named, well, *inner join*; for union we have a *union* or preferably the *union all* statement; and for aggregation the *group by* statement is used.

HANA Changing the OLTP vs. OLAP Game

I am far from a database expert. Therefore, it is with a heavy heart that I touch on this topic. Please be gentle with me. Conditions require that I say a few words about the impact the HANA database has had on the way we BI experts do our jobs. The impact it has on the development of SAP's BI tools is huge.

But let's start with a bit of history. In the old days, users could run queries in an ERP system. The impact of read actions for queries on database tables often conflicted with write actions for transaction input, the primary purpose of an ERP system. So-called runaway queries could even lead to system crashes. At the time, it seemed like a good idea to separate write actions from read actions, with write actions staying in the OLTP ERP system, and read actions being moved away to a separate OLAP system. This made it possible to optimize an OLTP database for write actions, and an OLAP database for read actions.

In 2006, the Hasso Plattner Institute started questioning this separation by studying the workloads of OLTP and OLAP systems and reached the conclusion that the workloads for the two types of systems are actually not that different (Figure 1-11).

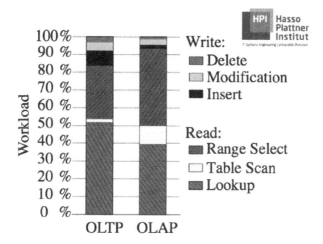

Figure 1-11. *OLTP access pattern myth: "Workload analysis of enterprise systems shows: OLTP and OLAP workloads are not that different"[4] ©SAP AG, 2014*

The Hasso Plattner Institute also concluded that a column store setup of the database would outperform the more commonly used row store setup, and this is true for OLTP as well as OLAP systems. Simply put, going through a dataset column by column is faster than going through it row by row. The third conclusion was that having data in memory instead of on disk makes everything go faster. Well, even I knew that.

SAP took the results of these studies and turned them into a concrete product: the HANA database. What does HANA stand for?

- *Option 1*: High-Performance Analytical Appliance

- *Option 2*: HAsso's New Architecture

I think it is the second one, but SAP invented the first one later to uphold the myth that Germans do not have a sense of humor. Nowadays, the HANA database is the workhorse beneath all of SAP's OLTP and OLAP systems—cloud as well as on-premise.

---

[4]Lecture: "Trends and Concepts in the Software Industry," Dr.-Ing. Jürgen Müller, Hasso Plattner Institute (2014)

With the HANA database, SAP introduced a new data tiering approach (Figure 1-12). Data can be subdivided into "hot," "warm," and "cold" data, depending on the frequency of its use. Hot data is stored in memory in the HANA database. Warm data is also stored in the HANA database, but on disk. Cold data is stored on disk in a "cheap" database, for instance SAP IQ, formerly known as Sybase IQ.

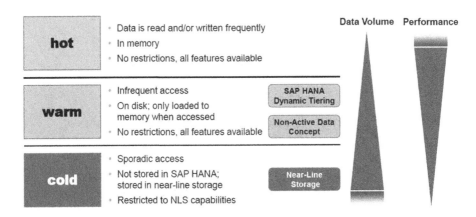

Figure 1-12. *SAP's data tiering approach: "Multi-Temperature Data Management" ©SAP AG*

But what is the impact of the HANA database on the work of an SAP BI specialist? First, all of SAP's OLTP systems have higher performance once the HANA database is shoved underneath them. The same is true for SAP's OLAP system, the data warehouse solution known as SAP Business Warehouse (BW). But more importantly, the historical shift of moving read actions from an OLTP system toward an OLAP system has been reversed by the HANA technology to a notable extent. Database read actions that were impossible to execute in an OLTP system in the pre-HANA era without running into issues can now be brought back into the OLTP system. This has all sorts of benefits, e.g., accessing real-time data instead of "yesterday evening's" data, which is typical for a data warehouse loaded overnight.

Initial enthusiasm among SAP representatives for S/4HANA, the new ERP system on the HANA database, was so great that it looked like SAP saw no future at all for separate OLAP systems like BW. Such systems were left out of system landscape overviews presented at the time. A short time later, two limited use cases were presented for BW with SAP ERP data, i.e., "historical" data, meaning data that is not in the original OLTP system anymore because it has been deleted or archived, and so-called snapshots of data stored at a certain point in time. Historical data and snapshots obviously cannot be delivered by a database in real-time mode. A third use case for a data warehouse is of course to combine SAP ERP data with data from other systems, SAP as well as non-SAP.

I agree that a lot more reporting can be done directly in the OLTP system thanks to HANA. But it also needs to be said that everything has its limitations, even the performance benefits of HANA. For instance, "consolidation" type of reports, financial data across all company codes, many years of data, and large data volumes with no interest in details on document level are difficult to build with a performance that is acceptable to modern computer users, spoiled by millisecond response times. In such cases, it makes sense to build the report on stored, aggregated data. OLAP systems are definitely not dead yet.

Cloud Flavors: SaaS vs. IaaS

It is without a doubt that the ICT world is pushing strongly toward various flavors of cloud deployment. The benefits are clear: reliability (I haven't lost a single file since I store my private administration in the cloud), pay per use and thereby lower thresholds for small companies, lower total cost of ownership, access from anywhere, security as a service, scalability, and more. SAP may have been late in jumping on this bandwagon but is now seriously doing so. Software development budgets are focusing on cloud versions, cloud versions are more regularly updated than on-premise versions, and all new functionalities are made available in a "cloud-first" fashion.

But there are various flavors of "cloud," differing by the level of control handed over to the party managing the cloud. SaaS, also known as the *public cloud*, is "total surrender." Software is consumed in a browser, and the organization using the software does not have access to the back end of the system. But on the bright side, the user organization does not need to worry about software installation and updates, as this is all taken care of by the cloud vendor. The back end (the applications and data) is controlled by the user organization in the platform-as-a-service (PaaS) flavor. In the third flavor, IaaS, only hardware, network, and such are controlled by the cloud vendor. This last option is also called a *private managed cloud* and usually involves cooperation with hyperscalers such as Amazon, Microsoft, or Google. Figure 1-13 gives an overview of the various cloud flavors.

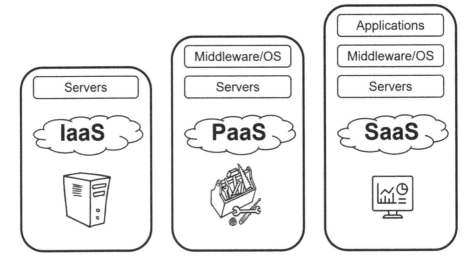

Figure 1-13. *IaaS, PaaS, and SaaS*

The S/4HANA software can be consumed in three ways: on-premise, IaaS, and SaaS. The current official name for the SaaS version of the software is S/4HANA Cloud Essential Edition. For the IaaS version, it is S/4HANA Cloud Extended Edition. The difference between on-premise and IaaS is of course huge for infrastructure types of technical consultants, but for functional consultants, like ERP module experts, or BI experts, IaaS is almost business as usual. In both situations, we have access to the back end of the system, and we can do whatever we were used to doing, although some limitations exist in the Extended Edition compared to on-premise. This is not the case for SaaS. Figure 1-14 demonstrates the difference between on-premise/IaaS and SaaS. On-premise/IaaS is like a piece cut from a pie (shown on the right). The filling can be reached from all sides. SaaS is like a "Berliner Pfannkuchen" (shown on the left): you have to eat partway through the dough to reach the filling (which is actually not that bad, come to think of it).

Figure 1-14. *On-premise/IaaS (full use) on the left versus SaaS (runtime) on the right. I don't know the source of this absolutely brilliant illustration; it's from a consultant I met at a training or conference. Please make yourself known, and I will reward you. Please note that I brew beer*

I have worked mainly with the on-premise version of S/4, but also briefly with IaaS and SaaS versions. Working with the SaaS version was quite frustrating. I felt like a repairman who left his toolbox at home. "I could fix this in a minute, ma'am, if I only I had the right tools." The BI system landscape I dealt with was SaaS version S/4 connected to SAP Analytics Cloud, which is only delivered as SaaS. The limited data-integration options in this setup were quite maddening. I will address this topic in Chapter 7. That is when SAP's PaaS solution, SAP Cloud Platform (SCP), will come in handy.

In conclusion, use SaaS version S/4 only for small, unambitious, and/ or cheap organizations or parts of organizations. Just kidding. Or am I?

Front End: Fiori and UI5

Again, I am far from a Fiori expert, but some basics about Fiori need to be introduced as they are relevant for the topics of this book. After all, the end results of our efforts in Chapters 2 to 5 will be Fiori tiles.

There was a lot of criticism on the UI technology SAP applied in previous versions of its ERP software. I never quite understood this, as I grew to be quite fond of the solid German look and feel of, for instance, the 4.6 GUI. But modern folk want to have an Internet-like experience everywhere they go. So, SAP developed a new UI named Fiori, which is Italian for "flowers." The goals of Fiori are to be role-based, responsive, simple, coherent, and delightful. They kind of lose me with the "delightful" bit, but the "responsive" property means Fiori works well for different devices such as desktop, tablet, and smartphone; in fact, it does an excellent job in scaling automatically to fit the screen size.

The screen an SAP user will see at the start of the workday will be filled with Fiori tiles. Most of them are just square push buttons to start a transaction or app, but others will show numbers, lists, graphs, pictures, or anything (Figure 1-15).

Figure 1-15.   *Example of a user screen with Fiori tiles (source: blog "Get Ready for SAP Fiori 3"[5] ©SAP AG, 2019)*

Below the tiles, three types of Fiori apps can be discerned: transactional, analytical, and fact sheet. From the point of view of decision support, or "insight to action" as it is often called, transactional and analytical apps are most important: find an issue with an analytical app, solve it with a transactional app, and check the solution with an analytical app. Some tiles even combine these steps in one app.

---

[5]Blog: "Get Ready for SAP Fiori 3," Margot Wollny, May 25, 2019, `https://blogs.sap.com/2019/05/25/get-ready-for-sap-fiori-3/`

Another way to divide Fiori apps is by the underlying technology. Most apps are built with a technology called UI5, but some rely on the older technologies Web Dynpro and SAP GUI for HTML. Now it is time to introduce new words into your vocabulary. In Dutch projects, the words are *fioriseren* or *verappen*, which would roughly translate to "to fiorize" or "to appify." Old ECC transactions can be "fiorized" into tiles without much effort. You'll learn more about this in the next chapter.

The UI5 technology is used by SAP to build its own apps and is also made available for use by customers to build extensions and custom apps. The use of UI5 by customers is not taking off to the extent that SAP intended. In my view, this is because the required skill set, mainly HTML and JavaScript, is quite different from what is available in the SAP community of developers, mainly ABAP programming. You'll learn more about UI5 and its role in extensibility in Chapter 7.

SAP's BI Portfolio

I once asked a guest speaker, who was experienced in nearly all existing BI software packages, which BI software was most successful in his view. The answer was Microsoft Excel. Most people already have it, those who have it mostly know how to use it, and it may not have been specifically developed for BI applications, but it has come a long way. I think the guest speaker was right. Therefore, SAP's initial choice to build its BI front-end tool as a plug-in for Microsoft Excel was quite clever. This front-end tool was named Business Explorer (BEx), and it worked on a BI back-end system or data warehouse named Business Warehouse.

In 2007, SAP acquired BusinessObjects (BO), a then-leading French BI software company. Integrating BO's front-end tools with SAP's BW back end turned out to be quite a challenge and was never fully successful. Tools from the pre-acquisition period, like Crystal Reports and WebIntelligence, are still used but do not integrate well with BW. Combining developers from both companies in joint teams to develop new front-end tools was more successful. From this cooperation, high-quality products emerged such as Lumira, Design Studio, and Analysis for Office. Analysis for Office is an Excel plug-in and can be seen as a modern successor of Business Explorer. But still, tagging along with salespeople to do sales support brought no great joy in this time period, as I had no idea what advice to give to customers with all these SAP products coming and going. Sometimes I secretly wished the customers would choose a non-SAP BI front-end tool, and often they did. At some point, SAP became aware of this problem and initiated a very welcome "convergence" of its BI front-end portfolio (see Figure 1-16).

Figure 1-16. *Convergence of SAP's client BI tools in 2014 (source: reference[6])*

---

[6]"Run Simple: Convergence of the SAP BusinessObjects BI Product Portfolio," Jayne Landry, June 25, 2014; https://blog-sap.com/analytics/2014/06/25/run-simple-convergence-of-the-sap-businessobjects-bi-product-portfolio/

The BI back-end portfolio has shown much more stability over the years. Business Warehouse may not be the most popular data warehouse in the world, but it shows a continuous flow of improvements in new releases, excellent integration with SAP transactional systems, and good adaptation to the HANA database. In addition, it has a steady customer base, although it's much smaller than that of SAP's ERP systems. Over many years, I managed to fulfill the majority of real-life business requirements with BW. In other words, it gets the job done.

With the HANA database, SAP introduced an alternative type of data warehousing called SQL data warehousing, native HANA, or simply calculation views. We saw some examples of calculation views in the "Operators for Data Integration" section. Combined with the column store setup of HANA, this type of data warehousing based on SQL gives better performance and better options for virtualization of data, or in other words "leaving the data where it is." But it did not succeed in replacing BW.

And then came the cloud and Big Data. HANA was developed further, and the BI portfolio was turned upside down once again. But it needs to be said that SAP now at least works from a clear vision of business software under the title of the "intelligent enterprise." See Figure 1-17.

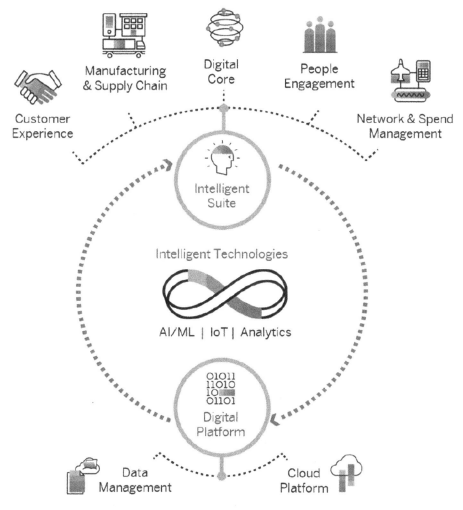

Figure 1-17. *The intelligent enterprise (source: openSAP training*
"SAP Leonardo – Enabling the Intelligent Enterprise" ©SAP AG, 2018)

The intelligent enterprise consists of these three parts:

- The "intelligent suite" corresponds to all of SAP's transaction systems, such as S/4HANA (ERP), C/4HANA (sales), Ariba (procurement), and SuccessFactors (HR). These systems are either SaaS only or SAP is pushing customers toward the SaaS version.

- The "workhorse" of the intelligent enterprise is the digital platform, consisting of data management and the cloud platform. Data management means... HANA. The SAP Cloud Platform (SCP) as it is called nowadays used to be called the HANA Cloud Platform (HCP) as it relies heavily on the HANA database underneath. It is a powerful PaaS offering for data storage, data modeling, and app development.

- The "intelligent technologies" are loosely coupled offerings grouped by the marketing term Leonardo. These offerings include functionalities in the following domains: the Internet of Things (IoT), artificial intelligence (AI)/machine learning (ML), data science/ predictive analytics, and blockchain. The analytics system SAP Analytics Cloud (SAC), with the Digital Boardroom on top and Big Data solution Data Hub, is also sometimes covered by the Leonardo umbrella.

Within this concept, there appears to be room for only one BI front-end tool: the SaaS offering SAP Analytics Cloud (SAC). SAP's entire BI front-end software development budget seems to be directed toward SAC. The ambitions of SAC are great. SAC already integrates well with S/4, BW, and other SAP systems, but it will also be built into all SAP applications, beginning with SuccessFactors and the SaaS version of S/4.

The situation for the BI back end is less clear. Recent presentations show three types of data warehousing: BW, native HANA or SAP SQL data warehousing, and a new SaaS offering named SAP Data Warehouse Cloud. See Figure 1-18.

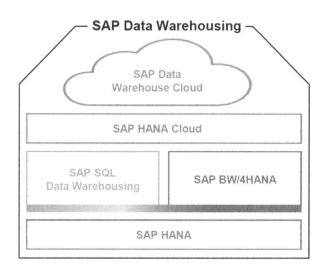

Figure 1-18. *Statement of direction for SAP data warehousing (source: presentation AIN208 at conference SAP TechEd Barcelona 2019 ©SAP AG, 2019)*

BW is far from dead, as it is still being improved on a regular basis. The latest version, BW/4HANA, works best with HANA technology; it has clearly been simplified compared to previous versions and is definitely to be preferred for greenfield implementations. "Native HANA" seems to have been side-tracked. This is a pity, as it has some clear advantages. Data Warehouse Cloud is still very immature and needs to prove itself in the coming years. The version I saw looks more like a limited data storage option for SAC than a genuine data warehouse. In a recent webinar, SAP called Data Warehouse Cloud "SAC on steroids," which is funny as well as proves my point. Somehow I believe that it is easier to properly offer a front-end tool in SaaS mode than a back-end system. But the future may prove me wrong.

SAP is struggling how to enter the world of Big Data. Unstructured data, e.g., from social media or IoT, is stored as a "data lake" in cheap databases like Hadoop and processed with open source tools. How does SAP compete with stuff that is free? Well, basically by embracing this stuff. See Figure 1-19.

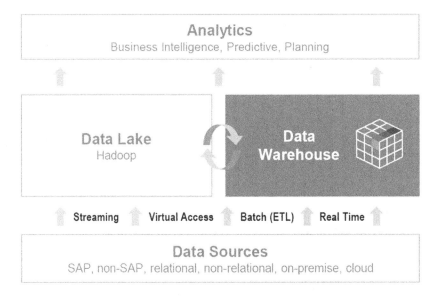

Figure 1-19. *Combining a data warehouse with a data lake (source: openSAP training "Modern Data Warehousing with SAP BW/4HANA" ©SAP AG, 2018)*

SAP is investing heavily in connectivity between Hadoop and other data lakes with SAP's data warehouse, in which structured business data resides. If you cannot beat them, join them! SAP's new product Data Hub is another example of SAP embracing popular non-SAP products. According to SAP, "SAP Data Hub provides data orchestration and metadata management across heterogeneous data sources." Data Hub is already being replaced by a SaaS product delivering comparable functionality named SAP Data Intelligence. See Figure 1-20.

SAP Data Intelligence
End to End Data Integration and Processing

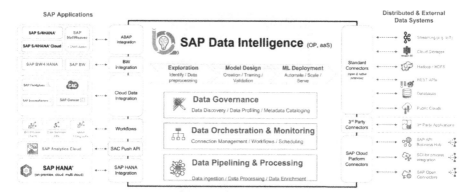

Figure 1-20. *Building blocks of SAP Data Intelligence (source:* `https://compamind.de/files/2019/11/Bild-1.png` *©SAP AG, 2019)*

Data Hub uses SAP Vora technology, is well integrated with other SAP systems, and is particularly good at "leaving the data where it is." It also cleverly integrates or orchestrates the darlings of the open source community such as Hadoop, S3, Kubernetes, Docker, Kafka, Spark, Python, Grafana, Kibana, and more. Again, good thinking! A former colleague of mine, who spent notably more years in the world of Big Data than I did, sees potential in this product, even though he is far from an SAP fan. But it will be hard to convince him and other representatives of the open source community to actually pay for software.

Which BI tools are advised nowadays in real life? Well, I happen to be a real-life consultant, and Figure 1-21 displays a BI system landscape I recently proposed to a real-life customer.

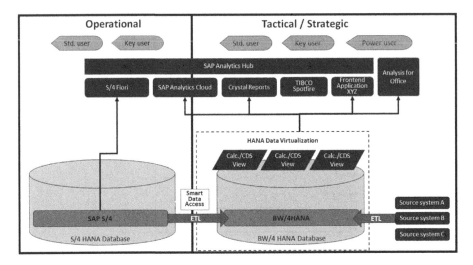

Figure 1-21. *Example BI system landscape (original version by my colleague Jeroen Keijzer, who is not family ©myBrand, 2020)*

It has an S/4HANA system, of course, with embedded analytics for operational reporting and a Fiori UI. We proposed on-premise version S/4, because…well, many reasons. We also proposed a BW data warehouse, version BW/4HANA, as it will be a greenfield implementation. Part of the S/4 data is loaded into BW via ETL, and part is made available in real time via Smart Data Access (SDA). We did not cover integration tooling, but SDA is an interesting one, as it "leaves the data where it is." Native HANA calculation views or CDS views are used between data and front-end tools. The front-end tools proposed were Business Objects heritage Crystal Reports for "pixel-perfect" reporting, choice of the future SAP Analytics Cloud, Analysis for Office for the Excel-lovers, and non-SAP tools like Spotfire, because this particular customer built up a lot of expertise in TIBCO software, so why not use that? To top it off, SAP Analytics Hub has uniform access to all these tools. In summary, it is a firm base of S/4HANA and BW/4HANA with some miscellaneous front-end tooling on top. This is what we will be advising for a few more years for a lot of customer situations.

The Latest Thing: CDS Views

What is a CDS view? Let's start with language: what does the abbreviation mean? Answer: Core data services. Does that explain much? No, at least not for me. But if you need help, there is always SAP Help: "Core data services (CDS) is an infrastructure for defining and consuming semantically rich data models in SAP HANA." Hmmm.

Let's look at a bit of history once again. The HANA database performs best when data consumption is pushed down to a database level instead of the application level. Native HANA views were the first to do this. SAP used this technology, mainly graphical calculation views, to build a virtual data model (VDM) named HANA Live in ECC on HANA. Then came S/4HANA with new tables, new code, and again a VDM, but now with a new underlying technology: CDS views. Why? The answer comes from SAP employees. "Previously, the VDMs were realized using the SAP HANA calculation views; in SAP S/4HANA, CDS views are realized using ABAP core data services. This was primarily done to provide the benefits of lifecycle management, authorization and translation."[7] These benefits are much appreciated. SAP's transport system may on occasion seem unnecessarily complicated, but having experience with transporting native HANA objects through the SAP system landscape taught me to appreciate it. In Chapter 6, we will see some examples of authorization and translation that would not have been that simple without the ABAP CDS technology.

What they do not tell you is the downside of this technology change. With Native HANA calculation views, I at least have the choice between a graphical or scripted version (see Figure 1-4). Graphical calculation views are fun. They're mostly just drawing lines and arrows and clicking little icons. A child could do it. With CDS views, there is only one option: "code until you drop." The first CDS-RSI victims are to be anticipated. Maybe I am one.

---

[7] *SAP S/4HANA Embedded Analytics: The Comprehensive Guide*, Butsmann, Fleckenstein and Kundu, Rheinwerk Publishing, 2018

Actually, there are two flavors of CDS views[8]: HANA CDS and ABAP CDS. HANA CDS was the first flavor to arise after the introduction of the HANA database. As it bypasses the ABAP application server, HANA CDS cannot make use of functions of the application server, like the ABAP dictionary. The benefits mentioned earlier in comparison with native HANA calculation views are not valid for HANA CDS. ABAP CDS is a way to work directly on the database and still make use of some functions of the application server. For the rest, the two technologies are quite similar. They both rely on a dialect of SQL as a coding language. The name "ABAP CDS" may be somewhat confusing, as there is no ABAP coding involved. Bottom line: for SAP S/4HANA Embedded Analytics, you need ABAP CDS.

In the SaaS version of S/4HANA, you have no access to the back-end system. Therefore, you cannot see structures (transaction SE11) or the content (transaction SE16) of tables or views. Remember how I shared my frustration as a repairman without a toolbox earlier in this chapter? Free beers go to the developer who adds tiles named SE11 and SE16 to the SaaS version of S/4. Expensive beers, like barrel-aged stouts. But, alas, until then, you need to analyze the content of a table by running a query on a part of the VDM that includes this table. It's not very direct, but it is your only option. Praise the VDM in SaaS S/4, as it is the only thing you have.

S/4HANA Embedded Analytics

By now, you should have some idea what S/4HANA is. But let me repeat: the newest version of SAP ERP is optimized for the HANA database, with the code rewritten and aggregated tables removed or replaced by views. It enables transaction input and analytics output simultaneously in one system and is an enabler of the intelligent enterprise. Wow again.

---

[8]Blog "CDS – One Concept, Two Flavors," Horst Keller, `https://blogs.sap.com/2015/07/20/cds-one-model-two-flavors/`, 2015

And SAP S/4HANA Embedded Analytics? What is that? Or better, what can it be, because it can mean many things? In summary, SAP S/4HANA Embedded Analytics can refer to any of the following:

- Standard reports and dashboards delivered with the S/4 software

- Virtual data model = standard (released) CDS views

- Option to create custom CDS views

- Option to create custom analytical queries

- User-defined KPI-based reports

We will revisit all these topics in the upcoming chapters. Once SAC is embedded in S/4, it is likely to also be called Embedded Analytics.

An interesting presentation at the latest TechEd conference in Barcelona[9] applies an even broader definition of SAP S/4HANA Embedded Analytics, including "intelligent technologies" and also throws SAC and BW into the mix. See Figure 1-22.

---

[9]Presentation "From Transaction to Insight with SAP Solutions...or how the SAP Analytics Cloud and SAP BW/4HANA solutions complement SAP S/4HANA," AIN201, SAP Teched Barcelona, 2019

SAP S/4HANA embedded analytics =

Analytics embedded in SAP ERP + SAP HANA + Intelligent Technologies

+ Content (Data Models and Applications) + Design Time Applications

Figure 1-22. *"What is SAP S/4HANA Embedded Analytics?" (source: presentation AIN201 at conference SAP TechEd Barcelona 2019 ©SAP AG, 2019)*

The same presentation gives a high-level architectural overview of this mix. See Figure 1-23.

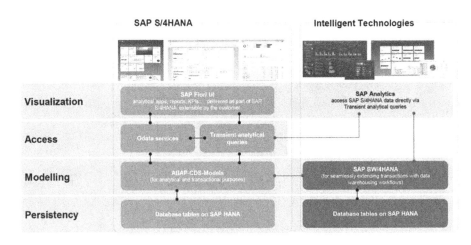

Figure 1-23. *Analytics with SAP S/4HANA, high-level architecture (source: presentation AIN201 at conference SAP TechEd Barcelona 2019 ©SAP AG, 2019)*

Modeling is done with ABAP CDS. OData services play a major role in connectivity. Using a CDS view of type analytical query in SAP Analytics Cloud is less complex than what it looks like in the figure. Just checking a box or adding a tag is sufficient to perform all the steps that are necessary under the hood. Indeed this is true for most SAP BI front-end tools.

As a BW veteran, I cannot help but compare real-time embedded analytics with reporting on data in a data warehouse. And I am enthusiastic about real-time analytics, not just because of the real-time character of the output, as for most reports people can afford to wait until the next day. I am enthusiastic because there is no intermediate data storage, thereby succeeding 100 percent in "leaving the data where it is." If virtual structures are built correctly, the report cannot show anything else but correct data. There is no dependency on loading processes being built with errors. There's no dependency on a support consultant with a hangover repairing a data load in the wrong order, thereby creating a "data hole" in a data warehouse cube that is likely to stay there forever. I have seen many examples of data warehouses where certain parts were completely useless because of such data errors. My philosophical statement: "what is not cannot be wrong."

You are right, philosophy is not my thing. So, let's get more down to Earth and move on to the next chapter.

CHAPTER 2

No Work: Use What Is Delivered

Why waste energy on building something that is already there? You would be surprised to know how often this happens in practice: a developer builds something that is standardly available, and often they build it worse than what is already available. So, at the beginning of a project, take some time to assess what is already available in your area for analytics.

For now, let's discuss how good SAP is at devising standard content for real-life organizations. The consultant's answer to any question is of course "It depends." In this case, it depends on where you live. In the early days of my career, I followed an SAP business intelligence (BI) training in Brussels, Belgium, for which an instructor was flown in from SAP India. This encounter revealed some cultural differences, one of them being the way in which companies are willing to accept standard BI content.

Our trainer described an SAP BI implementation in India as follows: "We fly to the customer, install the software, activate the standard content, demonstrate it to the customer, the customer is satisfied, and we fly back home." Overall, the experience of Belgian and Dutch implementation consultants in the classroom was like this: "We drive to the customer (much smaller countries), install the software, activate the standard content, demonstrate it to the customer, we all have a good laugh, and then we start discussing what the customer really needs to run the business." What causes this cultural difference? Probably a combination

© Freek Keijzer 2021
F. Keijzer, *SAP S/4HANA Embedded Analytics*, https://doi.org/10.1007/978-1-4842-7017-2_2

of admiration by companies in the new economies for the Western-world companies for which the standard content was developed and an overestimation of uniqueness among the Western-world companies. I am not choosing sides here. I do know, however, that I have built a lot of special KPI-type reports for European companies that seemed unnecessarily complex to me and where the added value compared with standard functionality was quite unclear. So, I sympathize with both parties.

In the previous chapter, I described how SAP had been struggling for a long time with consistency in its BI front-end offerings, thus leaving space for competitors such as Tableau, QlikView, and EveryAngle in the Netherlands to fill this gap. The initial popularity of these products was mainly based on that they were earlier in applying in-memory technology than SAP. Currently, these products are being replaced by SAP HANA-based BI at a rapid pace. However, during this process, another advantage of these products is encountered: non-SAP vendors are frequently better at developing standard BI content on top of SAP ERP than SAP itself. But once again, how satisfied a customer is with SAP's standard BI content depends strongly on the situation.

Which Tiles Are Shown, and How Are They Grouped?

Now it's time for something completely different. Let's spend some time in the world of tiles. Any user entering the Fiori Launchpad will see a bunch of tiles grouped in a certain way. But who decides which tiles are shown to the user and how they are grouped? As an example, take the group of tiles shown in Figure 2-1. I as a user see this group in all systems of the customer Dutch Railways. Note that Figure 2-1 was taken while being logged in with the English language, which I did especially for this book. All tiles showing an English description are standard SAP apps and therefore have a description in all languages. The two tiles showing a Dutch description are custom-made. In fact, they are custom-made analytical queries using the technology described in Chapters 5 and 6. As Dutch is the only target language in the Dutch Railways project, the descriptions of custom-made objects are strictly in Dutch, and no effort has been made for multilingual descriptions. In Fiori, descriptions from the development language are shown in case there are no descriptions in the logged-in language. By the way, we will revisit multilingual descriptions in Chapter 6.

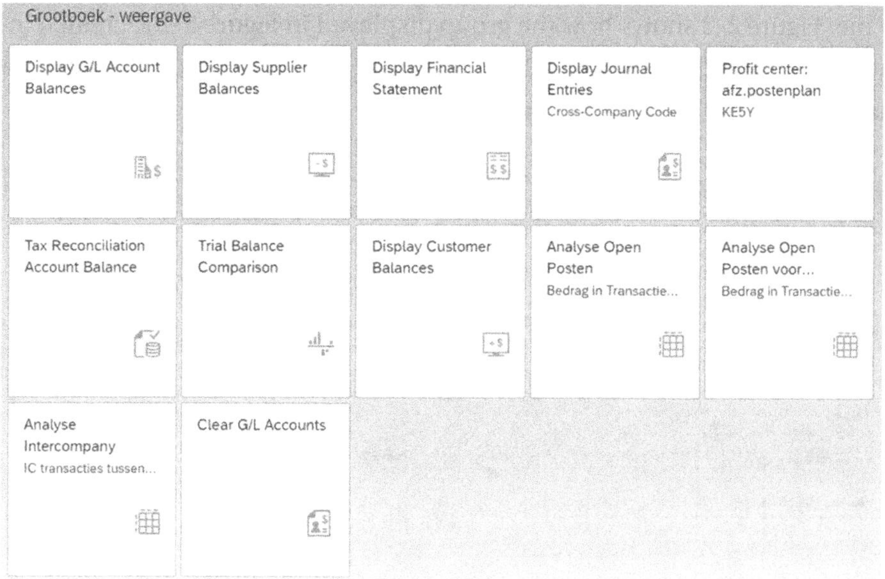

Figure 2-1. *Example of Fiori tiles in a group*

Let's get back to the main question: who decides which tiles are shown to the user and how they are grouped? To understand this in detail, we need to run the back-end transaction /UI2/FLPD_CUST, which brings you to the Fiori Launchpad Designer in the Fiori front end. When was it that SAP transactions were nice four-character abbreviations like FB03 or MB5B without slashes and stuff? Never mind.

Five types of objects are relevant for the answer to this question: technical catalogs, business catalogs, tile groups, business roles, and user IDs. The catalogs and groups can be managed within the Fiori Launchpad Designer. Business roles and user IDs belong to traditional authorization work with transactions PFCG or Role Maintenance and SU01 or User Maintenance, respectively. Technical catalogs are important in the development of Fiori tiles and other objects. Business catalogs and business roles define which tiles are available for a user. A tile must be in a business catalog that is within a business role that is assigned to me before I can see the tile. Tile groups define the structure in which tiles are shown to me. Figure 2-2 shows how the group displayed in Figure 2-1 is created in the Fiori Launchpad Designer. Both technical and business catalogs can be managed via the button Catalogs in the upper-left corner.

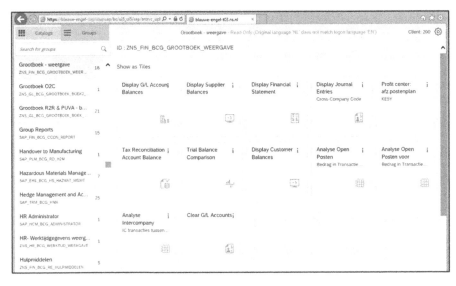

Figure 2-2. *Fiori Launchpad Designer to manage catalogs and groups*

If you are wondering what a Blauwe Engel is, it is Dutch for "Blue Angel," the name of a diesel railcar in operation from 1953 to 2002 that traveled from Marienberg to Almelo, which is where I happen to live. What a coincidence.

Warning: Do not make the mistake as a developer to give yourself all the existing business roles in a Fiori development system. The initial loading of all tiles after each login will take a serious amount of time, maybe indefinitely. If you did make this mistake, there is only one setting that can save you, besides deleting roles. Click the pawn-shaped icon and select Settings ➤ Home Page ➤ Home Page Display ➤ Show one group at a time (Figure 2-3).

Figure 2-3. *Fiori setting Show one group at a time*

Discover Analytical Apps

For the discovery of analytical apps, we need to go to the interweb, as some people my age erroneously call it. The two most useful URLs are the following:

- *SAP Best Practices Explorer*: `https://rapid.sap.com/bp/` (S-user required)

- *SAP Fiori Apps Reference Library*: `https://fioriappslibrary.hana.ondemand.com/`

As a BI consultant, you will start with the Best Practices Explorer. Or better put, your functional consultant project teammates will start with the Best Practices Explorer. By requesting activation of best practices or scope items, they will order chunks of functionality within their domains of expertise. These chunks will often include analytical apps. As an analytics consultant, you can lay back and relax until they are finished. Or even more likely, you will not be around when they do this type of work, as BI consultants tend to arrive late in an ERP implementation project. This makes perfect sense, as ERP customizing needs to have reached some sort of steady state, and somewhat representative development data needs to be present before a BI consultant can start. On the positive side, BI consultants also tend to be the last ones to leave a project.

In the case of a SaaS version S/4HANA implementation project, requesting best practices means sending a list of scope items to SAP, and SAP experts will take care of the activation. That is how SaaS works. No one has access to the system back end, except for SAP. In the case of an on-premise S/4HANA implementation, the list with scope items can be sent to a technical consultant within the project team.

Scope items are three-character abbreviations like 1HB, which in this case stands for "Profit and Loss Plan Data Load from File." This is just a random example. After a while, a project team will communicate in these three-character abbreviations, thus bonding internally but alienating itself from the rest of the world. A particularly useful scope item in the context of this book is BGH, which stands for "Embedded Analytics with SAP S/4HANA." This will activate all tiles to be used in upcoming chapters.

So, first you let your colleagues activate the big chunks of functionality and thereby numerous analytical apps. Second, you assess these apps before concluding that some apps are missing. Third, you go back to the interweb to look for individual analytical Fiori apps in the Reference Library. After entering the URL, SAP explains and shows the search categories (Figure 2-4).

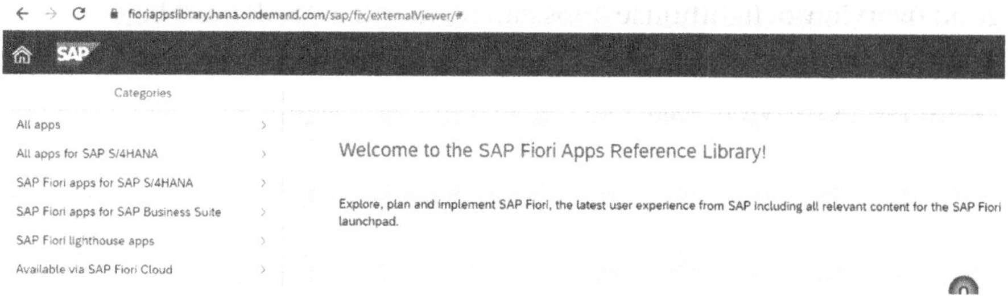

Welcome to the SAP Fiori Apps Reference Library!

Figure 2-4. *SAP Fiori Apps Reference Library*

You will find various types of apps. SAP uses the same tools for its own application as the tools made available to the community of developers. You will therefore find apps looking like the predefined Fiori page types displayed in Figure 2-5.

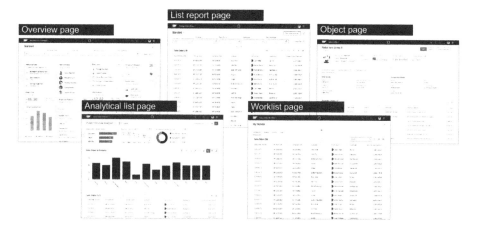

Figure 2-5. *Predefined Fiori page types (source: presentation UX101 at conference SAP TechEd Barcelona 2019 ©SAP AG, 2019)*

SAP draws special attention toward so-called Fiori lighthouse apps. Lighthouse apps are seen as the apps in which Fiori brings the most benefit compared with old-school GUI transactions. They are usually overview pages with multiple tiles and a lot of graphical elements.

A good overview of lighthouse apps can be found in "SAP Fiori Lighthouse Scenarios."[1] Figure 2-6 shows an example of a lighthouse app, the Procurement Overview Page.

Figure 2-6. *Example of a Fiori lighthouse app, the Procurement Overview Page (source: Fiori Apps Library ©SAP AG, 2020)*

Let's check what the Fiori Apps Library has to say about this app. Figure 2-7 shows, among other things, an icon indicating that it is a lighthouse app, the application type, and the SAP Fiori elements: the overview page and an app ID consisting of the letter *F* followed by a number. This app ID is extremely useful in communication with technical experts concerning the app, as it is the clearest identifier available. Additional information given by the Fiori Apps Library includes product

[1]Presentation "SAP Fiori Lighthouse Scenarios," April, 2020, https://www.sap.com/corporate/en/documents/2018/01/12b3dec4-ec7c-0010-82c7-eda71af511fa.html

features, a link to documentation on the SAP Help Portal, a screenshot of the output of the app (shown in Figure 2-6), the scope item to which the app belongs, and a list of related apps. Also, implementation information is given, but this will be addressed in the next section.

Figure 2-7. *Information on lighthouse app Procurement Overview Page in the Fiori Apps Library*

In my current project, lighthouse apps were often considered but not often selected for implementation. More down-to-Earth apps were frequently chosen by representatives of the business. Let's scroll over to the other end of the spectrum and take a look at an app with almost no added value compared with a GUI transaction, as it basically still is a GUI transaction. To be exact, it is the GUI transaction given by the app ID in the Apps Library: FB03. SAP fiorized transaction FB03 in the same way it appified many more transactions. Figure 2-8 compares the output for an identical dataset via the GUI transaction versus the Fiori app.

Figure 2-8. *Example output of GUI transaction FB03 (top) versus Fiori app FB03 (bottom) for the same dataset*

There is not a spectacular difference other than the bottom one being in a browser and the top one not being in a browser. Well, the top one is grayish, and the bottom one being more bluish, as e-book readers can verify, but hard-copy book readers cannot. The Fiori Apps Library tells us that this app is of application type SAP GUI (Figure 2-9). The first comment in the product features is as follows: "This app is a SAP GUI for HTML transaction. These classic transactions are available in the SAP Fiori theme to support a seamless user experience across the SAP Fiori Launchpad."

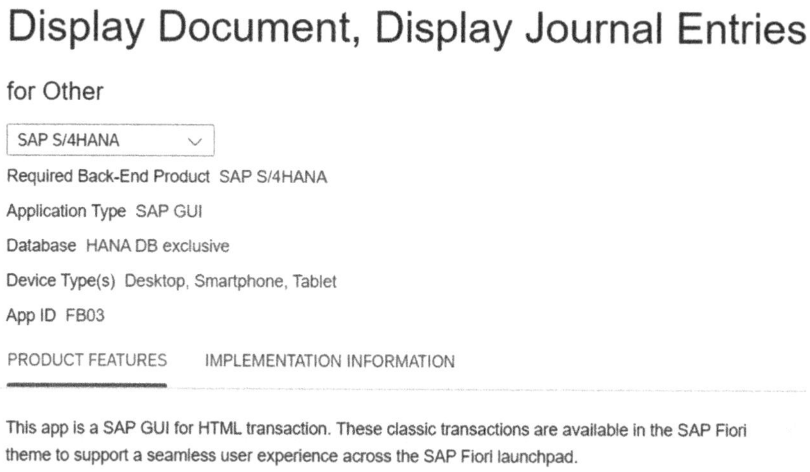

Display Document, Display Journal Entries

for Other

SAP S/4HANA ⌄

Required Back-End Product SAP S/4HANA

Application Type SAP GUI

Database HANA DB exclusive

Device Type(s) Desktop, Smartphone, Tablet

App ID FB03

PRODUCT FEATURES   IMPLEMENTATION INFORMATION

This app is a SAP GUI for HTML transaction. These classic transactions are available in the SAP Fiori
theme to support a seamless user experience across the SAP Fiori launchpad.

Figure 2-9. *Information on app Display Document, Display Journal Entries in the Fiori Apps Library*

Two other examples in the financial domain I would like to present are Display G/L Account Balances and Trial Balance. To start with the former, its output will look like Figure 2-10.

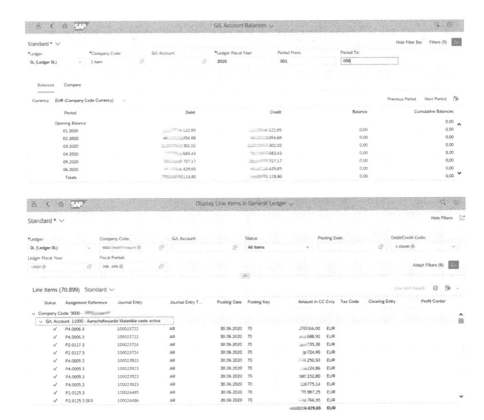

Figure 2-10. *Example output of app Display G/L Account Balances. When clicking one of the amounts at the top, the follow-up app Display Line Items in General Ledger automatically opens (bottom)*

Figure 2-11 shows information given about this app in the Fiori Apps Library. The application type is Transactional (SAP Fiori (SAPUI5)). The fact that it is a UI5 app explains why it has a selection bar integrated with the output and actionable links in the output. It also means that you will not learn how to build an app like this in the context of this book. Sorry. Such apps can, however, have underlying CDS views to collect the data, so if they need to be modified, ABAP CDS expertise can be required.

Display G/L Account Balances

for General Ledger Accountant

SAP S/4HANA ⌄

Required Back-End Product SAP S/4HANA

Line of Business Finance

Application Type Transactional (SAP Fiori (SAPUI5))

Database HANA DB exclusive

Device Type(s) Desktop, Tablet

App ID F0707

Figure 2-11. *Information on UI5 app Display G/L Account Balances in the Fiori Apps Library*

The second example of a down-to-Earth app in the financial domain is Trial Balance. Figure 2-12 shows some example output. There's no integrated selection bar in this app, but a selection screen with prompts that needs to be filled in before output is generated.

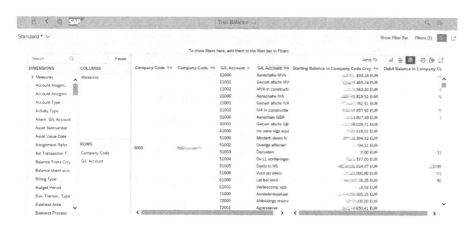

Figure 2-12. *Example output of app Trial Balance*

This is a very different looking app of indeed a different type. Figure 2-13 shows the information that the Apps Library gives.

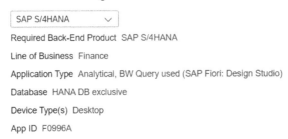

Trial Balance (Design Studio)

for General Ledger Accountant

SAP S/4HANA ∨

Required Back-End Product SAP S/4HANA

Line of Business Finance

Application Type Analytical, BW Query used (SAP Fiori: Design Studio)

Database HANA DB exclusive

Device Type(s) Desktop

App ID F0996A

Figure 2-13. *Information on Design Studio app Trial Balance in the Fiori Apps Library*

This version of Trial Balance is a so-called Fiori Design Studio app. It has a separate selection screen, measures, and dimensions in columns and rows to be dragged and dropped, as well as many more features we will investigate in detail in upcoming sections and chapters. The attentive reader may remember that Design Studio is one of the SAP BI tools described in Chapter 1 and may worry this implies that additional tooling is to be installed. Not to worry. The technology originates from a combination of Design Studio, BW/BEx, and Fiori a long time ago, but it now stands on its own with only CDS views and Fiori required.

Please note, dear reader, that this Fiori Design Studio type of app is something you will be able to build after you have reached the end of this book. I promise you.

Activate Them

Your functional colleagues have requested all best practices or scope items they deem necessary, technical experts have made these available, you as a BI expert have spent numerous hours on the Fiori Apps Library website to discover apps that are still missing, and you drafted a list of app IDs. Now what? In a SaaS situation, you are at the mercy of an SAP specialist, who needs to implement these while maintaining his balance in the cloud. In a on-premise situation, you will probably send your list of app IDs to a project team member who has been given the task of implementing apps. But what will this colleague do?

Basically, they will also go to the Fiori Apps Library and follow the instructions on the Implementation Information tab. In Figure 2-14 you will find such instructions for one of the apps presented in the previous section, i.e., Display G/L Account Balances. The Installation section shows technical details regarding SAP notes, front-end components, and back-end components required for this app.

PRODUCT FEATURES   IMPLEMENTATION INFORMATION

Please select a delivery date. The implementation information below only applies for the app version delivered on this date.

SAP S/4HANA 2020   ⌄

SAP Fiori Overview

⌄   Important SAP Notes

System	Note Number	Description
General Note	2058320	
Front-End Server	2935911	Release & Information Note: SAP Fiori for SAP S/4HANA 2020 - SPS Initial Shipment Stack
Back-End Server	2912253	Release & Information Note: SAP S/4HANA 2020 - SPS Initial Shipment Stack

Show additional notes in SAP Support Portal

⌄   Installation

The app consists of front-end components (such as the user interfaces) and back-end components (such as the OData service). The back-end and front-end components are delivered with separate products and have to be installed in a system landscape that is enabled for SAP Fiori.

Front-End Components

Product Version	SAP FIORI FOR SAP S/4HANA 2020 SAP Fiori for SAP S/4HANA 2020
Support Package Stack	Initial Shipment Stack
Software Component Version	UIAPFI70 800 - SP 0000
Prerequisite for installation	SAP FIORI FOR SAP S/4HANA 2020 - SPS Initial Shipment Stack is an *Add On* to SAP FIORI FES 2020 FOR S/4HANA - SPS Initial Shipment Stack

Back-End Components (ABAP)

Product Version	SAP S/4HANA 2020 SAP S/4HANA 2020
Support Package Stack	Initial Shipment Stack
Software Component Version	S4CORE 105 - SP 0000

Figure 2-14. *Fiori Apps Library information for installation*

Scroll down to reach the Configuration part of the implementation information (Figure 2-15). Earlier in this chapter, five object types were mentioned that play a role in which tiles are shown to a user and how they are grouped. For four of these object types, the standard SAP object is named: technical catalog, business catalog, group, and business role. In the productive phase of a project, these will probably be replaced by custom-made objects, adapted to the specific needs of the organization. But in the earliest phases of a project, these standard objects can be used to explore and test certain apps. For instance, if I were to give myself the role General Ledger Accountant (SAP_BR_GL_ACCOUNTANT) in a demo system, this app would automatically become available to me for assessment, and I would be able to find it in the group Analytics for General Ledger.

∨ Configuration

The following sections list app-specific data required to configure the app:

SAPUI5 Application

The ICF nodes for the following SAPUI5 application must be activated on the front-end server:

Component	Technical Name	Path to ICF Node	SAP UI5 Component
SAP UI5 Application	FIN_GL_BALANCES	/sap/bc/ui5_ui5/sap/fin_gl_balances	fin.gl.balances.display

OData Service(s)

The following OData services must be activated on the front-end server
Users require PFCG authorization for the front-end and back-end systems.

OData Service	Version	Software Component Version	Back-End Authorization Role (PFCG)
FAC_GL_ACCOUNT_BALANCE_SRV	0001	S4CORE 105	

SAP Fiori Launchpad

You require the following data to give users access to the app in the SAP Fiori launchpad. Note that additional fields or parameters may be required that are not listed here. For an overview of the required data, see Setting Up Content With the Launchpad Designer in the SAP Fiori launchpad documentation.

Technical Configuration

Technical Catalog	SAP_TC_FIN_ACC_COMMON
Technical Catalog Description	SAP
SAPUI5 Application	FIN_GL_BALANCES

Target Mapping(s)

Semantic Object	Semantic Action	Parameter Key	Parameter Value
GLAccount	displayBalance	BusinessArea	%%userdefault.extended.businessarea%%

App Launcher(s)

Title	Subtitle	Information	Parameter-Value
Display G/L Account Balances			

Business Catalog(s)

Catalog Name			Extend Apps Selection
SAP_SFIN_BC_GL_ANALYTICS	Catalog Description	General Ledger - Analytics	

Business Group(s)

Business Group	Group Description
SAP_SFIN_BCG_GL_ANALYTICS	Analytics for General Ledger

Business Role(s)

Role Name		Extend Apps Selection
SAP_BR_GL_ACCOUNTANT	Role Description	General Ledger Accountant

Figure 2-15. *Fiori Apps Library information for configuration*

Furthermore, the Implementation Information tab of the Fiori Apps Library gives information on extensibility, support, and related apps. As we saw earlier, it is possible to go from the app Display G/L Account Balances

to the more detailed app Display Line Items in General Ledger. Figure 2-16
shows the way in which this is reflected in the Fiori Apps Library. The
detailed app is listed here with Relation Type equal to Navigation Target. In
this navigation, the Target Mappings option listed in the Configuration part
of the implementation information (Figure 2-14) plays an important role.
Under Where Used, it can be seen which apps use the Display G/L Account
Balances as a navigation target.

Related Apps		
Related Apps		Extend Apps Selection
App Name	App ID	Relation Type
Display Line Items in General Ledger	F2217	Navigation Target
Where Used		
App Name	App ID	Relation Type
Balance Sheet/Income Statement - China	F1698	as Navigation Target

Figure 2-16. *Fiori Apps Library information on related apps*

Finally, let's step back almost to the top of the implementation
information (Figure 2-14). The link under the text "SAP Fiori Overview"
leads to useful information on the SAP Help Portal with details how the
implementation activities are to be carried out (Figure 2-17). It is not by
accident that I am showing you the part on activating OData services.
Colleagues doing this type of work day-in and day-out assure me that
activating OData services is the majority of their work. The OData
services to be activated can be found in the configuration section of the
implementation information (Figure 2-15).

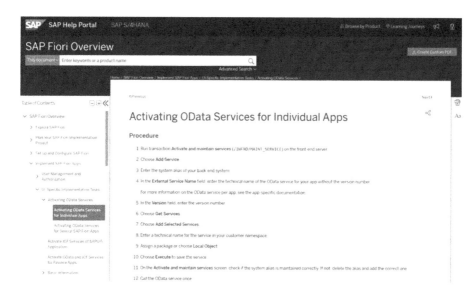

Figure 2-17. *SAP Fiori overview on the SAP Help Portal*

Use Them

Browser-based applications are supposed to be self-explanatory, and indeed many of them are. A UI5 app, like Display G/L Account Balances described in previous sections, is pretty easy to use. The selection bar on top contains input boxes that can be filled in. If such a box is marked with an asterisk, it needs to be filled in. And if you click something blue in the output part of the app (sorry, hard-copy book readers), you can jump to a more detailed level of information.

Although the same is true for an app of Design Studio type, I do want to dive deeper into the details of how such an app is used and can be used to its full extent. The reason is that we will be creating apps of this type ourselves in upcoming chapters. Let's get started using the Trial Balance app as an example.

Any app, including a Fiori Design Studio app, can be started by clicking a tile (Figure 2-18).

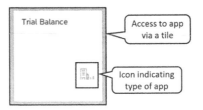

Figure 2-18. *Tile to access the Trial Balance Fiori Design Studio app*

A selection screen will appear (Figure 2-19). Different types of parameters can be present: optional or mandatory, single value, multiple values, interval, hierarchical, etc. Default values can be proposed, but these can be overwritten. At the right side of the input fields, icons indicate if value lists are available, e.g., calendars in the case of date parameters.

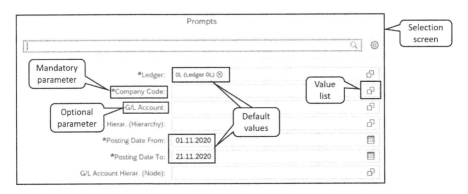

Figure 2-19. *Selection screen of the Trial Balance app*

Entering the selection options of a field like Company Code leads to two tabs: "Select from list" and "Define conditions" (Figure 2-20). On the "Select from list" tab, single or multiple values can be selected, depending on the type of parameter. On the "Define conditions" tab, more complex from-to conditions can be entered for inclusions, as well as conditions for exclusions.

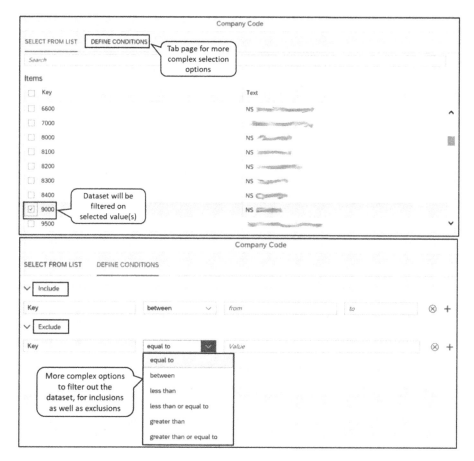

Figure 2-20. *Selection options for a dimension in the selection screen. Top: "Select from list." Bottom: "Define conditions"*

Once all the mandatory parameters are filled, the OK button becomes active (Figure 2-21). But please enter more restrictions on the dataset if you can, as this will improve the performance of the analytics session you are about to start.

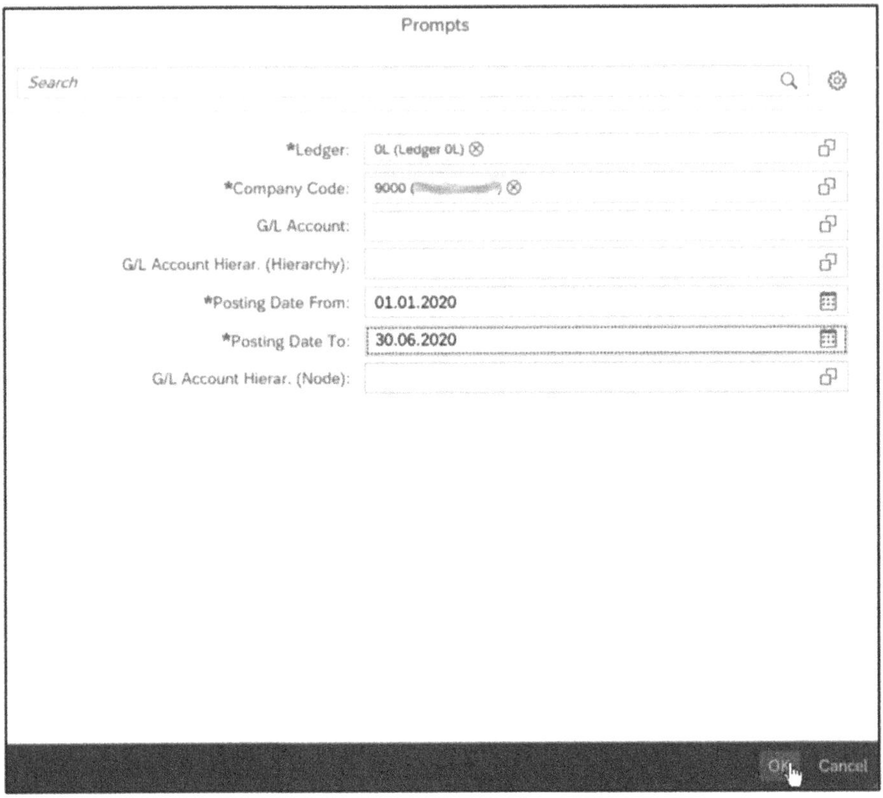

Figure 2-21. *Selection screen completed; analytics session can be started*

The initial view of a Design Studio app will be like what is shown in Figure 2-22. There are three areas for navigation: Columns, Rows, and Dimensions. The left half of the result area is dedicated to the dimensions, the right half to the measures. Both sections have their own scroll bar at the bottom. Measures are initially always in the columns, but dimensions can be in columns as well as rows. On the left side, there is a potentially long list of dimensions available that can be included in the output. Dimensions already used are indicated by a marker. Dimensions can be moved by dragging and dropping between the navigation areas. Such a navigational step is immediately reflected in the result area.

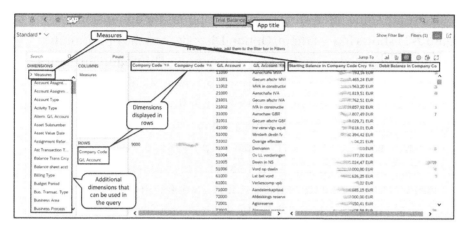

Figure 2-22. *Initial view of the Trial Balance app*

Adding or removing measures works a bit differently. To do this, the ➤ icon in front of Measures as the first line in the Dimensions navigational area needs to be clicked to display all the available measures (Figure 2-23). For the Trial Balance app, this is also quite a long list. Measures already in use are indicated by a marker. Measures can be added or removed by a right-click operation.

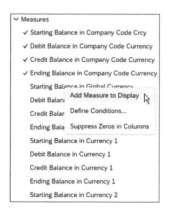

Figure 2-23. *Measures available for display*

There are some interesting right-click options for dimensions. Figure 2-24 shows four of them. Option Display gives the opportunity to display dimensions as either key, text, or both. The option Attributes presents a list of attributes that can be displayed in a column immediately to the right of the dimension. Attributes differ from dimensions in a sense that it is not possible to filter or navigate on attributes, so you can display them only. The option Hierarchy makes it possible to show the dimension in a hierarchical fashion, at least if a hierarchy is available. Jump To is an option so interesting we will dive into it in detail in the upcoming chapters. For now, it is sufficient to know the following: that it enables jumping to other apps usually giving more detailed information, that the list with jump targets shown depends on authorizations, and that it is extremely useful.

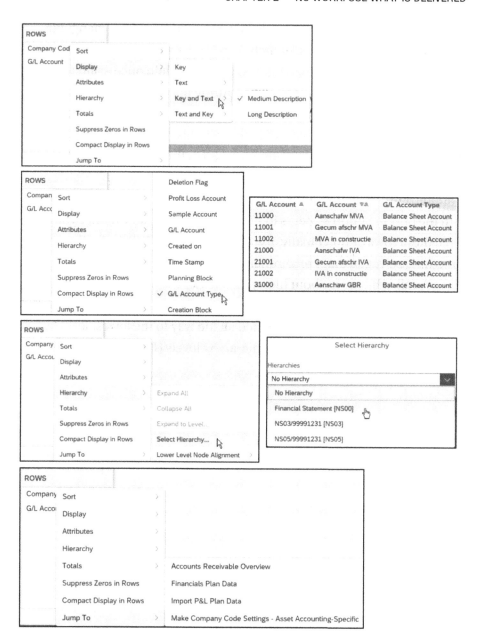

Figure 2-24. *Right-click options for the dimension G/L Account. From top to bottom: Display, Attributes, Hierarchy, and Jump-to*

Furthermore, the option Sort does the same thing as the triangular icons in the column headers, namely, sort. The option Totals can be used to switch on/off summarizations. Let me explain once again (boy did I have to explain this a lot to others during my career): if you want to see totals per dimension #1, you do not need to switch on totals for dimension #1, but for #2, if you want to see totals per dimension #2, you need to switch on totals for #3, and so on. So in this example, the totals per company code means switching on totals for G/L Account. Sigh. Let's continue. Rows with only zeros as measures can be either of interest or not. With the option Suppress Zeros in Rows, you can decide whether you want to see these rows or not. Finally, the option Compact Display in Rows does something so vague that I recommend you not use it.

Let's talk a bit more about hierarchies. After the hierarchical display has been switched on, the hierarchy usually presents itself as "collapsed" to the highest level and can be opened all the way to the lowest level by clicking the ➤ icons in front of the hierarchy levels (Figure 2-25).

G/L Account ⌅	G/L Account ⍗⌅	Starting Balance in Company Code Crcy ⍗⌅
> 0NS00	Financial Statement	0,00 EUR

G/L Account ⌅	G/L Account ⍗⌅	Starting Balance in Company Code Crcy ⍗⌅
∨ 0NS00	Financial Statement	0,00 EUR
∨ 01	Balans	0,00 EUR
∨ 010	Vaste activa	.995,96 EUR
∨ 0101	Materiële vaste acti	.791,12 EUR
∨ 00011	Materiële vaste acti	791,12 EUR
11000	Aanschafw MVA	.693,16 EUR
11001	Gecum afschr MVA	.465,24 EUR
11002	MVA in constructie	.563,20 EUR
211001	Tussenrek activa	0,00 EUR
> 0103	Immateriële vaste ac	.914,92 EUR
> 0104	Gebruiksrechten vast	.777,78 EUR
> 0105	Investeringen verwer	.618,01 EUR
> 0106	Ov fin vaste activa,	.700,90 EUR
> 0107	Latente belastingvor	.193,23 EUR
> 011	Vlottende activa	.936,23 EUR
> 012	Eigen vermogen	.685,15 EUR
> 014	Langlopende verplich	.413,43 EUR
> 015	Kortlopende verplich	.961,15 EUR
> 02	Resultaatsbijdrage	0,00 EUR

Figure 2-25. *Hierarchical display of dimension G/L Account collapsed to the highest level (top) and partially opened to the lowest level (bottom)*

Filtering is of course of crucial importance in any analytical application. We already saw one method of filtering, i.e., the selection screen appearing as soon as the app is started. Let me emphasize once again that any restriction on the dataset entered in this selection screen will have a positive impact on query performance for the entire analytics session that is to follow. This is lesson #1 for users complaining about query performance after neglecting the filtering options in the selection screen altogether. Once the analytics session has been started, clicking the button Filters in the top-right corner of the screen leads to the same type of filtering options shown in the selection screen, but now for all available dimensions (Figure 2-26). As in the selection screen, values can be typed into the entry field box or selected after clicking the icon for the value list. Also, more complex inclusions and exclusions are available in a Define Conditions tab. A new feature as compared with the selection screen is the option to mark dimensions for display on a separate Filter Bar. This Filter Bar is hidden by default, but the Show/Hide Filter Bar toggle button takes care of that. The Filter Bar is displayed and can be used simultaneously with the result set of the query.

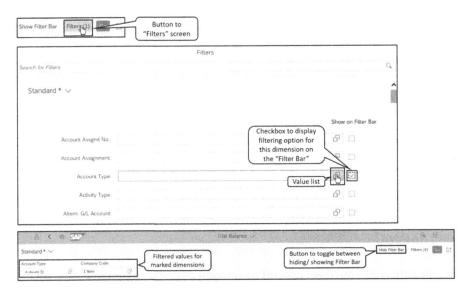

Figure 2-26. *Interactive filtering options for a Fiori Design Studio app. Values can be entered in a field box or after pressing the icon for a value list. Dimensions can be marked for display on a separate Filter Bar*

An even more interactive option to filter data is available as a right-click option on a dimension value (Figure 2-27). The options Filter Member and Filter Member and Remove from Axis differ in a sense that the former option leaves the dimension in display, whereas the latter option takes the dimension out, which can be a useful way to take two navigational steps at the same time. A limitation of this method of filtering is that it can be used to filter on only one dimension value, which is one of the drawbacks of doing analytics in a browser.

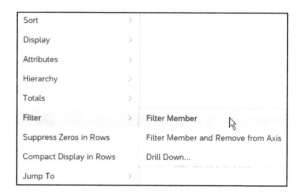

Figure 2-27. *Interactive filtering options after right-clicking a dimension value*

So far, we checked a number of right-click options on a dimension, but there are also interesting right-click options on measures. Figure 2-28 shows three of them. Like columns for dimensions, columns for measures have triangular sorting icons, and the Sort option here does the same. The option Number Format gives the opportunity to change the number of decimal places as well as introduce and display a scaling factor, e.g., to show the amounts in kEURs instead of eurocents.

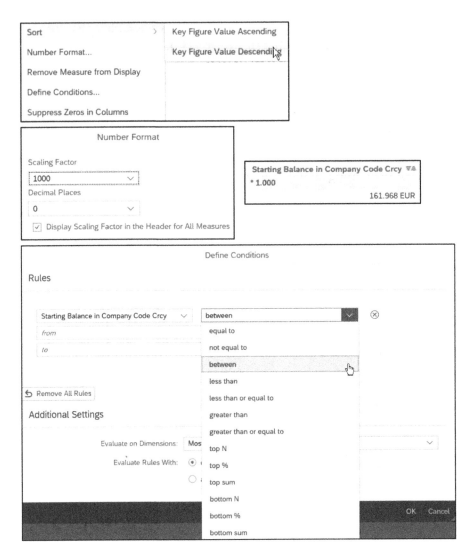

Figure 2-28. *Right-click options for a measure. From top to bottom: Sort, Number Format, and Define Conditions*

The options I skipped are Remove Measure from Display and Suppress Zeros in Columns, as these should be self-explanatory by now.

Last but not least, I want to explain some general-purpose buttons spread across the top part of the screen (Figure 2-29). If you plan on doing multiple navigational steps at the same time and you are not interested in the output while you are doing so, then the Pause button comes in handy. This will stall the response of the output area until you click the same button once again, which meanwhile received the name Refresh. Jump To is the same option as described previously, but now on a dataset level instead of row level. Option Settings ➤ Show Prompts brings back the selection screen filled in at the beginning of the analytics session. Two main applications of this setting are to remind the user what has been entered and to broaden the dataset in case this is necessary. Note that it is not necessary to leave the app and start over in order to broaden the dataset. The option Settings ➤ Totals provides settings for summarization on a dataset level, such as Show All, Hide All, and the position of the totals. The option Settings ➤ Information gives, well, information.

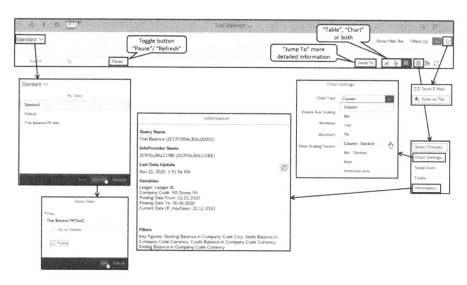

Figure 2-29. *General-purpose buttons*

Via three buttons, it is possible to switch between various modes of display: Table, Chart, or both. Table display is the default and also the most often used. Clicking the Chart button at a random point during a analytics session usually leads to a confusing graph, but clicking it after some careful preparation can lead to meaningful graphical information. Figure 2-30 shows an example in Graph and Table modes. Via Settings ➤ Chart Settings, the chart type and properties of the axes can be modified.

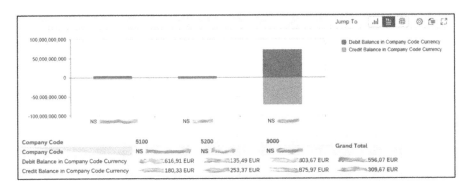

Figure 2-30. *Display mode Graph and Table*

The option Settings ➤ Swap Axes moves dimensions and measures from rows to columns and vice versa. It does so in Graph mode as well as in Table mode. We are used to measures being in columns and (most) dimensions being in rows, but in a situation with many measures, like in Profitability Analysis, it can be better to have measures in rows. In Figure 2-31, an example of the Trial Balance app is shown with a large number of measures displayed as rows. This example also demonstrates what happens to a measure in case of mixed currencies or units. In such a case, asterisks are displayed.

Transaction Currency	EUR	NOK	Grand Total
Starting Balance in Company Code Crcy	4,75 EUR	0,00 EUR	784,75 EUR
Debit Balance in Company Code Currency		,44 EUR	896,89 EUR
Credit Balance in Company Code Currency		,72 EUR	787,13 EUR
Ending Balance in Company Code Currency	.366,79 EUR		UR
Starting Balance in Global Currency	.784,75 EUR		UR
Debit Balance in Global Currency	.841,45 EUR		UR
Credit Balance in Global Currency	259,41 EUR		UR
Ending Balance in Global Currency	.366,79 EUR	,72 EUR	EUR
Starting Balance in Balance Currency	784,75 EUR	0,00 NOK	.
Debit Balance in Balance Currency	UR	,26 NOK	.
Credit Balance in Balance Currency	UR	,13 NOK	.
Ending Balance in Balance Currency	.366,79 EUR	.13 NOK	.
Starting Balance in Transaction Currency	.784,75 EUR	0,00 NOK	.
Debit Balance in Transaction Currency	.841,45 EUR	,26 NOK	.
Credit Balance in Transaction Currency	259,41 EUR	,13 NOK	.
Ending Balance in Transaction Currency	.366,79 EUR	,13 NOK	.

Callouts in figure: "Dimension(s) in columns"; "Asterisks are shown in case of mixed currencies or units"; "Measures in rows"

Figure 2-31. *Example output of the Trial Balance app with measures in rows*

I saved the two features shown in Figure 2-29 for last, as these are important in providing "self-service" to end users. The Actions button in the upper-right corner leads to the options Send E-Mail and Save as Tile. These options make it possible to store properties of the analytics session for oneself as a tile or to share it with others via email. Note that no data is stored, only the navigational state: selected dimensions and measures in rows and columns, filters, data formats, etc. The button Views in the upper-left corner provides the option to store a navigational state as a view for personal use or to share it with colleagues. For the latter, the checkbox Public needs to be marked. The view is then available for all users with access to the app. Needless to say, strict agreements and naming conventions are in order to avoid proliferation. Both the Actions button and the Views button make it easier for users to create and save their own version of the query. This will reduce the pressure on developers and the support organization to deliver multiple versions of the same query. One basic version should suffice; the users themselves can do the rest.

Export to Excel...Please Don't

By now, you are probably wondering why I put so much effort in describing the various functions of a Fiori Design Studio app. Also, there is one more option I did not cover yet. I will explain myself later, but first let me describe how this last option works.

The feature I skipped is a button in the top-right corner of the screen leading to the options Export to MS Excel and Export to MS Excel (Basic) (Figure 2-32). Both options do more or less the same thing, i.e., create an XLSX-file with data in the navigational state at the time the export was requested. The two options differ in the metadata sent along with the output data.

Figure 2-32. *Options to export to Microsoft Excel*

To be honest, this feature does not work well. If the output in the browser contains more than 10,000 rows, a warning message appears in the lower-left corner, advising the user among other things to "use the Excel Export functionality to view all results." Once a user does that, a new message appears warning the user against "memory and performance issues" and disclaiming that everything "will be at your own risk" (Figure 2-33). Hmm.

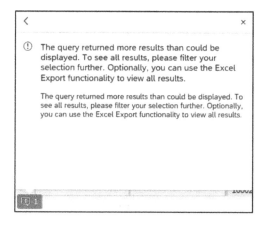

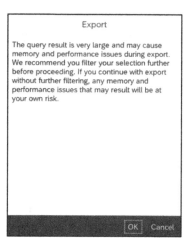

Figure 2-33. *Warning massages while displaying more than 10,000 rows in the browser (left) or exporting this data volume to Excel (right)*

The performance of the download is poor indeed. In the early stages of a project, we decided to fill a demo system using this type of download. A download of 30 columns times 25,000 records took 30 minutes, and I had to make several of such downloads. (Luckily, there was Champions League football on TV.) Please note that this is true only for Fiori Design Studio apps. Fiori UI5 apps like Display G/L Account Balances have much better performance when downloading to Excel.

Nonetheless, I feel the urge to speak out in defense of SAP. What is the point in displaying more than 10,000 records in a browser or downloading them to Excel? Is it humanly possible to oversee such a volume of data and draw conclusions from it? I know that I cannot. The way to use a BI tool is to start with a high-level overview and to drill down to a more detailed level only after filtering on a subset of data, and to do this step by step. All the while, there should be no more than a few screens of output. SAP's repeated advice "please filter your selection further" in my view makes all the sense in the world.

As stated in Chapter 1, Microsoft Excel is probably the most successful tool in the history of business intelligence. People are used to it and know how to use functions like pivot tables. Being introduced to new BI tooling, the thoughts of users usually go like this: "Hey, this is all very new. If only there was a button to export to Ex…. Ahh, thank God, there it is." End of brain activity. I am convinced that data analysis and decision support can be done well in a BI environment such as S/4HANA Embedded Analytics without exporting to Excel. The benefits of working directly on tables with reliable, real-time data outweigh any downsides there may be.

To summarize this section, there is an option to export to Excel. Please do not use it. You bought yourself an automobile. Stop using it as a dog cart!

Retrospective

One of the great artifacts of the Scrum methodology is the "retrospective": taking one's time to look back and draw conclusions. I will do so after each chapter in which embedded analytics functions or tools are presented.

What about the standard analytics content presented in this chapter? As stated, the appreciation of standard content is heavily influenced by cultural aspects. However, one should never skip the step of checking whether a business requirement can be fulfilled by standard content. If there is a shortcut, take it.

In Chapters 4 to 6, we will focus on creating custom-made analytical queries. The reason why I put so much effort into introducing you to all the features of a Fiori Design Studio app is that these analytical queries will be of the same type and will have the same features. An app like Trial Balance gives you the opportunity to organize a user training for custom-made analytical queries even before the first query has been created.

CHAPTER 3

Some Work: Smart Business Service

Some more work than using SAP-delivered apps, but still far from an expert tool: Smart Business Service. What is it? The SAP Help Portal tells us that it is "…a framework for exposing strategic (key) and operational performance indicators (KPIs, OPIs) as SAP Fiori applications without the need to write any code."[1] As shown in Figure 3-1, it is a codeless, menu-driven user interface, facts from which SAP draws the conclusion that the tooling is suitable for end users. The end product of a design session with the Smart Business Service is an actionable tile showing a figure or graph or, with some more effort, multiple tiles assembled in an overview page or analytical list page. Take a second look at Figure 2-5 in Chapter 2 to see what these Fiori page types are.

---

[1]SAP Help Portal on Smart Business Service: https://help.sap.com/viewer/ 352c8328eab24b80be4bf876355d340c/Cloud_Dev/en-US/b5aedca2bb934453a 51215f042f997d7.html

F. Keijzer, *SAP S/4HANA Embedded Analytics*, https://doi.org/10.1007/978-1-4842-7017-2_3

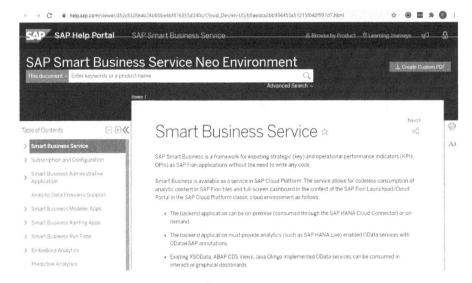

Figure 3-1. *SAP Help Portal on Smart Business Service*

Smart Business Service is often presented as an offering on the SAP Cloud Platform, but it is also available as a Fiori tile in S/4HANA. The tooling has been around for a while. The first demo I saw of it was in an online Fiori training in 2014.[2] And it apparently has been on the move ever since: changing tiles, changing functions, changing names. Recently, there has been a restructuring of the design-time tiles, from eleven tiles divided into two groups to only one tile (Figure 3-2).

---

[2]openSAP course "Introduction to SAP Fiori UX," September 2014, week 3 unit 8:
`https://open.sap.com/courses/fiori1`

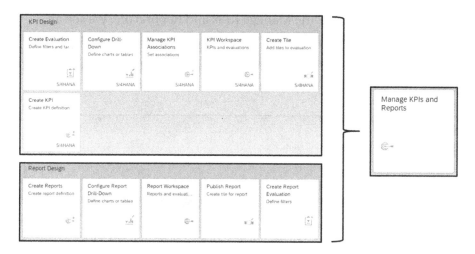

Figure 3-2. *Restructuring of tiles for Smart Business Service*

The Manage KPIs and Reports tile is part of business role SAP_BR_ANALYTICS_SPECIALIST. The same role provides access to the tile View Browser discussed in the previous chapter and the tiles Custom CDS Views and Custom Analytical Queries that will be discussed in the next chapter.

Demo

I felt somewhat reluctant to present a demo of the Smart Business Service tooling, as there are already so many demos available. An example is the excellent 2018 openSAP course called "Analytics with SAP Cloud Platform."[3] However, due to the continuous changes in the tooling, most of these demos are outdated. Add to this the fact that a colleague of mine was willing to set up such a demo on our example system, and *voila*, in this section you'll get a demo.

---

[3]openSAP course "Analytics with SAP Cloud Platform," June 2018, week 4 unit 1: https://open.sap.com/courses/cp6

For starters, let's click the Manage KPIs and Reports tile. We see an overview screen with separate KPI and Reports buttons (Figure 3-3). The KPI screen has Groups and KPIs tabs. With the + button, we can get to work by creating or editing a group.

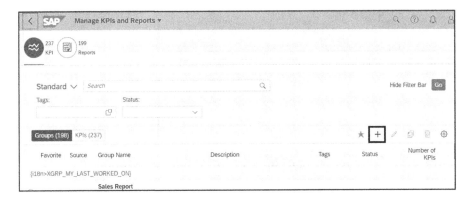

Figure 3-3. *Manage KPIs and Reports screen: initial view*

The next step is to create or edit a KPI (Figure 3-4). The most important step here is to select the data source. Various objects with the ability to generate an OData service can serve as a data source, e.g., a HANA calculation view, but in the context of this book, the option CDS view is the obvious choice. You'll learn more about OData services in Chapter 7. It took me a while to figure out which CDS views appear as a selection option on the Create KPI screen. One could expect that it has to do with a CDS view being "whitelisted" or not, but apparently the only criterion is the annotation odata.publish being present with the value true (Figure 3-5). As this implies that custom CDS views with the proper annotation can be selected, we chose the custom CDS view Z_SalesReport for the demo, and from this CDS view, we chose the key figure Net Value for the KPI.

Figure 3-4. *Creating or editing a KPI: selecting a data source*

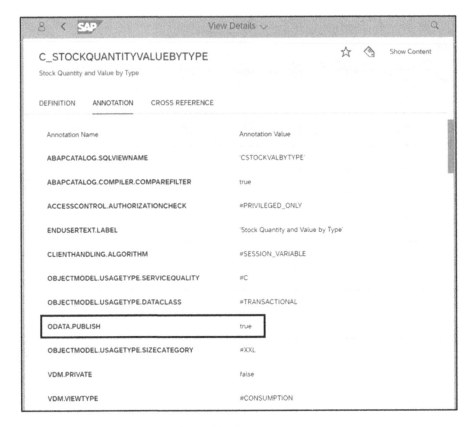

Figure 3-5. *CDS views selectable for a KPI*

Now comes the fun part: graphics. The screen in Figure 3-6 is quite colorful, but in the black-and-white version of the book you will not notice. The grayish color below 5200000 is red, the grayish color above 7000000 is green, and the grayish color in between is orange. You can choose fixed limits or limits relative to other key figures.

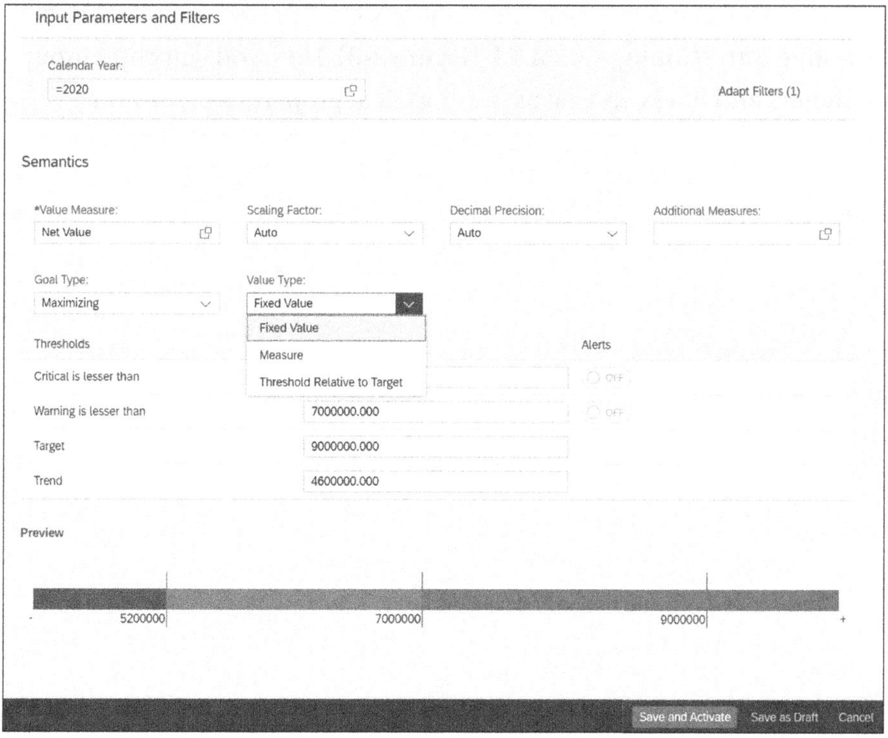

Figure 3-6. *Input parameters and filters*

As mentioned in the introduction, the end product will be an actionable tile showing a figure or a graph. The action behind the tile will be a report, either tabular or graphical. To start building such a report from the KPI Details screen, click Create Report and then select Generic Drilldown (Figure 3-7).

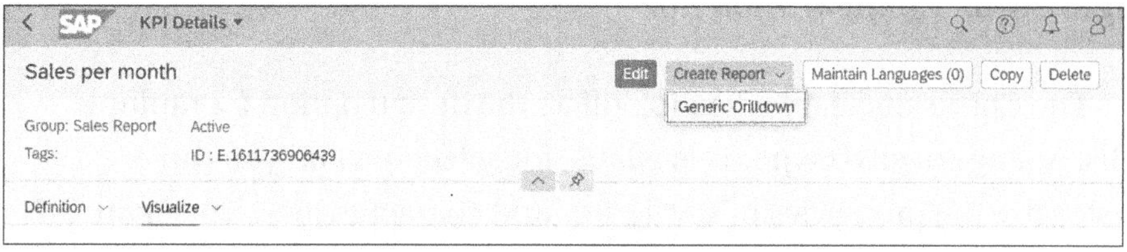

Figure 3-7. *Create Report screen*

On the Definition tab, enter descriptions for Title and Subtitle. More interesting is the Configuration tab (Figure 3-8). Here you can enter input parameters and filters, as well as the graphical properties of the end product.

Figure 3-8. *Configuration tab*

The Charts and Tables section offers the design option for multiple tabs. A range of chart types is available for selection, and you can customize the properties of key figures and characteristics. See Figure 3-9 for details.

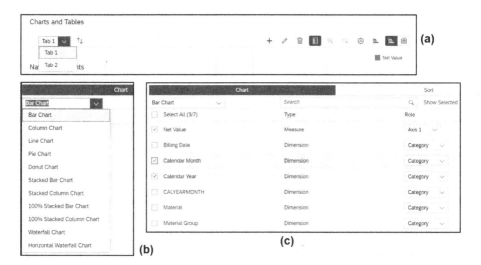

Figure 3-9. *Charts and Tables section: (a) multiple tabs, (b) chart types, (c) properties of key figure and characteristics*

The Visualize tab of the KPI Details screen allows us to lay out the properties of the tile, as shown in Figure 3-10. Clicking the + here allows us to select the tile type options shown in Figure 3-11. We selected the bottom-right option.

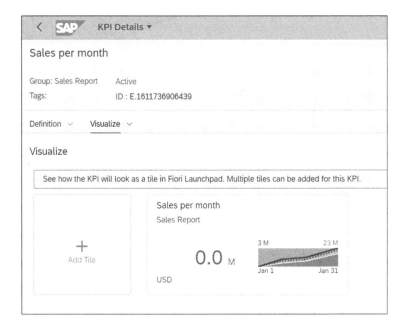

Figure 3-10. *Selecting KPI details on the Visualize tab*

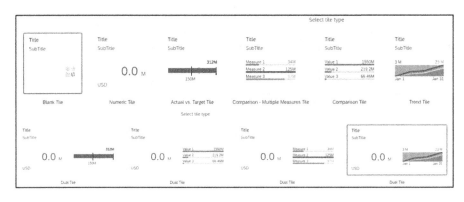

Figure 3-11. *Selecting the tile type*

The final step in the design process is the Create Application screen. Figure 3-12 shows what kind of data needs to be entered here, e.g., technical catalog. Not shown is the Target Mapping screen. You'll learn more about target mapping in Chapter 6.

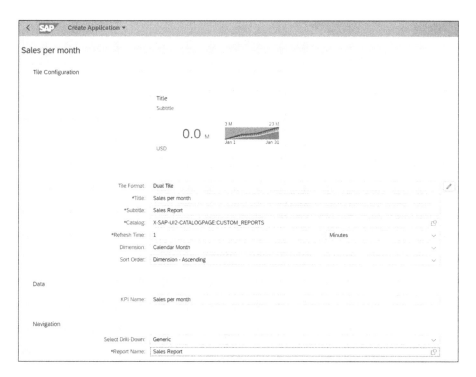

Figure 3-12. *Creating an application*

Figure 3-13 shows the end result of the design process. The actionable tile leads to a tabular report and a graphical report. The Refresh icon of the tile shows Now as the tile was recently refreshed.

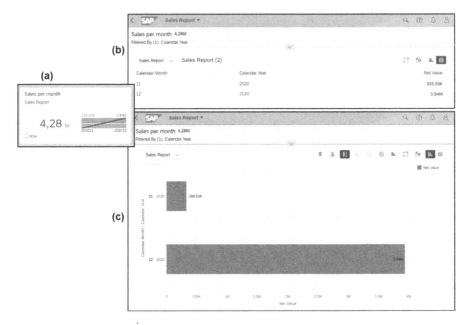

Figure 3-13. *End product: (a) KPI tile, (b) drilldown to tabular report, (c) drilldown to graphical report*

There are some more options not explored in this demo (e.g., navigational intents and combining Smart Business Service with the Analysis Path Framework[4]), but I am sure you get the general idea for what this tooling can bring.

Retrospective

By now you are probably wondering about two things: why does this chapter present a demo example and not a productive example, and also, why is this chapter so short?

---

[4]SAP Help Portal on Analysis Path Framework: https://help.sap.com/viewer/
468a97775123488ab3345a0c48cadd8f/7.40.15/en-US/1c457c53595a6655e10
000000a423f68.html

Good questions. Let me start by answering the first one. The project in which I am currently involved is the largest S/4HANA implementation in the Netherlands, so there are plenty of opportunities to apply all sorts of tooling. I was not involved from the start of the project, and when I arrived, a proactive functional consultant had already built an analytical application with Smart Business Service, i.e., a financial application named Debtors Top 10. This was great! In Chapter 1, I shared my opinion that SAP has the tendency to either overestimate the ability of its user groups or underestimate the user-friendliness of its software, leading to the situation in which a tool is often used by a user group "one level higher" than the target audience as intended by SAP. SAP positions Smart Business Service as a user tool, which raised my expectations that the tool would be suitable for functional consultants, such as finance consultants building financial analytical applications, MM consultants building MM apps, PM consultants building PM apps, and me binge-watching Netflix. I therefore put time and effort into promoting this tool with all the functional consultant involved in the project. To no success. No one followed. But what happened to the financial application already built by the proactive project team member? Its sad fate was that it somehow "got lost" during the journey through DTAP. No business user cared enough to test it, so it was overwritten by system copies and buried in the graveyard of unused developments. Here's the short answer to the question: there was no productive example in this chapter because I do not have any.

Now for the second question: why is this chapter so short? Could it be that I have little confidence in the future of this tooling? I am afraid it could. The fact that no application designed with Smart Business Service made it to the finish line in the largest S/4HANA implementation in the Netherlands is a bad sign. In a project, the priority lies with fulfilling concrete business requirements. Smart Business Service applications will at best partially overlap with certain business requirements but will rarely fulfill them completely. In my experience, Smart Business Service has all the characteristics of a "prom queen of the demo ball."

CHAPTER 4

More Work: Building Analytical Queries Using Tiles

It's time to build our first custom analytical query (aka multidimensional report aka analytical app) of type Design Studio. In S/4HANA Embedded Analytics, this is the real thing.

For this chapter, let's pretend we are in a SaaS-version S/4HANA environment. Why? There are two reasons to pretend we are in a SaaS-version S/4HANA environment. First, we really might be in a SaaS-version S/4HANA environment. Second, even if we are not, we want to stay compatible with SaaS version S/4 by using only the development methods allowed for SaaS S/4. Such compatibility has, of course, clear advantages if there are concrete plans to move to SaaS version S/4 on short notice, but even if this is not the case, there is the advantage that testing efforts after upgrades can be reduced. System updates can involve database and process changes that impact the overall data model. For a SaaS system, it is the responsibility of the software vendor to correct for these changes in such a way that there is no impact on the virtual data model (VDM) made available for users. In other words, if in an on-premise situation you make use of the access to the system back end by bypassing the VDM, the update problems are yours to solve; if not, the update problems are SAP's.

© Freek Keijzer 2021
F. Keijzer, *SAP S/4HANA Embedded Analytics*, https://doi.org/10.1007/978-1-4842-7017-2_4

As mentioned, in SaaS version S/4, tiles are all you have. For the work described in this chapter, the four tiles shown in Figure 4-1 are your friends.

Figure 4-1. *Tiles for apps used in the process of developing analytical queries in a SaaS-compatible manner*

The app View Browser is the best way to explore SAP-delivered CDS views of all types. The view Query Browser can be used in many ways such as to discover SAP-delivered analytical queries and to test-drive analytical queries, either SAP-delivered or custom. However, the app can also be used to give access to analytical queries in a productive environment. The apps Custom CDS Views and Custom Analytical Queries are the SaaS options for developing custom analytical queries and underlying composite views. All these apps will be covered in the upcoming sections of this chapter.

Discovery of SAP-Delivered CDS Views with Tiles View Browser and Query Browser

I definitely have spent a lot of time browsing for standard SAP views, and I have reached the conclusion that the app delivered by SAP for this purpose is the best way to do this. Clicking the View Browser tile leads to the initial view shown in Figure 4-2. Nothing is in the search bar yet, so the list and the statistics shown are for all CDS views in the system, standard as well as custom. Views are ordered alphabetically by name, which is why the first ones are funny ones starting with slashes. The Release Status column specifies whether the view can be used in a SaaS environment. Views with the release status Yes are also called *whitelisted*.

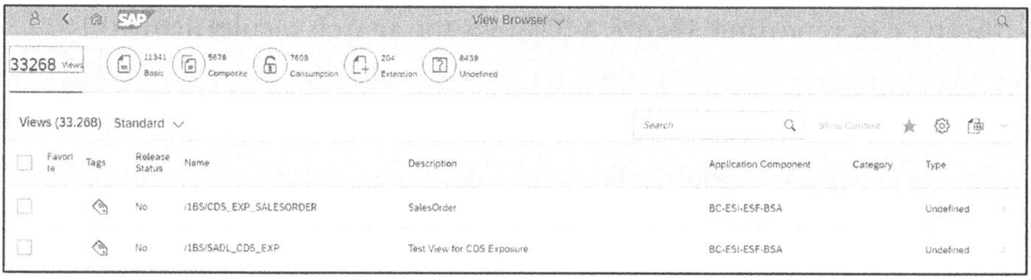

Figure 4-2.   *Initial view after opening the app View Browser*

But now, how do we effectively use the search bar? Let me start with a practical pointer for SAP dinosaurs like me: do not use asterisks. It took me several months to break this habit. It is a Google-like search method: the search string is looked for in all parts (beginning, middle, end) of all aspects (name, description, properties) of the CDS view. The result set of the search is often larger than what you might have hoped for, but on the bright side, it is hard to miss something this way.

Then what do we put into the search bar? You can of course use the old-school German abbreviations for table names, like BKPF (Belegkopf für Buchhaltung) or BSEG (Belegsegment Buchhaltung), or field names, like BUKRS (Buchungskreis) or GJAHR (Geschäftsjahr). Yes, with old-school SAP it helps a lot if you speak a little German. But then you will mainly find more basic CDS views that still use the original table and field names. The SAP developers of CDS views seem to have a tendency to replace the short, German-based abbreviations for table and field names with longer English-based names like CompanyCode or FiscalYear. To find less basic CDS views, it is therefore better to use such English-based names.

Let's jump to the search method I like most. Your interest will usually be in a specific reporting domain like Inventory or General Ledger

Accounting. During initial searching on field names and other terms, you will find results within a specific application component. For CDS views within the General Ledger Accounting domain, for example, you will notice that the views lie within an application component named FI-GL-IS. Entering this in the search bar gives you all the CDS views relevant for this type of reporting. Figure 2-3 shows the search results using this method; there are 847 views of which 542 are Basic, 149 are Composite, and 19 are Consumption. That's a large number of views, but user-friendly filtering options are available. For example, clicking the Consumption icon and filtering on a column Category equal to Query gives the result set of the five views shown in Figure 4-3.

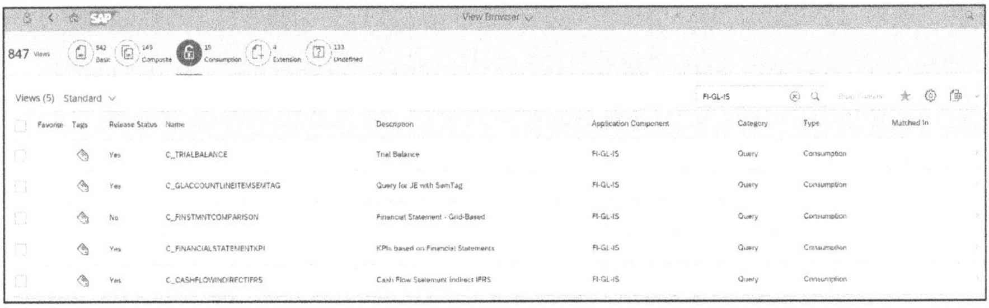

Figure 4-3.   *Search results in the View Browser app using the application component as a search term*

Let's take a moment to plot all the different types of CDS views in the data modeling layers of Figure 1-3 in Chapter 1. Remember the raw-data layer, data-integration layer, cube layer, and query layer? What SAP calls Basic views can be plotted in the lowest part of the data-integration layer, directly above the physical tables. Composite views are also in the data-integration layer, except for composite views of type Cube, which belong in the cube layer. Finally, Consumption views of type Query constitute the query layer. For brevity, I will often use the term *query view* for Consumption views of type Query, and *cube view* for Composite views of type Cube.

SAP applies the following naming convention for the standard CDS views: Basic and Composite views start with I_, where the I stands for "interfacing" referring to the role these views play between physical tables and queries. Consumption views start with C_, where the C stands for... well, "consumption," of course. There is a group of standard CDS views starting with P_, where P stands for "private." These are not meant to be reused, so I propose not to reuse them. Finally, there are views of type Consumption starting with A_, with A standing for "API." These views are meant for external use. In the final chapter, APIs are covered in more detail. Figure 4-4 shows a graphical overview of these different types of views including their naming conventions.

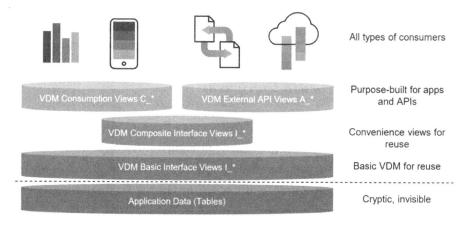

Figure 4-4. *Naming convention of SAP-delivered CDS views (source: S4H220 – Implementation Patterns for Core Data Services Views in SAP S/4HANA;* `https://www.sap.com/documents/2018/01/0a2348e2-ee7c-0010-82c7-eda71af511fa.html` *©SAP AG, 2017)*

The standard CDS views of type Consumption and category Query are particularly interesting, as they are ready-to-use analytical queries. If one exists that matches your requirements, you are done! You do not even have to transport anything, as the SAP-delivered CDS views are part of the software and exist all through your DTAP system landscape. For SAP newbies, DTAP means Development, Testing, Acceptance, and Production. So, please always check if you can take this shortcut. The tile Query Browser can be used to open and test-drive these queries, as shown in Figure 4-5.

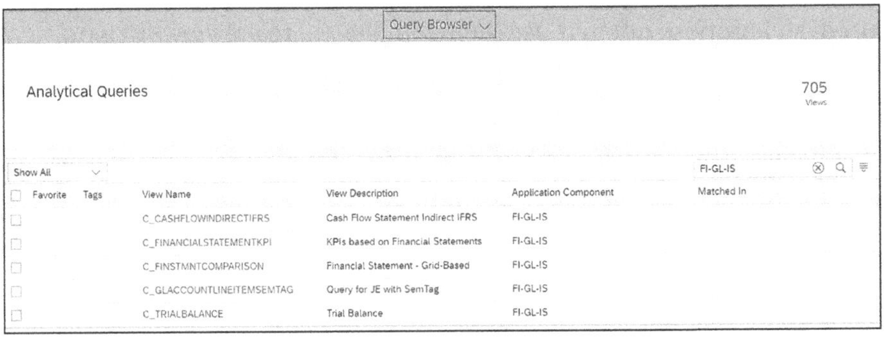

Figure 4-5. *Search results in the Query Browser app using the application component as a search term*

Not by accident, this is the same result set of five views as obtained with View Browser and shown previously in Figure 4-3. Apparently, queries that are not released are available for the app Query Browser and can be used productively. Once again, we bump into a Trial Balance. Let's focus on this query for a moment.

In Figure 4-6, information details obtained via the app View Browser and the app Query Browser are compared. Both apps present a list of field names with some properties and annotations. The information tab Cross Reference is available only for View Browser. View Browser has a Show Content button, which to be honest does not always work. Query Browser has a Open for Analysis button, which does always work and which kicks off the query as an app of type Design Studio in an environment described extensively in Chapter 2.

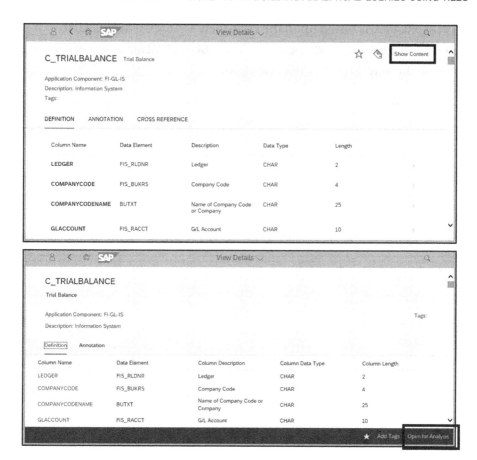

Figure 4-6. *Information for a CDS view of type Consumption in the category Query via the app View Browser (top) versus Query Browser (bottom)*

The information in the Cross References tab via the app View Browser is quite interesting, as shown in Figure 4-7. Usually, there is a long list of views with a master data relation. For a query view, a master data relation is denoted with Relation equal to Left Outer Join, for other views a master data relation is denoted as Association with a certain cardinality. But the most interesting information is the CDS view with Relation equal to From, as this is the underlying view on which the view is primarily based. Using the app View Browser, you can find out that the query view

99

C_TRIALBALANCE is based upon the cube view I_GLACCTBALANCECUBE, which on its term is based upon the view I_GLACCTBALANCE, and so on, and so on, all the way down to the basic views.

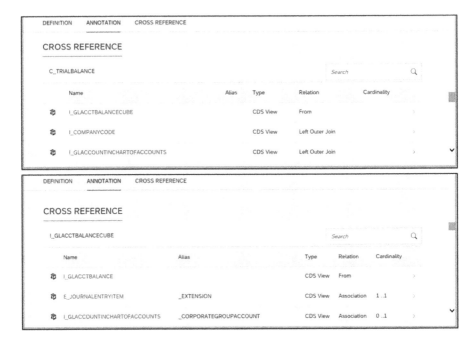

Figure 4-7. *Information in the tab Cross References via the app View Browser for a query view (top) and an underlying cube view (bottom)*

In conclusion, the tiles View Browser and Query Browser can be used to explore the available SAP-delivered CDS views. Query Browser can also be used to test-drive standard query views. In an ideal world, a standard query view exists that matches your requirements, and you are done. If not, you can use View Browser to identify cube views as potential candidates to build custom analytical queries on top of. That brings us to the next section of this chapter.

Custom Analytical Query in an Almost Ideal Situation: Part 1

In an ideal situation, a ready-to-use SAP-delivered query view exists that matches your requirements. In a slightly less ideal situation, no such query view exists, but there is a strong standard cube view upon which a custom query view can be based. I will present that example in this section.

The example involves the most popular business case of all: actual-plan comparison in the financial domain. It is hard to find an SAP ERP system without actual financial amounts, and often planned amounts are also present. The purpose of the latter is to compare the actuals to check whether the income and/or expenses are still within the prediction or budget. The application component for this type of financial data is FI-GL-IS, not coincidentally the example used in the previous section. By now we know we need to search for composite views of type Cube not starting with P_ but with I_. While the app Query Browser can work with unreleased query views, the app Custom Analytical Queries cannot work with unreleased cube views. Applying all relevant filters to the search in View Browser leads to an overseeable list of 17 views, one of which has the promising description "Actual Plan Comparison for Journal Entry Item" and technical name I_ActualPlanJournalEntryItem. Inspecting this cube view via View Browser gives a long list of available fields, which is always a good sign; all the right annotations; and also a long list of associations, which means that the cube view is heavily enriched with master data.

We can now also do the exercise described in the previous section, i.e., using the app View Browser repetitively to find the underlying views via the information on the Cross References tab all the way down to the physical tables. You know you are at the end of this exercise when you see something like what is shown in Figure 4-8.

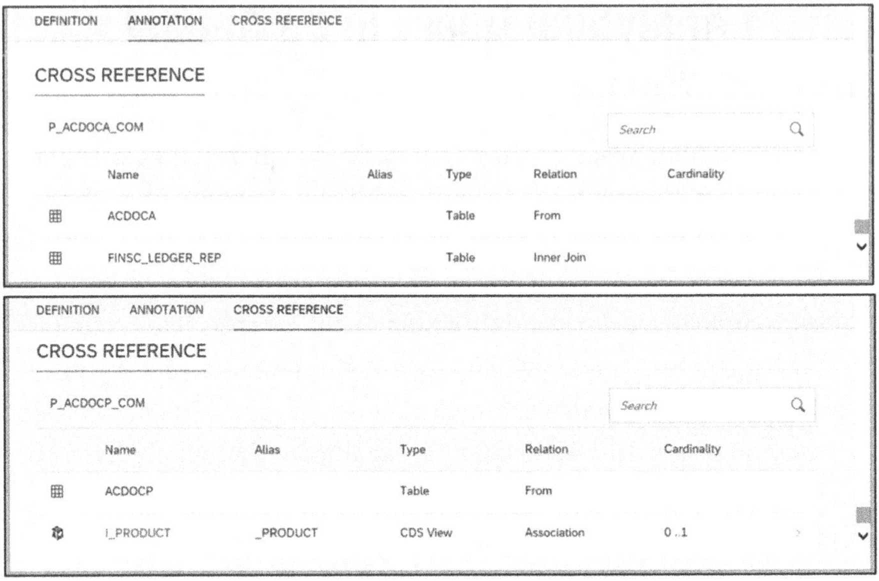
DEFINITION
ANNOTATION
CROSS REFERENCE
CROSS REFERENCE
P_ACDOCA_COM
Search
Name
Alias
Type
Relation
Cardinality
ACDOCA
Table
From
FINSC_LEDGER_REP
Table
Inner Join
DEFINITION
ANNOTATION
CROSS REFERENCE
CROSS REFERENCE
P_ACDOCP_COM
Search
Name
Alias
Type
Relation
Cardinality
ACDOCP
Table
From
I_PRODUCT
_PRODUCT
CDS View
Association
0..1

***Figure 4-8.** Information on the tab Cross References via the app View Browser for two basic views*

Now I want to show you something that will make it absolutely clear that I already was an adolescent during the early days of the computer era. I like to make overviews such as the one shown here:

```
I_ActualPlanJournalEntryItem
|- P_ActualPlanJrnlEntryItm (union)
   |- I_GLAccountLineItem
   |  |- P_Acdoca_Cube
   |     |- P_ACDOCA_COM
   |        |- acdoca
   |        |- finsc_ledger_rep
   |- I_FinancialPlanningEntryItem
      |- P_ACDOCP_COM
         |- acdocp
```

You can laugh if you want. But this text-style overview does have the advantage that you can add it to all kinds of documents as well as inline comments in your code. By the way, it works best with a monospaced font. The overview clearly – yes, clearly - demonstrates the layered structure of CDS views from the cube view down to tables. The main tables in this setup are the relatively new Simple Finance tables Universal Journal Entry Line Items (ACDOCA) and Plan Data Line Items (ACDOCP). Simple Finance is a term we are not allowed to use anymore by SAP, but I am a rebel. Universal Journals combine information from various types of financial documents (Finance, Controlling, Profit Center Accounting, etc.) from the pre–Simple Finance era, which implies that ACDOCA combines data from tables such as Accounting Document Segment (BSEG), CO Object: Line Items (by Period) (COEP), and more. Planning data also used to be scattered across the entire database but is now neatly combined in the table ACDOCP. In conclusion, the table content, on which this cube view is based, is excellent for our purposes.

We can also see that this stack of CDS views is not something we can build ourselves with tile Custom CDS Views. The only data modeling option this app has to offer is adding associations, which technically are left outer joins. This stack of CDS views has a view applying the union operator to combine the Actuals and Plan key figures, and inner join clauses are applied as well, e.g., to join the ACDOCA and FINSC_LEDGER_REP tables. If unions, inner joins, or aggregations via the GROUP BY clause are required in the data model, the only thing you can do in a SaaS environment is hope that SAP has done this for you in one of its standard CDS views or will do so in future releases.

But this time we are lucky. The cube view I_ActualPlanJournalEntry Item looks like an excellent basis for our financial actuals-plan comparison report. So, let's get started. First we'll see how far we get using only the tile Custom Analytical Query. Click the tile, and a screen appears as shown in Figure 4-9. It contains a list of existing views of type Consumption in the category Query, most of which are SAP-delivered. As we want to build a new query, click New. A mandatory prefix is something like YY1_ or ZZ1_, depending on the system settings. As the data source is named I_ActualPlanJournalEntryItem, I would have preferred to name the analytical view ZZ1_ActualPlanJournalEntryItem, but that is too long. The name ZZ1_ActPlanJEItem works. Click OK to continue.

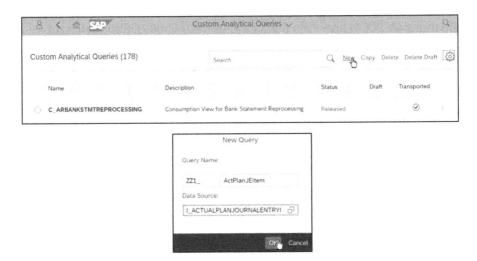

Figure 4-9. *Custom analytical queries: starting and entering the basics*

The next screen is explains the development process with arrows urging us to go from left to right: General >>> Field Selection >>> Display >>> Filters. On the General tab, we only need to fill in a label for the query (Figure 4-10).

8	<	SAP	Custom Analytical Queries
Actual Plan Comparison for Journal Entry Item (ZZ1_ACTPLANJEITEM)			Status: Draft
General >>> Field Selection >>> Display >>> Filters			
Label:	Actual Plan Comparison for Journal Entry Item		
Name:	ZZ1_ACTPLANJEITEM		
Data Source:	Actual Plan Comparison for Journal Entry Item (I_ACTUALPLANJOURNALENTRYI...		
Changed At:	01/09/2021,09:09:48		

Figure 4-10. *Custom analytical queries: General tab*

The tab Field Selection is where we can pick our fields (Figure 4-11). The standard cube view offers 170 (!) fields to choose from. I want to keep it simple and high level, so I pick only two amounts and the high-level characteristics Company Code, Fiscal Year and Fiscal Period, Ledger, and Profit Center. The characteristic Category (`PlanningCategory`) is used in table `ACDOCP` for a planning version, so I need that as well. I had some difficulties finding the field for Account, so I used the available search bar on the left.

Figure 4-11. *Custom analytical queries: Field Selection tab*

The tab Display shows that by default key figures are placed in columns and characteristics as free characteristics (Figure 4-12). Without modifications, the initial display of the query will show one record with two columns with amounts and no dimensions. I want the initial display to show GL Account in rows, so I change that. Other things I could do in this tab are change the label, add a results row, or change the default display format (key, text, or both), but I will leave everything at the defaults for the moment. For key figures there are other options, but I will leave these at the defaults as well.

Figure 4-12. *Custom analytical queries: Display tab*

Onward to the next tab: Filters (Figure 4-13). There are a few things I need to do here. First, I need to filter on one specific ledger; otherwise, all the amounts are doubled or tripled. I also add user input filters on Company Code and Fiscal Year, using different options: single value or interval, single or multiple selection, optional or mandatory, with or without default value. Let's see how these filters work out in practice.

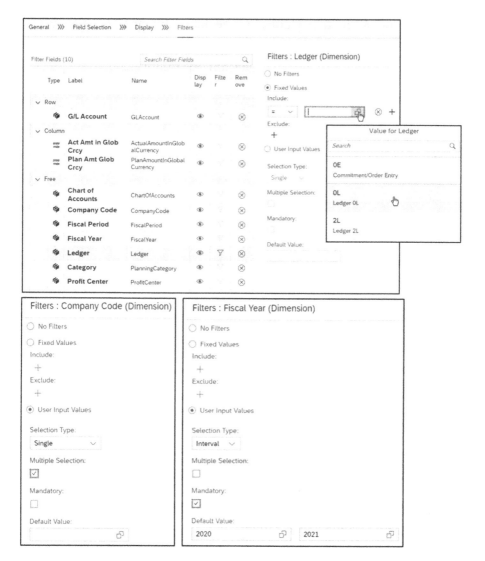

Figure 4-13. *Custom analytical queries: Filters tab*

We can now test-drive the analytical query with the tile Query Browser. The View Details screen gives an overview of all the selected fields with some metadata (Figure 4-14). As mentioned earlier, the column name in standard SAP cube views or query views is always different from the technical name of a field in a table, but the data element often gives away the source of the field, as this does not change when traveling from the table via the basic view to the cube view and the query view.

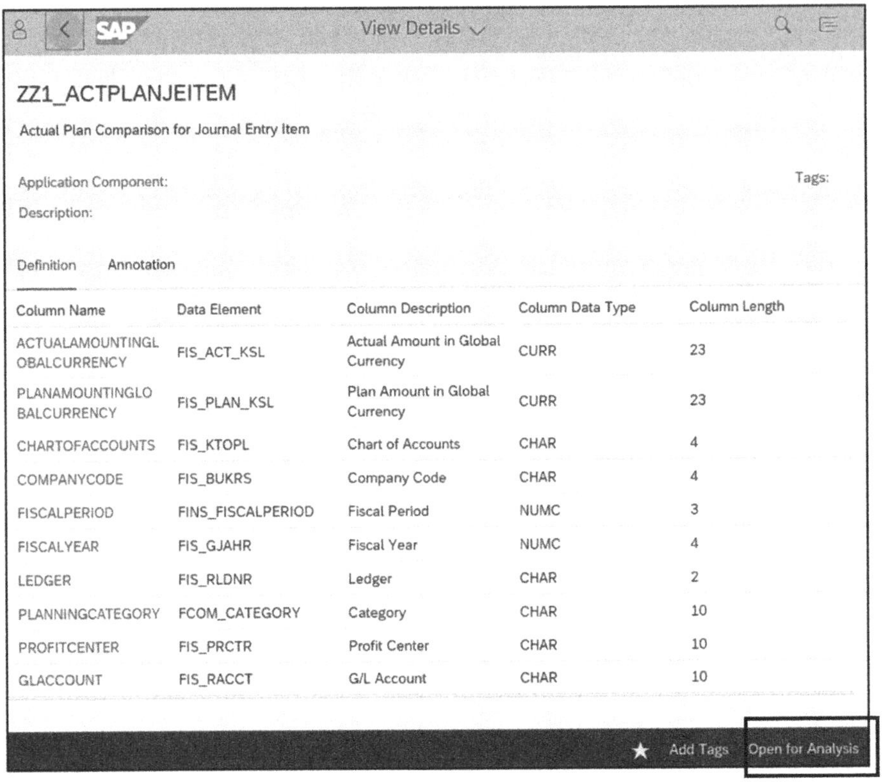

Column Name	Data Element	Column Description	Column Data Type	Column Length
ACTUALAMOUNTINGLOBALCURRENCY	FIS_ACT_KSL	Actual Amount in Global Currency	CURR	23
PLANAMOUNTINGLOBALCURRENCY	FIS_PLAN_KSL	Plan Amount in Global Currency	CURR	23
CHARTOFACCOUNTS	FIS_KTOPL	Chart of Accounts	CHAR	4
COMPANYCODE	FIS_BUKRS	Company Code	CHAR	4
FISCALPERIOD	FINS_FISCALPERIOD	Fiscal Period	NUMC	3
FISCALYEAR	FIS_GJAHR	Fiscal Year	NUMC	4
LEDGER	FIS_RLDNR	Ledger	CHAR	2
PLANNINGCATEGORY	FCOM_CATEGORY	Category	CHAR	10
PROFITCENTER	FIS_PRCTR	Profit Center	CHAR	10
GLACCOUNT	FIS_RACCT	G/L Account	CHAR	10

Figure 4-14. *Test-driving the custom analytical query via the app Query Browser: View Details screen*

Clicking the button Open for Analysis brings us to the next step: the selection screen (Figure 4-15). It looks perfect. Filter on Fiscal Year has a star, meaning it is mandatory. The default values are filled in, but these can be overwritten. You can select multiple single values for Company Code. There's nothing to improve here. Let's click OK and move on.

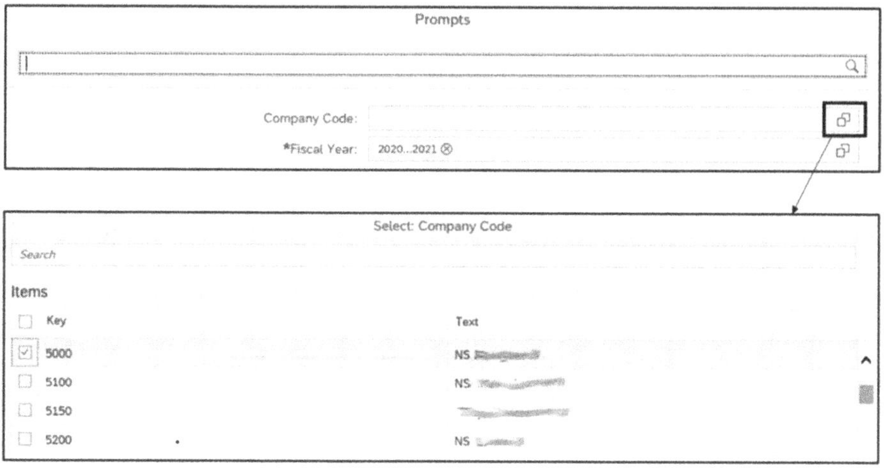

Figure 4-15. *Test-driving the custom analytical query via the app Query Browser: selection screen*

The next screen shows the initial display of the query result: Actual and Plan amounts in the columns and G/L Account in the rows—so far so good (Figure 4-16). But there are some features I do not like. Apparently the default format option for characteristics is the key only. A user can switch that to key and text, but it would be preferable to have that format as an initial display for G/L Account, Company Code, and Profit Center.

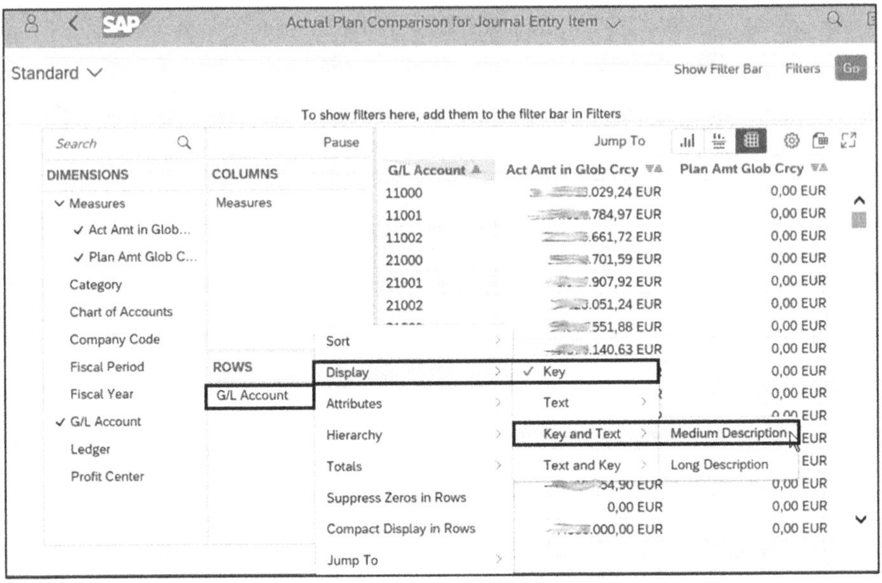

Figure 4-16. *Test-driving the custom analytical query via the app Query Browser: initial query output*

For the key figures, I also see some potential optimizations. First, I would like to get rid of the euro cents. Second, let's work on the labels. The actual amount is named Actual Amount in Global Currency on the View Details screen, and Act Amt in Glob Crcy in the query output itself. The latter is an ugly name. Figure 4-17 shows where these descriptions come from. Unless a description is overwritten between the table and cube view or query view, descriptions are delivered by the data element. The View Details screen shows the property Short Description of the data element, and the query output shows the Field Label version of length 20. Overwriting the label in the custom analytical query only affects the query output, not the View Details screen.

Data element	FIS_ACT_KSL		Active
Short Description	Actual Amount in Global Currency		

Attributes	Data Type	Further Characteristics	Field Label

	Length	Field Label
Short	10	Act Amt GC
Medium	20	Act Amt in Glob Crcy
Long	40	Actual Amount in Global Currency
Heading	40	Act Amt in Glob Crcy

Figure 4-17. *Source of field descriptions in CDS views*

I also need to do something about the planning versions. The dimension Category has the value ACT01 for Actuals and values like PLN or similar for Plan. I need to filter on ACT01 plus one of the planning versions to avoid all planning versions being summed up.

Checking the attributes of G/L Account, I find two of them particularly interesting: Account Group and the indicator Profit Loss Account (Figure 4-18). These are already available as attributes in this version of the query thanks to all the master data associations in the standard cube view, but I would like to use them more dynamically for filtering and separate drilldown, in other words, as a dimension. The query output now starts with balance accounts, and users will often not be interested in those accounts, only in profit and loss accounts. The indicator Profit Loss Account can be used to filter this out. Up to this point, all optimizations I had in mind could be dealt with in the app Custom Analytical Query, but for adding the attributes as dimensions, we need the app Custom CDS View.

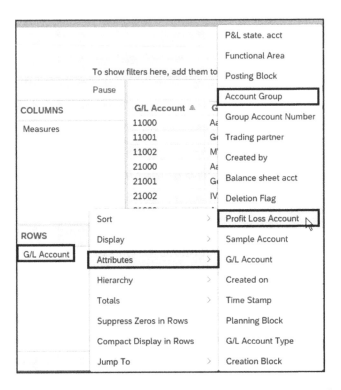

Figure 4-18. *Test-driving the custom analytical query via the app Query Browser: checking the attributes of G/L Account*

Custom CDS View in an Almost Ideal Situation

We are hands-on types of people, so let's click the tile Custom CDS View to see where this brings us. It brings us to the screen shown in Figure 4-19: a list of existing CDS views and a Create button.

Figure 4-19. *Custom CDS Views screen: starting the app for a new CDS view*

Once again, the first screen explains the development process with arrows going from left to right: General >>> Field Selection >>> Field Properties >>> Parameters >>> Filters. On the General tab, we need to fill in a label, decide whether this view is for external (OData API) or internal (Analytical) use, decide whether the view will be of type Cube or Dimension, and choose a primary data source to start with (Figure 4-20). In this app we can build a cube view connecting facts to dimensions. But in this almost ideal situation with a very rich standard cube view being available, I only want to slightly modify this cube view for our purpose. I therefore choose the cube view we used for the first version of the custom analytical query as a primary data source, I_ActualPlanJournalEntryItem.

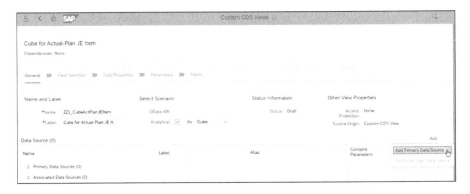

Figure 4-20. *Custom CDS Views screen: General tab, adding the primary data source*

On the next screen, Field Selection, we are in for a surprise (Figure 4-21). Building a cube view on top of a rich standard cube view, we apparently have a staggering number of 48,492 (!) fields and associations to choose from. Most of these are fields via associations (via associations...via associations...), so you may want to use the search bar on the left side. On the right side, you see some key fields that cannot be left out of the custom cube view. These are the key fields of the ACDOCA and ACDOCP tables. Not to worry: they can be left out of the query view.

Figure 4-21. *Field Selection tab: using the search bar*

There are a couple of things we need to do:

1. Find and select all the characteristics we need for the query. Ledger, Fiscal Year, and Company Code are already in as they are key fields. Profit Center, Category, and G/L Account need to be added. G/L Account has Chart of Accounts as a compounding key, and it's the same for Profit Center and Controlling Area, so these need to be added as well.

2. Select not only the required key figures but also the accompanying currency and unit fields. In our case, this means also select the currency field Global Currency.

3. Select Account Group and the indicator Profit Loss Account from the association I_GLAccountInChartOfAccounts, renamed as _GLAccountInChartOfAccounts. The same association appears on many levels in cube views like this one, so it is important to use the association directly below the primary data source. In Figure 4-22 this means the bottom one for Account Group, not the top one.

4. In the version of the analytical view built directly on top of the standard cube view, we had attributes and text available for Company Code, Profit Center, and G/L Account. But we will lose this functionality, unless we propagate the accompanying associations further in our custom cube view. To achieve this, we need to select the associations _CompanyCode, _ProfitCenter, and _GLAccountInChartOfAccounts. Once again, be careful to pick the right ones (Figure 4-22).

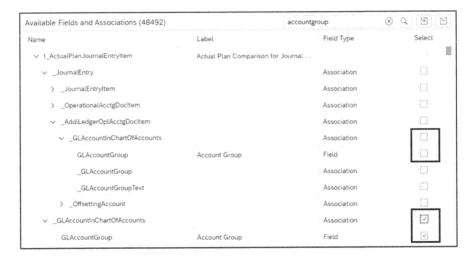

Figure 4-22. *Field Selection tab: selecting associations and fields from associations*

The next step in the development process is the screen Field Properties. Figure 4-23 shows the things you can do in this screen. The column Aggregation is required for all key figures. Usually you fill in the sum for amounts and quantities and the max for things like prizes. The columns Semantics and Semantic Value couple the field to useful metadata, e.g., a couple of key figures to the appropriate currency or unit field. In the column Master Data View, the accompanying view for attributes or text needs to be entered to have attributes or text available in the query.

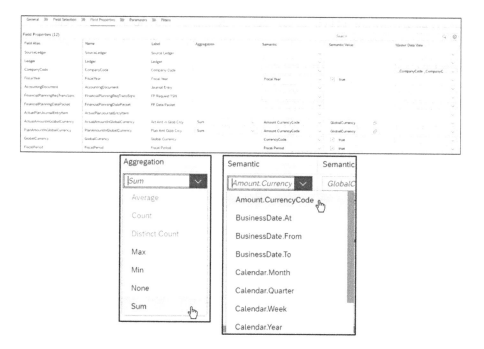

Figure 4-23. *Field Properties tab: options for Aggregation and Semantic*

There are two more steps in the development process to cover: Parameters and Filters. As we do not need parameters, and I want to do the filtering in the query view, so we can skip these steps for now.

In hindsight, we did not need the option Add Associated Data Source. This is of course because the primary data source in this case already had so many associations—rather too many than too little.

Custom Analytical Query in an Almost Ideal Situation: Part 2

Let's go back to tile Custom Analytical Query to implement the optimizations. Ideally, we would change the data source for query ZZ1_ACTPLANJEITEM from I_ActualPlanJournalEntryItem to ZZ1_CubeActPlanJEItem, but as this is not possible, we will build a new query, ZZ1_ACTPLANJEITEM2, on top of cube ZZ1_CubeActPlanJEItem. The number of available fields is now 19 instead of 170, which makes it rather easy to find the required fields. The new field Account Group and the indicator Profit Loss Account are indeed available. On the screen Field Properties, we make the desired changes: set the standard display format of G/L Account to Key and Text and change the label and number of decimals for the two amounts. See Figure 4-24.

Figure 4-24. *Field Properties tab: changing the properties of characteristics and key figures*

On the Filters screen, we introduce a filter on the new indicator Profit Loss Account. The indicator has a value of X for profit and loss accounts versus ' ' for balance accounts (Figure 4-25). I choose the filter to be mandatory and multiple single values with a default value of X. This way, if the user does not change this in the selection screen, only profit and loss accounts will be shown, but the user has the option to change this to only balance accounts or to both types of accounts. We also introduce a fixed values filter on the dimension Category.

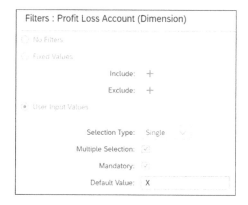

Figure 4-25. *Filters tab: filter on indicator Profit Loss Account*

It's time to test-drive the optimized query by starting Query Browser. The selection screen now has an additional entry for the indicator Profit Loss Account, which does what it is supposed to do (Figure 4-26).

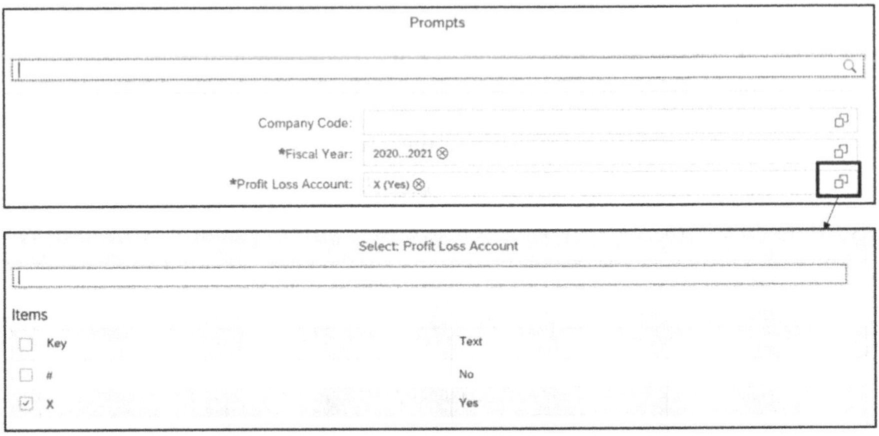

Figure 4-26. *Test-driving the optimized custom analytical query via the app Query Browser: selection screen*

The output of the optimized query looks good as well. All the optimizations are there: key and text for G/L Account, Company Code, and Profit Center; simplified labels for the amounts; no more euro cents; and new dimensions Account Group and Profit Loss Account (Figure 4-27). We are done!

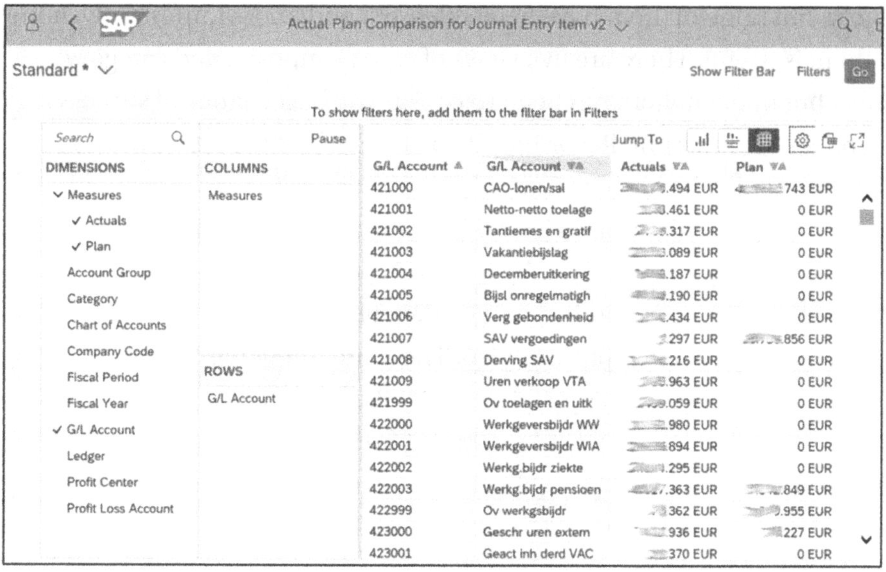

Figure 4-27. *Test-driving the optimized custom analytical query via the app Query Browser: query output*

Custom CDS View in a Not-So-Ideal Situation

We are not always lucky. Not always is a rich standard cube view available to modify and build a query upon. In such a not-so-ideal situation, we can try to build a cube view ourselves starting from facts and dimensions. In this section, I describe such an example from practice involving the process of time recording.

The first stop is View Browser. The source of time recording transaction data is the table CATS: Database Table for Time Sheet (CATSDB). Entering the table name in the search bar of View Browser teaches us that the application component for this type of data is CA-TS-S4. This application component has 54 views, including 7 basic, 38 composite, and 8 consumption. There are five views of type Consumption and category

121

Query, but none of them have been released, and, more importantly, none of them is useful. There are five views of type Composite and category Cube, but none of them has been released. The best chance of success is the released view Time Recording Data (I_TimeSheetRecord), with the type Basic and the category Fact.

The output of this basic view will also be quite basic: involved employee with personnel number (catsdb.pernr), sending cost center (catsdb.skostl) as a number, and work date (catsdb.workdate) only as a day but not the week, month, or year. These are things we can fix in the app Custom CDS View. So let's just do that. By the way, denoting fields in this fashion—catsdb.pernr, [table name].[field name] in small letters—is the exact notation in ABAP CDS as inherited from SQL. You'd better get used to it for the remainder of this book.

This time we do need to add associated data sources, i.e., the standard CDS views I_CostCenter, I_CalendarDate, and I_WorkforcePerson. While adding a data source, you may need to ignore a warning about adding an access-protected data source. After adding an associated data source, a broken link icon appears (Figure 4-28).

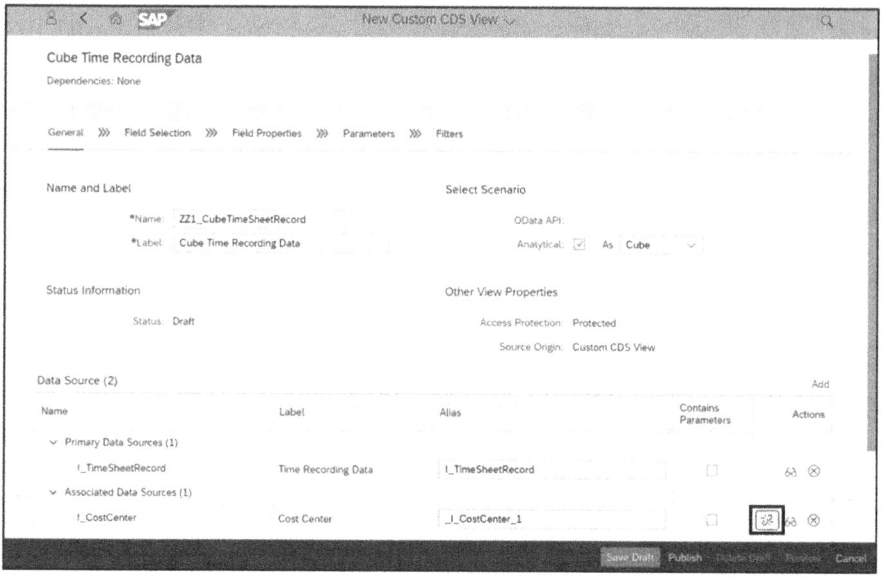

Figure 4-28. *General tab: broken link icon after adding an associated data source*

This can be solved by entering the correct association properties information. This is shown for Sender Cost Center in Figure 4-29. Do not forget the compounding keys. For the data source I_CalendarDate, the field I_CalendarDate.CalendarDate is connected to I_TimeSheetRecord. TimeSheetDate. For the data source I_WorkforcePerson, the field I_WorkforcePerson.PersonExternalID is connected to I_TimeSheetRecord.PersonWorkAgreement. This may cause a problem, as the field I_WorkforcePerson.PersonExternalID is not a key field, which may influence cardinality.

Figure 4-29. *General tab: Association Properties section*

Once all the associated data sources are neatly coupled to the primary data source (Figure 4-30), we can move on to the next tab.

Figure 4-30. *General tab: all associated data sources successfully coupled to the primary data source*

On the Field Selection tab, I select from the primary data source only the fields relevant to demonstrate the enrichment. I also select the association for Cost Center, the field Year/Month via the work date, and the full name of the employee (Figure 4-31).

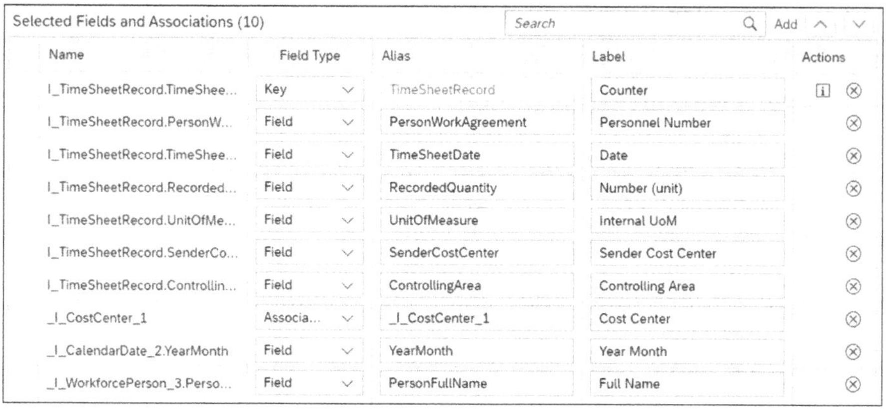
Selected Fields and Associations (10)
Search
Add
Name
Field Type
Alias
Label
Actions
I_TimeSheetRecord.TimeShee...
Key
TimeSheetRecord
Counter
I_TimeSheetRecord.PersonW...
Field
PersonWorkAgreement
Personnel Number
I_TimeSheetRecord.TimeShee...
Field
TimeSheetDate
Date
I_TimeSheetRecord.Recorded...
Field
RecordedQuantity
Number (unit)
I_TimeSheetRecord.UnitOfMe...
Field
UnitOfMeasure
Internal UoM
I_TimeSheetRecord.SenderCo...
Field
SenderCostCenter
Sender Cost Center
I_TimeSheetRecord.Controllin...
Field
ControllingArea
Controlling Area
_I_CostCenter_1
Associa...
_I_CostCenter_1
Cost Center
_I_CalendarDate_2.YearMonth
Field
YearMonth
Year Month
_I_WorkforcePerson_3.Perso...
Field
PersonFullName
Full Name

Figure 4-31. *Field Selection tab*

The Field Properties tab of the Custom CDS View app has no secrets for us anymore (Figure 4-32).

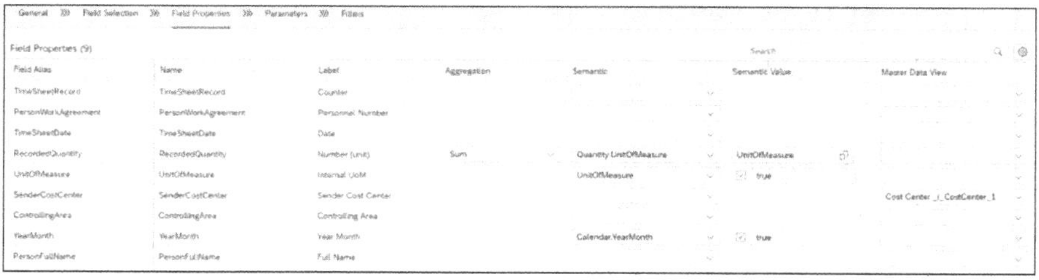
General
Field Selection
Field Properties
Parameters
Filters
Field Properties (9)
Field Alias
Name
Label
Aggregation
Semantic
Semantic Value
Master Data View
Sum
Quantity.UnitOfMeasure
UnitOfMeasure
true
Cost Center _I_CostCenter_1
Calendar.YearMonth

Figure 4-32. *Field Properties tab*

We can now save and publish this custom cube view, which is our first one built from scratch. Well, it was almost from scratch since it was built on top of the basic views of the VDM. While saving, we receive the warning "The association _I_WorkforcePerson_3 can modify the cardinality of the result set," which is not totally unexpected. Such warnings should be taken seriously. You will learn more about these types of issues in the next chapter.

Am I allowed to show my archaic overview for the last time in this chapter? Here is the layered structure of CDS views down to the (main) tables of what we built in this section:

```
ZZ1_CubeTimeSheetRecord
|- I_TimeSheetRecord
|  |- catsdb
|  |- E_TimeSheetRecord
|  |  |- catsdb
|- I_CostCenter
|  |- csks
|  |- ...
|- I_CalendarDate
|  |- scal_tt_date
|  |- I_YearMonth
|  |  |- scal_tt_month
|  |  |- scal_tt_year
|- I_WorkforcePerson
   |- I_BusinessPartner
   |  |- but000
   |  |- ...
   |- I_HrRelation
      |- hrp1001
      |- ...
```

Proof of the pudding for the new custom cube view is of course building an analytical query on top with the app Custom Analytical Query and test-drive it with the app Query Browser. Let's go through the necessary steps with some shortcuts. In the app Custom Analytical Query, I select only the relevant fields. On the Display tab, I change the label of quantity RecordedQuantity from Number (unit) to Hours. I also change the initial display format of Sender Cost Center to Key and Text and add it to the rows. I change the label of Year/Month to Month and add it to the columns. See Figure 4-33 for the result of these actions.

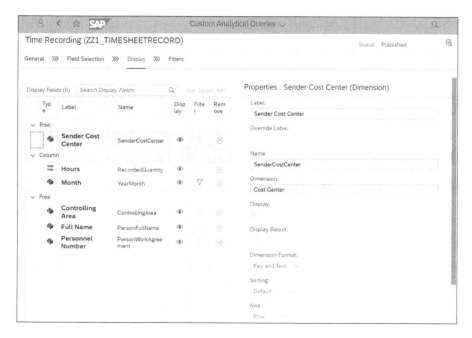

Figure 4-33. *Display tab*

Selecting the analytical query in Query Browser and bringing in Full Name as the second dimension in the rows leads to the output shown in Figure 4-34. For the second time in this chapter, we are done!

8 < ⌂ SAP		Time Recording ⌄							Q

Standard ⌄						Show Filter Bar	Filters (3)	**Go**	

To show filters here, add them to the filter bar in Filters

Search Q	Pause				Jump To	.ıl ⌷ ⊞ ⊙ ⌷ ⌷

DIMENSIONS	COLUMNS				Hours			
⌄ Measures	Measures	Sender Cost Center ⌃	Sender Cost Center ⌄⌃	Full Name | Month ⌃	06.2019	07.2019	08.2019
✓ Hours	Month	940030010	Communicatie Algeme3	E. Externvijftien	25 H	10 H	
Controlling Area				V. Externveertien	31 H	54 H	23 H
✓ Full Name	**ROWS**	940040020	Procurement 1	P. Externe tijdschrijver 1	1 H	1 H	2 H
✓ Month	Sender Cost Center	940059600	NSG HR BP Operatie D	E. Externzestien			2 H
Personnel Number	Full Name	940071140	NSG SC Finance NS St	A. Manager Azziz		6 H	4 H
✓ Sender Cost Center				E. Eerstemans	40 H	133 H	197 H
		940071600	NSG TOP Finance	P. Externe tijdschrijver 1	3 H		
				Z.A. Zevendemans	40 H		3 H

Figure 4-34. *Test-driving the custom analytical query for the not-so-ideal situation via the app Query Browser: query output*

Transporting Custom CDS Views and Analytical Queries

Earlier, I mentioned the DTAP system landscape, with DTAP meaning Development, Testing, Acceptance, and Production. This is the most often used setup for an on-premise SAP system. A SaaS system usually has only two versions: one for DTA and one for P.

Transporting custom CDS views and custom analytical queries built via tiles following the D > T > A > P route for on-premise or the DTA > P route for SaaS systems involves two more tiles: Configure Software Packages and Register Extensions for Transport (Figure 4-35).

Figure 4-35. *Tiles required to transport custom CDS views and custom analytical queries: Configure Software Packages and Register Extensions for Transport*

These tiles are used for all S/4HANA extensions. Custom CDS views and custom analytical queries belong to the so-called In-App Extensions, just as for instance Custom Fields and Logic. You'll learn more about In-App Extensions in Chapter 7.

Custom CDS views and custom analytical queries are originally created as local objects, assigned to package $TMP. The tile Configure Software Packages connects an open transport with a task assigned to the developer to a real software package via the Add Registration button (Figure 4-36).

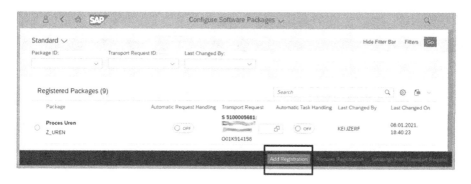

Figure 4-36. *The Configure Software Packages tile*

The tile Register Extensions for Transport connects the extensions to the package via the Reassign to Package button. The extensions are then automatically included in the open transport (Figure 4-37).

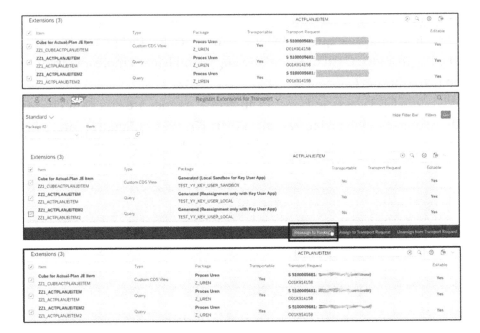

Figure 4-37. *The Register Extensions for Transport tile*

The best way to check the transport for completeness is to check the objects under Data Definition Language Source. Figure 4-38 shows the output of the back-end transaction Transport Organizer (SE01).

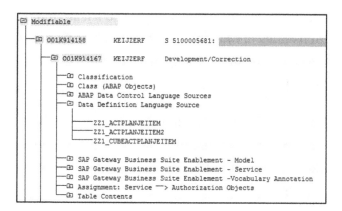

Figure 4-38. *Contents of a transport including custom CDS views and custom analytical queries (back-end transaction SE01 output)*

The objects are now ready to follow the normal transport process of the project.

Retrospective

Allow me to spend some time looking back at what we did in this chapter and drawing some conclusions regarding the usability of the tools presented.

First, let's look at the not-so-ideal situation example. This example is actually based on a real-life business requirement in a SaaS environment. To be honest, I had a hard time bending the demo around all the issues, e.g., by focusing on the sending side of the data. In reality, we were more interested in the receiving side, but the fields in CATSDB required to report on the receiving side were missing in the basic view. We also wanted to combine the time-recording data with financial data. This required the use of a union operator, which is not possible in a SaaS-version S/4HANA environment. Bummer. The idea back then was to focus on side-by-side extensibility outside of the S/4HANA system. You'll learn more about this type of extensibility in Chapter 7. And then, all the team members including myself left to do other things, like happens ever so often. So, no, it's not a success story.

Second, let's talk about the almost ideal situation example. I started off by explaining the benefits of building analytical queries in this SaaS-compatible way, even in an on-premise environment. Not only are you a goody-goody, but also, as you build the custom objects on top of SAP's virtual data model of CDS views, upgrade issues are not likely to occur, and if they are, they are SAP's to solve and not yours. I then shared my enthusiasm regarding this particular SAP-delivered cube view, `I_ActualPlanJournalEntryItem`. But does this mean that the resulting analytical query is now used in a real-life productive system? I am afraid not. A version of the query similar to what is described in this section is indeed transported into the productive system, but only to compare the performance of this query with that of a similar query built in an IDE (covered in the next chapters). The following are some reasons why the standard cube view in the end did not meet requirements. These reasons are typical for this customer project situation, but the type of mismatches will give you an idea what type of disappointments to expect in your experience with SAP's VDM:

- An extremely useful field like Debit/Credit Indicator (`acdoca.drcrk`) is renamed to `DebitCreditCode` in view `I_I_GLAccountLineItem`, disappears in view `P_ActualPlanJrnlEntryItm,` and is thus not available in our cube view `I_ActualPlanJournalEntryItem`. Do you see now how handy my overview is?

- In the current project, the process of time recording is done on the level of Network Activity. The following fields in the `ACDOCA` table are involved in this process: Network Number for Account

Assignment (`acdoca.nplnr`) and Network
activity (`acdoca.nplnr_vorgn`), renamed to
`ProjectNetwork` and `RelatedNetworkActivity` in
view `I_I_GLAccountLineItem`, disappearing in view
`P_ActualPlanJrnlEntryItm`, and not available in our
cube view. For the real-life requirements of the current
project, this was a blocking issue.

- Some other fields from table ACDOCA were also
  missing in the cube view; not all of them were critical,
  but some were.

- In principle, table ACDOCA should include an
  alternative for all the fields from tables like BSEG and
  BKPF. In reality, some fields from BKPF were required
  for which there was no alternative in ACDOCA. These
  fields were also not included in the standard cube view.

- Complex logic was required for numerous purposes,
  e.g., filtering of the dataset on complex conditions
  involving multiple fields. There was no way this could
  have been possible within the limitations of the
  two tiles Custom CDS Views and Custom Analytical
  Queries.

But I have to admit, for the almost ideal situation example, the
SaaS development options have come a long way. And if SaaS is all you
have, you are more likely to stretch the available options to the limit
than when you can easily move to the on-premise tooling described in
upcoming chapters. My final advice to fellow developers working within
a SaaS-version S/4 environment is to take a short course in expectation
management.

CHAPTER 5

Most Work (Basic): Building Analytical Queries in an IDE

If you are dealing with a SaaS-version S/4HAHA environment, then this chapter and the next are not for you. Sorry. Do not blame me, but blame the person who decided that SaaS was good enough for your organization. Go back to Chapters 3 and 4 to squeeze every last drop of functionality out of the tiles. You also may want to take a look at the section on side-by-side extensibility in Chapter 7.

If you are a hardcore developer dying to start typing code and you decided to skip Chapter 4, then you made a mistake. The functions explained in the previous chapter for the SaaS situation will not be explained again in the chapters about the IDE (or will be only briefly). See Chapter 4 for an explanation of what the coding in this chapter does.

Getting Started with an IDE

An integrated development environment (IDE) is a software application providing facilities to computer programmers for software development. For SAP software, there are basically two IDEs to consider: WebIDE, which is part of the SAP Cloud Platform (SCP), and Eclipse. WebIDE

© Freek Keijzer 2021
F. Keijzer, *SAP S/4HANA Embedded Analytics*, https://doi.org/10.1007/978-1-4842-7017-2_5

is cloud-based and thereby the future-proof choice. But at this point in time Eclipse is a more mature platform. I had the opportunity to compare both IDEs when developing HANA calculation views (Chapter 1) and indeed found Eclipse to be much more intuitive for graphical user interface actions such as drawing arrows and connecting dots. CDS view development is mainly typing code, so I can imagine the difference in functionality between the two IDEs being much smaller in that case. The examples presented in this chapter come from an implementation project in which Eclipse is used as IDE.

To create custom CDS views in Eclipse, you first need to install the Eclipse software with required the SAP plug-ins or submit an application to the support organization. Once this is done, you can do some preparations, as shown in Figure 5-1. The Eclipse perspective for developing ABAP CDS is the ABAP perspective. Connecting to the S4/ HANA development system is done by creating a new project of type ABAP Project, entering the system connection details, and then entering your SAP user credentials. Single sign-on probably does not work, so you may need to change your password in the dev system. The resulting folder structure is [System] ➤ [Package] ($TMP or a real one) ➤ Core Data Services ➤ Data Definitions. Building a custom CDS view comes down to creating a new data definition.

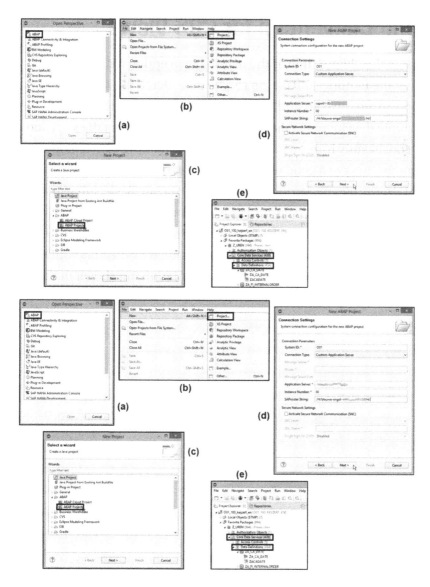

Figure 5-1. *Getting started with Eclipse: (a) opening an ABAP perspective, (b) creating a new project, (c) selecting type ABAP project, (d) entering system connection details, and (e) viewing the folder structure*

Naming Convention for CDS Views

Referring to the chapter title, is the naming convention for CDS views basic? Yes, the naming convention can be considered basic. It is important to have one from the start and use it consistently, especially when working with multiple developers in the same project. Using it from the start and using it consistently is more important than the naming convention itself. If you cannot think of a good one, then use the naming convention in Table 5-1. Views of type Attribute and Text are mostly Basic, but can also be Composite. View type Data-integration has the Category fact between parentheses, which is not necessarily the case by default. View type Text has the category Text in italics as this is determined by the annotation @ObjectModel.dataCategory, which is an annotation not shown in the app View Browser.

Table 5-1. *Proposed Naming Convention for Various Types of CDS Views*

View Type	Type in View Browser	Category in View Browser	Example of a Standard SAP View Name	Example of a Custom View Name	Example of a Custom View Description
Query	Consumption	Query	C_MaterialStockTimeSeries	ZQ_MM_RetList	MM: Return List
Cube	Composite	Cube	I_MaterialStockTimeSeries	ZC_MM_RetList	MM: Return List (cube)
Attribute	Basic	Dimension	I_Material	ZA_MM_Material	MM: Material attributes
Text	Basic	*Text*	I_MaterialText	ZT_MM_Material	MM: Material texts
Data-integration	Composite	(Fact)	P_MaterialStockTimeSeries	ZP_MM_RetListUn	MM: Return List (union)
Basic	Basic		I_MaterialDocumentRecord	ZB_MM_RetListLIPS	MM: Data from LIPS for Return List

The proposed naming convention for CDS views, also used in the current project, is ZX_YY_QqqQqqq. Here, Z is commonly used for custom objects, X indicates the type of CDS view, YY an indicator of the reporting domain (as an SAP veteran I tend to use abbreviations for old-school modules), and QqqQqqq is a unique identifier. In the technical name of the CDS view, it is better to use technical names of tables or fields, for example, rather than language-dependent descriptions. The LIPS part of ZB_MM_RetListLIPS is, for example, the technical name of a table. For a custom description, we chose to start with the indicator of the reporting domain followed by a colon and a functional description, e.g., MM: Data from LIPS for Return List.

Documentation and Data Lineage

So, referring again to the chapter title, is documentation basic? Again, yes it is. If I see a piece of programming, I want to see when it was written, by whom, and why. Often I cannot. The most reliable method of documenting is inline documentation, also known as *comments*. Documents or spreadsheets have a tendency of getting lost, in spite of or especially in a SharePoint-like environment. Inline documentation is always connected to the code. Just write some information at the start of the code, for instance when it was written, by whom, and why. If you do that, the world will be a better place.

Another important fact often forgotten, but important to be taken into account right from the start, is the data lineage. This is also basic information to include. After 10 layers of CDS views, numerous renamings of fields, and countless transformations, everyone has lost track of the source of the data displayed in an analytical query. A great help would be to add the source of a field as a comment in the lowest basic view and copy that through all the layers up to the query view. It's surprisingly little work if you do it from the start.

But how can one introduce comments in ABAP CDS? There are two methods.

- With /* ... */, everything in between becomes a comment and is ignored as code.

- After //, everything on the same line becomes a comment.

Examples of comments for documentation and data lineage will be presented in the "Embedded Analytics from Scratch" sections.

Getting Started with ABAP CDS

How do you learn ABAP CDS coding? Well, this book should be a good start. But as I am the one currently writing it, I had to do without when I started doing this type of work.

The first thing you need is some basic knowledge regarding the SQL language. There are excellent tutorials online, most of them for free (important for Dutchmen, Scots, and so on). The tutorial from w3schools[1] is very hands-on and allows you to try things yourself with a database filled with pretty good test data. In fact, I still use it from time to time to explore standard SQL functions.

But regarding ABAP CDS, to be honest I learned most from analyzing existing code and copying parts of it to my custom code. The existing code could be SAP-delivered CDS views. But just as importantly, it could be code generated by the system when building CDS views and analytical queries in a SaaS fashion, in other words, using the tools described in the previous chapter. To show you how instructive this can be, I imported the generated code from the time-recording example in the previous chapter into Eclipse, renamed it in accordance with the proposed naming

---

[1]SQL-tutorial from w3schools: https://www.w3schools.com/sql/

convention, removed the redundant coding (of which there is quite a lot), reorganized it a bit, and added some structure with comments. I also added the annotation @VDM.viewType, as this annotation is missing after building custom CDS views in a SaaS fashion, which makes the views appear as Undefined in the app View Browser. The following is the result for the cube view:

```
@EndUserText.label: 'CA: Time Recording (cube)'
@AbapCatalog.sqlViewName: 'ZCCATIMESHEETREC'

@VDM.viewType: #COMPOSITE
@Analytics.dataCategory: #CUBE
@AccessControl.authorizationCheck: #CHECK
@AbapCatalog.compiler.compareFilter: true
@DataAging.noAgingRestriction: true
@Search.searchable: false

define view ZC_CA_TimeSheetRecord as select from
I_TimeSheetRecord
  association[0..*] to I_CostCenter as _I_CostCenter_1
    on _I_CostCenter_1.ControllingArea = I_TimeSheetRecord.
    ControllingArea and
      _I_CostCenter_1.CostCenter = I_TimeSheetRecord.
      SenderCostCenter
  association[0..1] to I_CalendarDate as _I_CalendarDate_2
    on _I_CalendarDate_2.CalendarDate = I_TimeSheetRecord.
    TimeSheetDate
  association[0..*] to I_WorkforcePerson as _I_WorkforcePerson_3
    on _I_WorkforcePerson_3.PersonExternalID = I_TimeSheetRecord.
    PersonWorkAgreement
{
//--Characteristics, key fields
key I_TimeSheetRecord.TimeSheetRecord,
```

```
//--Key figures, currencies, units
    @Semantics.quantity.unitOfMeasure: 'UnitOfMeasure'
    @Aggregation.default: #SUM
    I_TimeSheetRecord.RecordedQuantity,
    @Semantics.unitOfMeasure: true
    I_TimeSheetRecord.UnitOfMeasure,

//--Characteristics, non-key fields
    I_TimeSheetRecord.PersonWorkAgreement,
    I_TimeSheetRecord.TimeSheetDate,
    @ObjectModel.foreignKey.association: '_I_CostCenter_1'
    I_TimeSheetRecord.SenderCostCenter,
    I_TimeSheetRecord.ControllingArea,

//--Fields via associations
    @Semantics.calendar.yearMonth: true
    _I_CalendarDate_2.YearMonth,
    _I_WorkforcePerson_3.PersonFullName,

//--Associations to be passed on to the query
    _I_CostCenter_1
}
```

Going back to Figure 4-29 and Figure 4-30, we recognize the code by the way the fact view I_TimeSheetRecord is connected to the associated data sources _I_CostCenter_1, _I_CalendarDate_2, and _I_WorkforcePerson_3 in the Custom CDS View app. We also recognize the input in the different columns of the Field Properties tab shown in Figure 4-32: Aggregation, Semantic, Semantic Value, and Master Data View.

The code starts with annotations. I separated the view-specific annotations from the annotations that are generic for a certain view type. There are two view-specific annotations. The annotation @EndUserText. label is the description of the view as shown before the query output. The annotation @AbapCatalog.sqlViewName is the name of the database view, in other words, the list of fields with properties. It is not allowed to have the technical name of the SQL view be identical to the name of the CDS view. As the naming convention for SQL views, we take the name of the CDS view, remove all the underscores, and abbreviate it a bit if necessary. Therefore, CDS view ZC_CA_TimeSheetRecord becomes SQL view ZCCATIMESHEETREC. You can check both views using the back-end transaction ABAP Dictionary Maintenance (SE11). Enter the name of the SQL view in the search field for View, and a list of fields included in the view will appear, along with other properties (Figure 5-2). The CDS view is shown as DDL source. Clicking the name of the CDS view brings you to a display of the code. Note that by using an S/4HANA back-end transaction you can only display ABAP CDS. To create or change the code, an IDE is required. Displaying the ABAP CDS code via SE11 is a useful method to check the code in a system not connected to the IDE, e.g., the productive system.

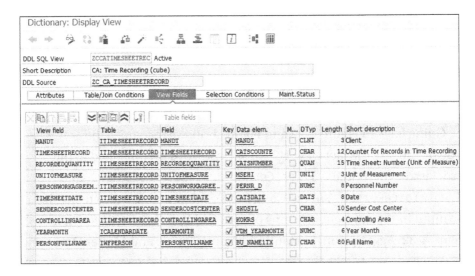

Figure 5-2. *Display of SQL view via back-end transaction "ABAP Dictionary Maintenance" (SE11)*

There are six annotations generic for this view type; five were generated by the system, and one was added by me. The first two, @VDM.viewType and @Analytics.dataCategory, identify the view type. I would not worry too much about the remaining four. You can look them up by Googling them, and you will probably end up in the "CDS Annotations" section of the SAP Help Portal.[2] But for me, I am leading a perfectly happy life just copying and pasting annotations without knowing what some of them mean. We will encounter exceptions to my general disinterest in Chapter 6.

Equally instructive, but with less code, is the query view. Again, the annotation @VDM.viewType is added manually.

```
@EndUserText.label: 'CA: Time Recording'
@AbapCatalog.sqlViewName : 'ZQCATIMESHEETREC'

@VDM.viewType: #CONSUMPTION
@Analytics.query: true
@OData.publish: true

define view ZQ_CA_TimeSheetRecord as select from ZC_CA_
TimeSheetRecord
{
//--Key figures
    @EndUserText.label: 'Hours'
    RecordedQuantity,
```

[2]SAP Help Portal, CDS Annotations: https://help.sap.com/viewer/cc0c
305d2fab47bd808adcad3ca7ee9d/7.5.9/en-US/630ce9b386b84e80bfade96
779fbaeec.html

```
//--Characteristics initially in columns
    @AnalyticsDetails.query.axis:#COLUMNS
    @Consumption.filter :{ selectionType: #SINGLE,
    multipleSelections: true, mandatory: false }
    @EndUserText.label: 'Month'
    YearMonth,

//--Characteristics initially in rows
    @AnalyticsDetails.query.display: #KEY_TEXT
    @AnalyticsDetails.query.axis:#ROWS
    SenderCostCenter,

//--Free characteristics
    ControllingArea,
    PersonFullName,
    PersonWorkAgreement
}
```

We need to compare this code to the actions carried out with the app Custom Analytical Query, as shown in Figure 4-33, and the result in Figure 4-34. We see the same two view-specific annotations as for the cube view. We also see a different set of annotations specific for the view type. The annotation `@Analytics.query: true` makes this view appear in the category Query via the app View Browser. The overwriting of labels is done with the annotation `@EndUserText.label`. The initial display in rows, columns, or neither is achieved with annotation `@AnalyticsDetails.query.axis`. To obtain an entry in the selection screen, annotation `@Consumption.filter` can be applied. Initial display as Key, Text, or both is achieved with annotation `@AnalyticsDetails.query.display`. "A child can do the laundry", we would say in Dutch.

In the next sections, we will see if we can apply these lessons learned to an end-to-end case based on real-life business requirements.

Embedded Analytics from Scratch: Requirements and Data Model

Sometimes business requirements are as vague as "I want a financial report," but on the other hand they can also be very specific, as shown in Figure 5-3. This is what a BI consultant can receive if a functional consultant acts as an intermediary. The spreadsheet has two tabs for two different "starting points." These tabs include a technical table and field names, table relations, and, yes, even input for the selection screen. Never before has a BI consultant been so spoiled! The business requirement had something to do with "clean" and "dirty" parts of trains being returned to a warehouse. Yes, I do like working for the "doink" industry.[3] Therefore, this requirement was named "Return List."

---

[3]The "doink" industry is a term introduced by Dutch former minister Andriessen in 1996 to indicate companies producing ships, trucks, planes, and other products generating a "doink" sound when dropped.

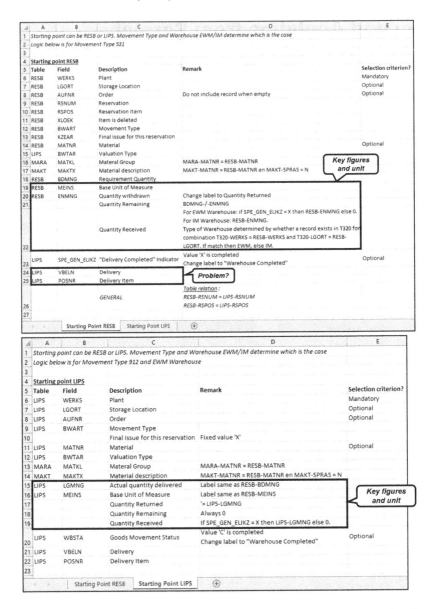

Figure 5-3. *Technical translation of business requirements for the "Embedded Analytics from Scratch" case covered in this chapter*

Let's first apply some acceptance criteria to this request. Is it operational information as opposed to tactical/strategic? It is a detailed work list, in which real-time data is much appreciated, so it's a definite candidate for Embedded Analytics. Does SAP standard content exist to satisfy the requirements or parts of the requirements? Well, as far as the transaction data is concerned, forget about it. But master data is probably available as standard CDS views. The conclusion is that we have to start building.

How do we translate these specifications into a data model? Well, in Chapter 1, we learned that we need to start by searching for the key figures. The data on the tab Starting Point RESB has fields mainly from the table Reservation/dependent requirements (RESB), including the key figures Requirement Quantity (`resb.bdmng`) and Quantity withdrawn (`resb.enmng`) and the unit field Base Unit of Measure (`resb.meins`). The key figure names are easier to memorize once you know that the German word for quantity is "menge." The tab Starting Point LIPS has one basic key figure, which is coming from table "SD document: Delivery: Item data" (`LIPS`), i.e., "Actual quantity delivered in stockkeeping units" (`lips.lgmng`) with the unit Base Unit of Measure (`lips.meins`).

Knowing only this, we already have a basic idea of what the data model should look like. Key figures are coming from two sources not having a one-on-one relation, so we will need a union operator to integrate the transaction data. The data model will therefore look like the one shown in Figure 5-4: two basic views immediately on top of the physical tables, a union view to integrate the transaction data, a cube view, and to top it all off a query view. We have, of course, some attribute and text views, preferably from the SAP standard items, connected to the cube view.

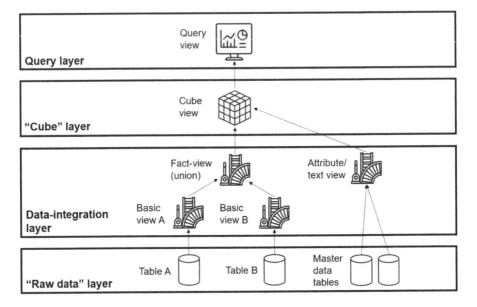

Figure 5-4. *Data model for a situation in which transaction data is coming from two sources*

There is one thing that worries me in the specifications for the starting point RESB. The requirement to display Delivery and Delivery Item also in relation with the key figures from RESB seems to be at odds with the table relation definition. The definition is that key fields of the primary data source (`resb.rsnum` and `resb.rspos`) are connected to nonkey fields of the associated data source (`lips.rsnum` and `lips.rspos`). This may lead to cardinality issues, mentioned in the previous chapter. But for now, let's focus on the basics and revisit this topic later.

Embedded Analytics from Scratch: Basic Views

To build a basic CDS view from scratch, nothing in your sleeve, you tell Eclipse you want to create a new data definition, fill in the technical name and description, click Next two times, select the first template you see, and

click Finish. The only things you need to do on the coding screen is change
the SQL view name from sql_view_name to something else, fill in the table
you want to select from, go to a position between the two braces, press
Ctrl+spacebar simultaneously (this is the hardest part), and choose the
option "Insert all elements" and click Activate (Figure 5-5). There you go,
you have created a basic CDS view in less than 10 seconds.

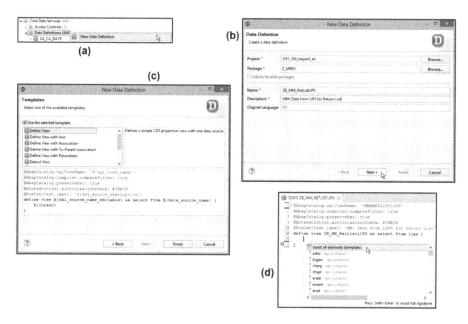

Figure 5-5. *Building a basic view from scratch the fast and easy way:
(a) create a new data definition, (b) enter the name and description,
(c) choose a template, (d) coding screen*

Such a CDS view will work, but it will not be pretty. And we also need
to add some filters, e.g., on Movement Type. The following is the prettified
coding of the basic view for the key figures from the LIPS called MM: Data
from LIPS for Return List (ZB_MM_RetListLIPS):

```
/* Freek Keijzer, myBrand, 17.01.2021
Basic view for key figures Deliveries.
Business requirement: user-story 34567
Source tables:
LIPS - "SD document: Delivery: Item data"
-----------------------------------------------------------
Change-log:
-----------------------------------------------------------
-----------------------------------------------------------*/
@EndUserText.label: 'MM: Data from LIPS for Return List'
@AbapCatalog.sqlViewName: 'ZBMMRETLISTLIPS'

@VDM.viewType: #BASIC
@AbapCatalog.compiler.compareFilter: true
@AbapCatalog.preserveKey: true
@AccessControl.authorizationCheck: #CHECK

define view ZB_MM_RetListLIPS as select from lips
{
    vbeln,                  //Delivery (lips.vbeln)
    posnr as vbelp,         //Delivery Item (lips.posnr)
    werks,                  //Plant (lips.werks)
    lgort,                  //Storage Location (lips.lgort)
    aufnr,                  //Order Number (lips.aufnr)
    bwart,                  //Movement type inventory
                            management (lips.bwart)
    matnr,                  //Material Number (lips.matnr)
    bwtar,                  //Valuation Type (lips.bwtar)
    lgmng,                  //Actual quantity delivered
                            (lips.lgmng)
    meins,                  //Base Unit of Measure (lips.meins)
    spe_gen_elikz,          //"Delivery Completed" Indicator
                            (lips.spe_gen_elikz)
```

```
    rsnum,                      //Reservation Number (lips.rsnum)
    rspos,                      //Reservation Item (lips.rspos)
    wbsta,                      //Goods Movement Status (lips.wbsta)
    1 as Counter                //Counter (for Delivery Items)
}
where lips.bwart  = '912' and   //--Only Movement Type '912' =
                                  'TR transfer in plant'
      lips.aufnr != ''          //--Order must be filled
```

On top, you see comments answering the when/who/what/why questions. There is room for a change log for future use. The annotations for the view type were inserted by the template, except for annotation @ VDM.viewType, which was entered manually. Data lineage comments are present for every field. This may look a bit redundant at this stage, but it will become more and more useful in the higher architectural layers. Field descriptions and other comments are in English for your convenience, but in the Dutch project they are in Dutch. I have a habit of entering a counter in all basic views and thus at the lowest level, for use during testing, but quite often also in the query. Last, filters are added outside of the braces with a where clause.

The basic view for the key figures from RESB is a bit more complex, as two tables need to be joined. The code for MM: Data from RESB for Return List (ZB_MM_RetListRESB) is shown here:

```
/* Freek Keijzer, myBrand, 17.01.2021
Basic view for key figures Reservations.
Business requirement: user-story 34567
Source tables:
RESB - "Reservation/dependent requirements"
LIPS - "SD document: Delivery: Item data"
--------------------------------------------------------
```

```
Change-log:
-----------------------------------------------------------
-----------------------------------------------------------*/
@EndUserText.label: 'MM: Data from RESB for Return List'
@AbapCatalog.sqlViewName: 'ZBMMRETLISTRESB'

@VDM.viewType: #BASIC
@AbapCatalog.compiler.compareFilter: true
@AbapCatalog.preserveKey: true
@AccessControl.authorizationCheck: #CHECK

define view ZB_MM_RetListRESB as select from resb
  left outer join lips
    on lips.rsnum = resb.rsnum and
       lips.rspos = resb.rspos and
       lips.bwart = '531'
{
key resb.rsnum,              //Reservation Number (resb.rsnum)
key resb.rspos,              //Reservation Item (resb.rspos)
    resb.werks,             //Plant (resb.werks)
    resb.lgort,             //Storage Location (resb.lgort)
    resb.aufnr,             //Order Number (resb.aufnr)
    resb.xloek,             //Item is deleted (resb.xloek)
    resb.bwart,             //Movement type inventory
                            management (resb.bwart)
    resb.kzear,             //Final issue for this
                            reservation (resb.kzear)
    resb.matnr,             //Material Number (resb.matnr)
    resb.bdmng,             //Requirement Quantity (resb.bdmng)
    resb.meins,             //Base Unit of Measure (resb.meins)
    resb.enmng,             //Quantity withdrawn (resb.enmng)
    lips.vbeln,             //Delivery (lips.vbeln)
```

```
      lips.posnr as vbelp,         //Delivery Item (lips.posnr)
      lips.bwtar,                  //Valuation Type (lips.bwtar)
      lips.spe_gen_elikz,          //"Delivery Completed" Indicator
                                   (lips.spe_gen_elikz)
      1 as Counter,                //Counter (for Reservation Items)
      case
        when lips.vbeln != '' then 1
        else                      0
      end as CounterDel,           //Counter for Delivery Items
      case
        when lips.vbeln != '' then concat(lips.vbeln,lips.posnr)
        else                      'XXXXXXXXXXXXXXXX'
      end as VbelnPos              //Concatenated Delivery
                                   Number+Item, special value when
                                   empty for testing purposes
}
where resb.rsart  = ''     and  //--Key field "Record type" must
                                be empty
      resb.bwart  = '531' and  //--Only Movement Type '531' =
                                'Receipt by-product'
      resb.aufnr != ''         //--Order must be filled
```

Most of the code will not be a surprise to you by now. This view introduces two SQL statements for the first time in this book: case and concat. The statement case is the SQL method to implement if ... then ... else ... logic. The statement concat is used to attach strings to one another. Please be aware that there is a special statement to attach strings separated by a space, i.e., concat_with_space (this took me a long time to figure out).

You are probably wondering why I am not only counting Reservation Items, but also Delivery Items, and why I am creating a concatenate object from delivery plus Delivery Item. This is preparation for logic we need to implement in the next layer: data integration.

Embedded Analytics from Scratch: Data Integration

For instructive purposes, let's act as if we are not aware of the potential cardinality issues in the part for key figures from RESB and continue implementing the data model shown in Figure 5-4. Figure 5-6 shows the result.

In general, left outer joins are used to connect data including key figures on the left side to master data without key figures on the right side. This works well as long as for every record on the left side only zero or one records on the right side are found via the join conditions. This is by definition the case if all key fields of the dataset on the right side are connected to fields on the left side. But our specifications require a left outer join connection between table RESB on the left side and table LIPS on the right side, in which we are not connecting to key fields of LIPS but to other fields. This means there can be more than one record on the right side connected to one record on the left side. In functional terms, for every Reservation Item, there can be more than one Delivery Item, which is very true.

The bottom part of Figure 5-6 gives a data example: Reservation Item 0000003510/0002 is connected to 0 Delivery Items, Reservation Item 0000003744/0008 to 1, and Reservation Item 0000003745/0002 to 3. The result is that the value of key figures from RESB, e.g., Requirement Quantity (resb.bdmng), are tripled for Reservation Item 0000003745/0002 in the basic view and will continue to be tripled all the way up to the query if we do not take action.

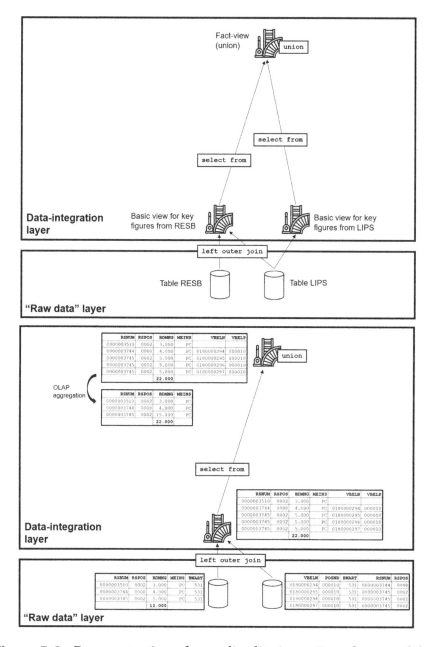

Figure 5-6. *Demonstration of a cardinality issue. Top: data model. Bottom: display of the data*

This can be fixed in the data-integration layer. After all, that is what the data-integration layer is for. In simple cases, it could be fixed with a group by statement in the union view for data coming from the basic view MM: Data from LIPS for Return List (ZB_MM_RetListLIPS). We could, for instance, only keep the highest value of Delivery Item for Reservation Item 0000003745/0002, which is Delivery Item 0180000297/000010, and remove the lines for the other two. But, in consultation with my functional colleague, we decided to not only show the highest value of Delivery Item, but also indicate the fact that there are more than one by counting the number of Delivery Items also for the dataset with key figures from RESB. This is where the preparations in the basic view for key figures from RESB come in handy.

Step 1 in this fix is building a view on top of the view with the cardinality issue to select only one value of the relevant characteristic. The concatenation of Delivery Number and Delivery Item prepared in the basic view is used in this action. Additionality, we want to keep count of the number of Delivery Items. For this we can use the counter that was also prepared in the basic view. The resulting code of view MM: Data LIPS aggr. to Reservation (ZP_MM_LIPSResAg) looks like this:

```
/* Freek Keijzer, myBrand, 17.01.2021
Preparation for data aggregation of Delivery Items to
Reservation Items.
There can be multiple Delivery Items for 1 Reservation Item.
In this view, 1 of these Delivery Items is selected for display
and the number of Delivery Items is counted.
-----------------------------------------------------------
Change-log:
-----------------------------------------------------------
----------------------------------------------------------*/
@EndUserText.label: 'MM: Data LIPS aggr.to Reservation'
@AbapCatalog.sqlViewName: 'ZPMMLIPSRESBAG'
```

```
@VDM.viewType: #COMPOSITE
@AbapCatalog.compiler.compareFilter: true
@AbapCatalog.preserveKey: true
@AccessControl.authorizationCheck: #CHECK

define view ZP_MM_LIPSResAg as select from ZB_MM_RetListRESB
{
    rsnum,                        //Reservation Number
                                  (resb.rsnum)
    rspos,                        //Reservation Item (resb.rspos)
    max(VbelnPos) as VbelnPos,    //Delivery Number+Item
    sum(CounterDel)  as CounterDel //Number of Delivery Items in
                                  Reservations
}
group by rsnum, rspos  //--Aggregation on Reservation Item
```

Step 2 is creating a composite view that is almost a copy of the basic view ZB_MM_RetListRESB. An inner join with the view ZP_MM_LIPSResAg removes two records as planned, while still counting the correct number of Delivery Items. The code of ZP-view MM: Data from RESB for Return List (ZP_MM_RetListRES) is shown here:

```
/* Freek Keijzer, myBrand, 17.01.2021
View for key figures Reservations.
Dataset for Delivery Item is being aggregated to level
Reservation Item.
For determination "Warehouse EWM/IM?" in next view, this table
is joined in this view:
T320 - "Assignment IM Storage Location to WM Warehouse Number"
--------------------------------------------------------
Change-log:
--------------------------------------------------------
-------------------------------------------------------*/
```

```
@EndUserText.label: 'MM: Data from RESB for Return List'
@AbapCatalog.sqlViewName: 'ZPMMRETLISTRESB'

@VDM.viewType: #COMPOSITE
@AbapCatalog.compiler.compareFilter: true
@AbapCatalog.preserveKey: true
@AccessControl.authorizationCheck: #CHECK

define view ZP_MM_RetListRESB as select from ZB_MM_RetListRESB
as _Resb
  inner join ZP_MM_LIPSResAg as _Ag
    on _Ag.rsnum    = _Resb.rsnum and
       _Ag.rspos    = _Resb.rspos and
       _Ag.VbelnPos = _Resb.VbelnPos
  left outer join t320
    on t320.werks = _Resb.werks and
       t320.lgort = _Resb.lgort
{
key _Resb.rsnum,        //Reservation Number (resb.rsnum)
key _Resb.rspos,        //Reservation Item (resb.rspos)
    _Resb.werks,        //Plant (resb.werks)
    _Resb.lgort,        //Storage Location (resb.lgort)
    _Resb.aufnr,        //Order Number (resb.aufnr)
    _Resb.xloek,        //Item is deleted (resb.xloek)
    _Resb.bwart,        //Movement type inventory management
                        (resb.bwart)
    _Resb.kzear,        //Final issue for this reservation
                        (resb.kzear)
    _Resb.matnr,        //Material Number (resb.matnr)
    _Resb.bdmng,        //Requirement Quantity (resb.bdmng)
    _Resb.meins,        //Base Unit of Measure (resb.meins)
    _Resb.enmng,        //Quantity withdrawn (resb.enmng)
```

```
_Resb.vbeln,           //Delivery (lips.vbeln)
_Resb.vbelp,           //Delivery Item (lips.posnr)
_Resb.bwtar,           //Valuation Type (lips.bwtar)
_Resb.spe_gen_elikz,   //"Delivery Completed" Indicator
                       (lips.spe_gen_elikz)
_Resb.VbelnPos,        //Concatenated Delivery Number+Item
_Resb.Counter as CounterRes,   //Number of Reservation Items
_Ag.CounterDel,                //Number of Delivery Items
t320.werks as werks_t320,      //IM Plant assigned to WM
                               Warehouse (t320.werks)
t320.lgort as lgort_t320       //IM Storage Location
                               assigned to WM Warehouse
                               (t320.lgort)
}
```

Step 3 is connecting the view with the removed records to the union view. Figure 5-7 shows the overall fix for the cardinality issue. Looking at the graph, you can probably understand why I call this solution a "triangle," but it may well be that I am the only person in the world who calls it like this. It is a standard concept taught to me by an experienced SQL programmer during a native HANA development project, but it is equally applicable to the development of CDS views.

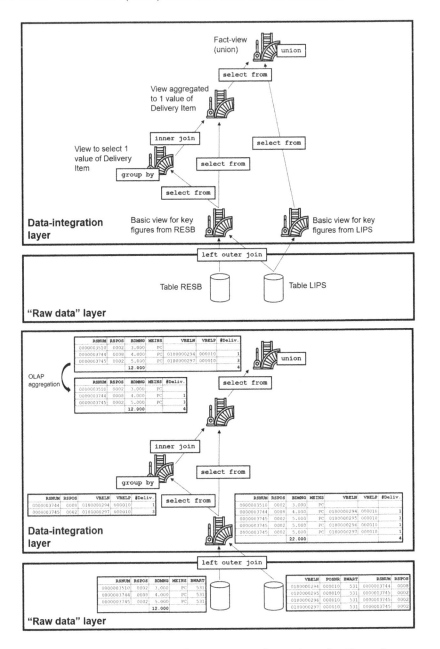

Figure 5-7. *Fix for a cardinality issue with a triangle. Top: data model. Bottom: display of the data*

```
define view C as
select from A
{
    field1,
    field2,
    field3
    ...
}
union all
select from B
{
    field1,
    field2,
    ' ' as field3
    ...
}
```

The list of fields for the combined views A and B needs to be identical. If a field cannot be mapped for one of the two views, a "zero" or "empty" needs to be inserted. Not only that, it needs to be the right type of "zero" or "empty." To give some examples, ' ' is the right type of empty for a CHAR-4 field, but 0000 is the right type of empty for a NUMC-4 field. 00000000 is the right type of empty for a date field, 0 is usually the right type of zero for a key figure, etc. It takes a while to get used to this, but the IDE will guide you through it with error messages.

It is important to note that the data format of a field is defined only by the first selection in the example before the selection from view A. For example, if a date field cannot be mapped for view A, but it can be mapped for view B, then it will not be sufficient to do this:

```
define view C as
select from A
{
    field1,
    '0000000' as date2,
    ...
}
union all
select from B
{
    field1,
    date2,
    ...
}
```

The date field B.date2 will be available in the query, but it will not behave like a date, e.g., be displayed as 17.01.2021 instead of 20210117. To achieve this, the cast expression from ABAP CDS needs to be applied like this:

```
define view C as
select from A
{
    field1,
    cast('0000000' as abap.dats) as date2,
    ...
}
union all
select from B
{
    field1,
    date2,
    ...
}
```

To bring this work to a minimum, select the view for which the highest number of fields can be mapped first. The cast expression is important, as it is used for all data format transformations.[4]

Standard SQL offers two union statements: union and union all. The difference lies in whether duplicates are allowed.[5] For our purpose, combining transaction data from multiple sources, the union all statement is to be preferred. It also gives much better query performance than the union statement. We learned that the hard way.

Let's get back to our Return List. Let me first present the code of the union view before discussing it in more detail:

```
/* Freek Keijzer, myBrand, 17.01.2021
Union-view for integration key figures Reservations & Deliveries.
Business requirement: user-story 34567.
Includes:
- Logic for key figure "Quantity Received?",
- Logic for characteristic "Warehouse EWM/IM?",
- Logic for characteristic "Warehouse Completed?".
--------------------------------------------------------
Change-log:
--------------------------------------------------------
------------------------------------------------------*/
@EndUserText.label: 'MM: Return List (union)'
@AbapCatalog.sqlViewName: 'ZPMMRETLIST'

@VDM.viewType: #COMPOSITE
@Analytics.dataCategory: #FACT
@AbapCatalog.compiler.compareFilter: true
```

---

[4]Documentation on the cast expression: https://help.sap.com/doc/ abapdocu_751_index_htm/7.51/en-US/abencds_f1_cast_expression.htm
[5]Documentation of the union and union all expression: https://www. w3schools.com/sql/sql_ref_union.asp

```
@AbapCatalog.preserveKey: true
@AccessControl.authorizationCheck: #CHECK

define view ZP_MM_RetListUn as
select from ZP_MM_RetListRESB
{
    'RESB' as Source,          //Source = 'RESB', 'LIPS'
    rsnum,                     //Reservation Number (resb.rsnum)
    rspos,                     //Reservation Item (resb.rspos)
    werks,                     //Plant (resb.werks)
    lgort,                     //Storage Location (resb.lgort)
    aufnr,                     //Order Number (resb.aufnr)
    xloek,                     //Item is deleted (resb.xloek)
    bwart,                     //Movement type inventory
                               management (resb.bwart)
    kzear,                     //Final issue for this
                               reservation (resb.kzear)
    matnr,                     //Material Number (resb.matnr)
    meins,                     //Base Unit of Measure (resb.meins)
    bdmng,                     //Requirement Quantity (resb.bdmng)
    enmng,                     //Quantity withdrawn (resb.enmng)
    case
      when werks_t320 != '' and spe_gen_elikz = 'X' then enmng
      else                                          0.0
    end as QuantRec,           //"Received" = "Quantity withdrawn"
                               (resb.enmng) with conditions
    vbeln,                     //Delivery (lips.vbeln)
    vbelp,                     //Delivery Item (lips.posnr)
    bwtar,                     //Valuation Type (lips.bwtar)
    @EndUserText.label: 'Warehouse EWM/IM?'
```

```
      case
        when werks_t320 != '' then 'EWM'
        else                        'IM'
      end as StorLoc_EWM_IM,    //"Warehouse EWM/IM?" = 'EWM' or
                                    'IM' based on table T320
      @EndUserText.label: 'Warehouse Completed?'
      case
        when werks_t320 = '' and bdmng  = enmng then 'X'
        when werks_t320 = '' and bdmng != enmng then ''
        else                    spe_gen_elikz
      end as StorLocCompl,      //"Warehouse completed?", based
                                    on table T320 and values resb.
                                    bdmng/enmng
      CounterRes,               //Number of Reservation Items
      CounterDel                //Number of Delivery Items
}
union all
select from ZB_MM_RetListLIPS
{
      'LIPS' as Source,         //Source = 'RESB', 'LIPS'
      rsnum,                    //Reservation Number (lips.rsnum)
      rspos,                    //Reservation Item (lips.rspos)
      werks,                    //Plant (lips.werks)
      lgort,                    //Storage Location (lips.lgort)
      aufnr,                    //Order Number (lips.aufnr)
      '' as xloek,              //Item is deleted
      bwart,                    //Movement type inventory
                                    management (lips.bwart)
      'X' as kzear,             //Final issue for this reservation
      matnr,                    //Material Number (lips.matnr)
      meins,                    //Base Unit of Measure (lips.meins)
```

```
  lgmng as bdmng,              //Actual quantity delivered
                               (lips.lgmng)
  lgmng as enmng,              //Actual quantity delivered
                               (lips.lgmng)
  case
    when wbsta = 'C' then lgmng
    else                  0.0
  end as QuantRec,             //"Received" = "Actual quantity
                               delivered" (lips.lgmng) with
                               conditions
  vbeln,                       //Delivery (lips.vbeln)
  vbelp,                       //Delivery Item (lips.posnr)
  bwtar,                       //Valuation Type (lips.bwtar)
  @EndUserText.label: 'Warehouse EWM/IM?'
  'EWM' as StorLoc_EWM_IM,     //"Warehouse EWM/IM?" =
                               'EWM' or 'IM'
  @EndUserText.label: 'Warehouse Completed?'
  case
    when wbsta = 'C' then 'X'
    else                  ''
  end as StorLocCompl,         //"Warehouse Completed?" based
                               on value "Goods Movement Status"
                               (lips.wbsta)
  0 as CounterRes,             //Number of Reservation Items
  Counter as CounterDel        //Number of Delivery Items
}
```

Here are some observations:

- The view is of type Composite, category Fact, as it is the
  last view with transaction data after the cube view.

- The list of fields starts with manual input for a field named Source. My best-practice advice is to always do this, even if it is only for testing purposes or for a power-user version of the query. In a query, it gives immediate insight into from which part of the data model data is coming. BW consultants will recognize this as a field standardly available in multiproviders and composite providers.

- We are lucky not to have "empties" or "zeros" in the first view selection, so no cast expression required.

- The fields bdmng and enmng have a straightforward mapping to resb.bdmng and resb.enmng, respectively, for the selection from ZP_MM_RetListRESB, but are mapped to a different field, in both cases to lips. lgmng, for the selection from ZB_MM_RetListLIPS. The union view is the ideal place to implement this type of mapping logic.

- Three new fields are introduced in this view: the key figure QuantRec and the characteristics StorLoc_EWM_ IM and StorLocCompl. Please take your time to compare the logic for these fields with the specifications of Figure 5-3. Coding when werks_t320 = '' or when werks_t320 != '' may require some explanation. In the view ZP_MM_RetListRESB, a left outer join was executed with table T320 for the fields Plant (werks) and Storage Location (lgort). If a match is found with table T320, the warehouse is of type EWM; if not, it is of type IM. We are therefore not interested in any of the values of the record found in T320, only if there is a match or not. Checking the value of werks_t320 is sufficient for this purpose.

- Labels can be introduced at any level in the stack of CDS views. The cube view makes the most sense, as all queries built on top of the cube view benefit from the label, but labels can also be introduced at a lower level. Here I chose to label the new fields StorLoc_EWM_IM and StorLocCompl in the union view using the @EndUserText.label expression. The labels are automatically propagated to the higher levels and do not need to be repeated.

As said before, the data-integration layer is where the real magic happens. But for now, it looks like we are done and can move on to the cube layer.

Embedded Analytics from Scratch: Cube View

Most of the hard work has been done in the data-integration layer. In the cube view, we optimize the data for multidimensional reporting. Again, let's look at the code first and then discuss it. The following is the code for cube view "MM: Return List (cube)" (ZC_MM_RetList):

```
/* Freek Keijzer, myBrand, 17.01.2021
Cube-view for Return List.
Business requirement: user-story 34567
Main source tables:
RESB - "Reservation/dependent requirements"
LIPS - "SD document: Delivery: Item data"
T320 - "Assignment IM Storage Location to WM Warehouse Number"
```

Layered structure of CDS-views:

```
ZC_MM_RetList                    - Cube-view
|- ZP_MM_RetListUn               - Union key figures Reservations
|                                  + Deliveries
|  |- ZP_MM_RetListRESB          - Transformed view key figures
|  |                               Reservations
|  |  |- ZB_MM_RetListRESB       - Basic view key figures
|  |  |  |                         Reservations
|  |  |  |- resb                 - Source table Reservations
|  |  |  |- lips                 - Source table Deliveries
|  |  |- ZP_MM_LIPSResAg         - Preparation for aggregation on
|  |  |  |                         Reservation Item
|  |  |  |- ZB_MM_RetListRESB
|  |  |  |  |- ...
|  |  |- t320                    - Table to determine Warehouse
|  |  |                            EWM/IM
|  |- ZB_MM_RetListLIPS          - Basic view key figures Deliveries
|     |- lips
|- I_Material                    - SAP std view attributes Material
|  |- mara, ...
|- I_Plant                       - SAP std view attributes Plant
|  |- t001w, ...
|- I_StorageLocation             - SAP std view attributes
|                                  Storage Location
|  |- t001l, ...
|- I_MaintenanceOrder            - SAP std view attributes
|                                  Maintenance Order
|  |- afih, ...
|- I_Movement_TypeText           - SAP std view texts Movement Type
   |- t156ht
```

```
-------------------------------------------------------
Change-log:
-------------------------------------------------------
-------------------------------------------------------*/
@EndUserText.label: 'MM: Return List (cube)'
@AbapCatalog.sqlViewName: 'ZCMMRETLIST'

@VDM.viewType: #COMPOSITE
@Analytics.dataCategory: #CUBE
@AccessControl.authorizationCheck: #CHECK
@AbapCatalog.compiler.compareFilter: true
@DataAging.noAgingRestriction: true
@Search.searchable: false

define view ZC_MM_RetList as select from ZP_MM_RetListUn as _Ret
  association[0..1] to I_Material as _Material
    on $projection.Material = _Material.Material
  association[0..1] to I_Plant as _Plant
    on $projection.Plant = _Plant.Plant
  association[0..1] to I_StorageLocation as _StorageLocation
    on $projection.Plant          = _StorageLocation.
    Plant              and
      $projection.StorageLocation = _StorageLocation.
      StorageLocation
  association[0..1] to I_MaintenanceOrder as _MaintenanceOrder
    on $projection.MaintenanceOrder = _MaintenanceOrder.
    MaintenanceOrder
  association[0..*] to I_Movement_TypeText as _MovementTypeText
    on $projection.MovementType = _MovementTypeText.
    MovementType
{
```

```
//--Key fields, currencies, units
    @Semantics.quantity.unitOfMeasure: 'meins'
    @DefaultAggregation: #SUM
    @EndUserText.label: 'Quantity'
    _Ret.bdmng,                     //"Quantity" = resb.bdmng or
                                    lips.lgmng

    @Semantics.quantity.unitOfMeasure: 'meins'
    @DefaultAggregation: #SUM
    @EndUserText.label: 'Returned'
    _Ret.enmng,                     //"Returned" = resb.enmng or
                                    lips.lgmng

    @Semantics.quantity.unitOfMeasure: 'meins'
    @DefaultAggregation: #SUM
    @EndUserText.label: 'Received'
    _Ret.QuantRec,                  //"Received" = resb.enmng or
                                    lips.lgmng with conditions

    @EndUserText.label: 'Unit'
    _Ret.meins,                     //Base Unit of Measure
                                    (resb/lips.meins)

    @DefaultAggregation: #SUM
    @EndUserText.label: 'Numb.of Reser.'
    _Ret.CounterRes,                //Number of Reservation Items

    @DefaultAggregation: #SUM
    @EndUserText.label: 'Numb.of Deliv.'
    _Ret.CounterDel,                //Number of Delivery Items
//--Characteristics
    @EndUserText.label: 'Source (RESB, LIPS)'
    _Ret.Source,                    //Source = 'RESB', 'LIPS'
```

```
@EndUserText.label: 'Res.nr'
_Ret.rsnum,                      //Reservation Number
                                 (resb/lips.rsnum)
@EndUserText.label: 'Res.pos'
_Ret.rspos,                      //Reservation Item
                                 (resb/lips.rspos)
@ObjectModel.foreignKey.association: '_Plant'
_Ret.werks as Plant,             //Plant (resb/lips.werks)
@ObjectModel.foreignKey.association: '_StorageLocation'
_Ret.lgort as StorageLocation,       //Storage Location
                                     (resb/lips.lgort)
@ObjectModel.foreignKey.association: '_MaintenanceOrder'
_Ret.aufnr as MaintenanceOrder,      //Order Number
                                     (resb/lips.aufnr)
_Ret.xloek,                      //Item is deleted (resb.xloek)
@ObjectModel.text.association: '_MovementTypeText'
_Ret.bwart as MovementType,      //Movement type inventory
                                 management (resb/lips.bwart)
_Ret.kzear,                      //Final issue for this
                                 reservation (resb.kzear)
@ObjectModel.foreignKey.association: '_Material'
_Ret.matnr as Material,          //Material Number
                                 (resb/lips.matnr)
@EndUserText.label: 'Del.nr'
_Ret.vbeln as EWMInboundDelivery,    //Delivery
                                     (lips.vbeln)
@EndUserText.label: 'Del.pos'
_Ret.vbelp,                      //Delivery Item (lips.posnr)
_Ret.bwtar,            .         //Valuation Type (lips.bwtar)
_Ret.StorLoc_EWM_IM,             //"Warehouse EWM/IM?" =
                                 'EWM' or 'IM'
```

```
    _Ret.StorLocCompl,                //"Warehouse completed?",
                                      see logic in union-view

//--Characteristics via associations
    _Material.MaterialGroup,          //Material Group (mara.matkl)

//--Associations to be passed on to a higher level
    _Plant,
    _StorageLocation,
    _Material,
    _MaintenanceOrder,
    _MovementTypeText
}
```

Let's go through the code from top to bottom:

- The cube view is the best place for more comprehensive inline documentation. It is for instance a good place to repeat the source tables used in the basic views and to insert the full layered structure of the underlying CDS views. You remember the old-school overview ridiculed earlier, right?

- The view is of type Composite and category Cube. It needs to be of category Cube to be able to build query views on top.

- We were lucky to find standard SAP CDS views for the required master data. The views I_Material, I_Plant, I_StorageLocation, and I_MaintenanceOrder were used for the attributes and text. The view I_Movement_ TypeText was used for text only. The part of the CDS view between the braces is called the *projection* area. In this area, we first renamed the involved characteristics from the German-based abbreviations to English-based names used in SAP standard views. An example is `_Ret.werks as Plant`. In the projection area, associations are coupled to characteristics via the annotations `@ObjectModel.foreignKey.association` and `@ObjectModel.text.association`.

- Renaming fields to the English-based names used in SAP standard views has the additional advantage that options to use the Jump To functionality from analytical queries will become available. This topic will be covered in the next chapter.

- For all key figures, the aggregation behavior needs to be entered in the cube view (or lower) with the annotation `@DefaultAggregation`. Again, use the value `#SUM` for quantities and amounts, `MAX` for things like prizes, and other values in exceptional situations.

- Key figures are coupled to currencies or units via the annotations `@Semantics.quantity.unitOfMeasure` and `@Semantics.amount.currencyCode`.

- Comments for data lineage can become more complex before a union view. Here's an example for a key figure: `//"Quantity" = resb.bdmng or lips.lgmng`. Here's an example for a characteristic: `//Plant (resb/lips.werks)`. And if it all becomes too complicated, use `//"Warehouse completed?", see logic in union-view`.

- To make an attribute from a master data view available as a dimension in the query, that is, with full navigational functionality, we need to include it explicitly in the projection area. Here's an example: `_Material.MaterialGroup`.

- To be able to use the associations for master data in a query, we need to pass them to a higher level. This is usually done at the end of the projection area.

Basically, this is all you need to know about cube views.

Embedded Analytics from Scratch: Query View and Final Result

And now for the grand finale: the query view. In the query layer, we reap what we sowed in the lower layers. Bring on the code:

```
/* Freek Keijzer, myBrand, 17.01.2021
Query-view for Return List.
Business requirement: user-story 34567
----------------------------------------------------------
Change-log:
----------------------------------------------------------
----------------------------------------------------------*/
@EndUserText.label: 'MM: Return List'
@AbapCatalog.sqlViewName: 'ZQMMRETLIST'

@VDM.viewType: #CONSUMPTION
@Analytics.query: true
@OData.publish: true

define view ZQ_MM_RetList as select from ZC_MM_RetList
{
//--Key figures
    bdmng,                      //"Quantity" = resb.bdmng or
                                lips.lgmng
    enmng,                      //"Returned" = resb.enmng or
                                lips.lgmng
```

```
    @DefaultAggregation: #FORMULA
    @AnalyticsDetails.query.formula: '$projection.bdmng -
    $projection.enmng'
    @EndUserText.label: 'Remaining'
    0 as QuantityRemaining,      //"Remaining" = "Quantity" -
                                 "Returned"
    QuantRec,                    //"Received" = resb.enmng or
                                 lips.lgmng with conditions
    @AnalyticsDetails.query.hidden: true
    CounterRes,                  //Number of Reservation Items
    CounterDel,                  //Number of Delivery Items

//--Characteristics initially in rows
    @Consumption.filter: {selectionType: #SINGLE,
    multipleSelections: true, mandatory: false}
    @AnalyticsDetails.query.variableSequence : 40
    @AnalyticsDetails.query.axis: #ROWS
    @AnalyticsDetails.query.display: #KEY_TEXT
    @AnalyticsDetails.query.totals: #SHOW
    Material,                    //Material Number
                                 (resb/lips.matnr)

//--Free characteristics
    Source,                      //Source = 'RESB', 'LIPS'
    rsnum,                       //Reservation Number
                                 (resb/lips.rsnum)
    rspos,                       //Reserveringspositie
                                 (resb/lips.rspos)
    @Consumption.filter: {selectionType: #SINGLE,
    multipleSelections: true, mandatory: false}
    @AnalyticsDetails.query.variableSequence : 10
    @AnalyticsDetails.query.display: #KEY_TEXT
    Plant,                       //Plant (resb/lips.werks)
```

```
@Consumption.filter: {selectionType: #SINGLE,
multipleSelections: true, mandatory: false}
@AnalyticsDetails.query.variableSequence : 20
@AnalyticsDetails.query.display: #KEY_TEXT
StorageLocation,                 //Storage Location
                                 (resb/lips.lgort)
@Consumption.filter: {selectionType: #SINGLE,
multipleSelections: true, mandatory: false}
@AnalyticsDetails.query.variableSequence : 30
@AnalyticsDetails.query.display: #KEY_TEXT
MaintenanceOrder,                //Order Number
                                 (resb/lips.aufnr)
xloek,                           //Item is deleted (resb.xloek)
MovementType,                    //Movement type inventory
                                 management (resb/lips.bwart)
kzear,                           //Final issue for this
                                 reservation (resb.kzear)
EWMInboundDelivery,              //Delivery (lips.vbeln)
vbelp,                           //Delivery Item (lips.posnr)
bwtar,                           //Valuation Type (lips.bwtar)
StorLoc_EWM_IM,                  //"Warehouse EWM/IM?" =
                                 'EWM' or 'IM'
@Consumption.filter: {selectionType: #SINGLE,
multipleSelections: true, mandatory: false, defaultValue: ''}
@AnalyticsDetails.query.variableSequence : 50
StorLocCompl,                    //"Warehouse completed?",
                                 see logic in union-view
MaterialGroup                    //Material Group (mara.matkl)
}
```

This is the final CDS view, and thus here are the final observations:

- A query view will pop up as being of type Consumption in the app Query Browser through the annotation @VDM.viewType: #CONSUMPTION.

- More important is the annotation @Analytics.query: true. This will assign it to the category Query in Query Browser, but, more importantly, it is conditional for the view to be used as an analytical query via the app Query Browser or in any other way.

- Operations on key figures such as add, subtract, multiply, or divide can be done in the underlying views and propagated to the query view, but they can also be done in the query view itself. BI specialists will recognize this as being the difference between a "before-aggregation" and "after-aggregation" calculation. We could have calculated the quantity QuantityRemaining as resb.bdmng - resb.enmng in a underlying view, and that would have been "before aggregation." We now choose to calculate it "after (OLAP) aggregation" using the @DefaultAggregation: #FORMULA annotation. This is an example of a situation in which I first built a similar object using the tile Custom Analytical Query in order to learn from the generated code. We want the key figure CounterRes to be available in the query, but not initially displayed. This can be arranged with the annotation @AnalyticsDetails.query.hidden: true.

- We saw an example of using the filter annotation
  @Consumption.filter earlier in this chapter, but in
  this code we see more options. The characteristic
  "Warehouse Completed?" indicates which part of the
  data is normally relevant for the operational report
  and which part is not. The requirement was to have
  a filter on the value ' ' by default but to give the user
  the opportunity to overrule this on the selection
  screen. This is an action that would lead to data for
  "Warehouse Completed?" being true, or value X, shown
  also. This is accomplished by following coding:
  @Consumption.filter: {selectionType: #SINGLE,
  multipleSelections: true, mandatory: false,
  defaultValue: ''}.

- The order in which dimensions appear in the selection
  screen is determined by following annotation:
  @AnalyticsDetails.query.variableSequence.

It's time to see what we have reaped. Please check out Figure 5-8.
A celebration is in order, I should think.

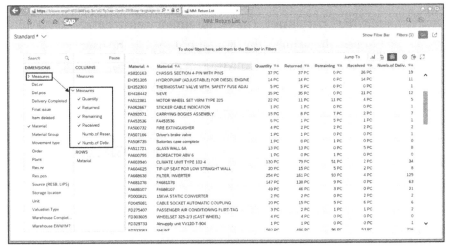

Figure 5-8. *The end result of the "Embedded Analytics from Scratch" case: selection screen (top) and query output area (bottom)*

As said, the "Embedded Analytics from Scratch" case presented in this chapter is based on real-life business requirements. The only differences with the actual stack of CDS views are a minor simplification of requirements and data model and a translation of descriptions and comments from Dutch to English. This actual stack of CDS views is currently being acceptance tested and will be live by the time this book is published.

Retrospective

I will give my final judgment regarding the tooling used in this chapter at the end of the next chapter. So far, my experiences are quite positive, and I hope you agree.

What I would like to do now is share experiences with fellow developers coming from a BW background, which may well be the majority of readers of this book. First, why do SAP's BI tools appear to become more and more primitive over time? BW had a nice development shell, native HANA was already more primitive but still with a graphical user interface, and now this? Typing code day-in and day-out is absurd. I'm glad to get this out of my system.

On the other hand, looking at it from some distance, there are quite a few similarities with BW development. The layered approach with a focus on a reusability of objects is of course familiar, as well as using standard content as much as possible. Also, there are some differences. For example, in BW the union (multiprovider, composite provider) is on top of multiple cubes, whereas in CDS view development the union usually is below a single cube. It's the same layers, but in a different order, causing differences in the data model. BW consultants are used to carry out aggregations by loading data into an "(advanced) Data Store Object" or "(a)DSO" with specific key fields. The SQL alternative is a view with the group by statement aggregating on specific fields. There's no loading here, of course. Connecting attributes and text to a cube is also a familiar concept. In query development, there are more similarities. Restricted key figures can be defined with a case statement, usually on the cube level. Calculated key figures are defined on a query level with the @DefaultAggregation: #FORMULA annotation, of which we saw an example in this chapter. Options for the selection screen will look familiar.

But coming from BW development, the exploding key figures phenomenon may come as a surprise to you. Every time you make a connection through a left outer join or an association, there is a risk of exploding key figures. In the section on data integration, we saw an example in which a key figure was multiplied by 3 because of a cardinality issue. Similar issues pop up all the time during ABAP CDS development. The high-score record within the current project is multiplication by a factor of 557. The cause was a left outer join to obtain a name for an SAP user ID via a nonkey field (`pa0105.usrid`, for those interested). If the SAP user ID is empty in the primary data source, the left outer join returns all people without SAP user IDs in the table. This was a varying number, but at the time the record was achieved it was apparently 557. Try explaining that to a business user: "The amount is €557,000 instead of €1,000 because the SAP user ID is empty." Good luck with that. The struggle against exploding key figures is a continuous struggle. I therefore became quite good at building "triangles." In many cases, the IDE warns you against potential cardinality issues. Please take these warnings seriously.

What you have learned in this chapter will probably earn you a Satisfactory at your next performance review. If you want to strive for Excellent, then move on to the next chapter.

CHAPTER 6

Most Work (Advanced): Building Analytical Queries in an IDE

The previous chapter was unusually structured, at least for me, as it was built around a well-defined end-to-end case. This chapter will be less structured, I am afraid. It contains a loosely coupled bunch of advanced topics brought together in one chapter. But you have grown. You can handle it.

Custom Master Data Views

Up to now, we were lucky to always find standard SAP attribute and text views to associate with the facts in our cubes. However, you cannot always be that lucky. In certain areas, SAP is still working on its content. In such cases, you need to build your own custom master data views.

Custom Text View

In HR, for instance, I could not find a standard text view for Employee Subgroup. Therefore, I built my own. It is not that hard, if you take a standard text view, like for instance I_MaterialText, as an example. Here is the code of my first custom text view, with many to follow:

```
@EndUserText.label: 'HR: Employee Subgroup text'
@AbapCatalog.sqlViewName: 'ZTHRPERSK'
@ObjectModel.representativeKey: 'Persk'

@VDM.viewType: #BASIC
@ObjectModel.dataCategory: #TEXT
@AccessControl.authorizationCheck: #NOT_REQUIRED
@ClientHandling.algorithm: #SESSION_VARIABLE
@Metadata.ignorePropagatedAnnotations: true

define view ZT_HR_Persk as select from t503t
  association[0..1] to I_Language as _Language
    on $projection.Language = _Language.Language
{
    @ObjectModel.foreignKey.association: '_Language'
    @Semantics.language
key sprsl            as Language,
key persk            as Persk,
    @Semantics.text
    ptext            as PerskName,
    _Language
}
```

The most important annotations for a text view are @ObjectModel. dataCategory: #TEXT, which makes it a text view, and @ObjectModel. representativeKey. All you need to do is find a suitable table storing the text (in this case t503t), figure out the field for the language (often spras

or langu, but here sprsl), and find the fields for the key (persk) and text
(ptext). Simply copy and paste and then modify. Do not forget to also modify
the value for the annotation @ObjectModel.representativeKey.

The end result is a multilingual text view. It can be attached to a
dimension using the @ObjectModel.text.association annotation. The
description of the dimension value shown will be automatically adapted to
the user's login language.

Custom Attribute View

Another area where SAP is still working on its standard content is real
estate, so this is good practice for a developer. One of the things we needed
was a text view called Region of Business Entity. The source table for these
text views is not multilingual, so we could do it a bit differently, i.e., as an
attribute view without attributes but with text. Hang on a bit, and you will
see what I mean. Here is the code of this attribute view without attributes:

```
@EndUserText.label: 'RE: Region of Business Entity attributes'
@AbapCatalog.sqlViewName: 'ZARESTDORT'
@ObjectModel.representativeKey: 'sstdort'

@VDM.viewType: #BASIC
@Analytics.dataCategory: #DIMENSION
@AbapCatalog.compiler.compareFilter: true
@AbapCatalog.preserveKey: true
@AccessControl.authorizationCheck: #CHECK

define view ZA_RE_StdOrt as select from tiv35
{
    @ObjectModel.text.element: 'xstdort'
key sstdort,                         //Regional location
(tiv35.sstdort)
    xstdort                          //Regional location,
    description (tiv35.xstdort)
}
```

The view type is defined by the annotation @Analytics.dataCategory: #DIMENSION. This type of view is primarily used for attributes, but text can also be squeezed in. Here the annotation @ObjectModel.text.element: 'xstdort' is linked to the field sstdort, which means that the field xstdort will be seen by the system as the text field for sstdort. The field xstdort will not be included in the list of attributes but will be the source of the Text display option. As a result, there are no attributes to display, and Attributes will not appear as a right-click option.

We also needed an attribute view that actually did include some attributes, i.e., for the field Business Entity. Besides the fields from the master data table vibdbe, we included a business partner, the name belonging to an SAP user ID, and the standard view for attributes of Company Code. We even used the freshly developed attribute view without attributes for Region of Business Entity. Behold the code:

```
/* Freek Keijzer, myBrand, 24.01.2021
Attribute view for Business Entity
Business requirement: user-story 56789

Layered structure of CDS views:
  ZA_RE_Swenr     - "Business Entity attributes"
  |- vibdbe       - "Business Entity"
  |- I_CompanyCode - Std view attributes CoCode
  |  |- t001      - "Company Codes"
  |- ZA_RE_StdOrt - "Region of Business Entity attributes"
  |  |- tiv35     - "Regional locations"
  |- vibpobjrel   - "Business Partner-Object Relationship"
  |- v_username   - "View for Reading User Name"
-----------------------------------------------------------*/
@EndUserText.label: 'RE: Business Entity attributes'
@AbapCatalog.sqlViewName: 'ZARESWENR'
@ObjectModel.representativeKey: 'REBusinessEntity'
```

```
@VDM.viewType: #BASIC
@Analytics.dataCategory: #DIMENSION
@AbapCatalog.compiler.compareFilter: true
@AbapCatalog.preserveKey: true
@AccessControl.authorizationCheck: #CHECK

define view ZA_RE_Swenr as select from vibdbe
  left outer join v_username
    on v_username.bname = vibdbe.responsible
  association[1..1] to I_CompanyCode as _CompanyCode
    on _CompanyCode.CompanyCode = $projection.CompanyCode
  association[0..1] to ZA_RE_StdOrt as _RE_StdOrt
    on $projection.sstdort = _RE_StdOrt.sstdort
  association[0..*] to vibpobjrel as _RE_Partner
    on _RE_Partner.intreno    = $projection.REKey
       and _RE_Partner.appl      = '0051'
       and //= Business Entity
       _RE_Partner.validfrom <= $session.system_date
       and _RE_Partner.validto   >= $session.system_date
{
    @ObjectModel.foreignKey.association: '_CompanyCode'
key vibdbe.bukrs as CompanyCode,
//Company Code (vibdbe.bukrs)
    @ObjectModel.text.element: 'xwetext'
key vibdbe.swenr as REBusinessEntity,
//Business Entity (vibdbe.swenr)
    @Consumption.hidden: true
    vibdbe.intreno as REKey,
    //RE Key (vibdbe.intreno)
    @Consumption.hidden: true
    vibdbe.objnr as StatusObject,
    //Object Number (vibdbe.objnr)
```

```
    vibdbe.imkey as RealEstateObject,
    //Real Estate Key (vibdbe.imkey)
    vibdbe.rerf as CreatedByUser,
    //Entered By (vibdbe.rerf)
    @EndUserText.label: 'Resp.Prs.SAP-id'
    vibdbe.responsible,
    //Person Responsible, SAP-user (vibdbe.responsible)
    @Semantics.text: true
    vibdbe.xwetext,
    //Business Entity Name (vibdbe.xwetext)
    @ObjectModel.foreignKey.association: '_RE_StdOrt'
    vibdbe.sstdort,
    //Regional location (vibdbe.sstdort)
    vibdbe.sverkehr,
    //Transport Connections (vibdbe.sverkehr)
    vibdbe.slagewe,
    //Location (vibdbe.slagewe)
    vibdbe.usgfunction,
    //Function (vibdbe.usgfunction)
    @EndUserText.label: 'Station Manager'
    _RE_Partner[1:role = 'ZR0014'].partner as StationManager,
    //Business Partner (vibpobjrel.partner) for Role 'ZR0014'
    @EndUserText.label: 'Resp.Prs.Name'
    v_username.name_text as ResponsibleName,
    //Person Responsible, name (v_username.name_text <- vibdbe.
    responsible)

//--Associations to be passed on to a higher level
    _CompanyCode,
    _RE_StdOrt,
    _RE_Partner
}
```

Let's once again go through this code from top to bottom, as it contains quite a few new things.

- As said earlier, technically left outer joins and associations are more or less the same thing, but there are some differences in use. Associations are preferred from a performance standpoint, as "uncalled" associations do not contribute to the overall query runtime, whereas left outer joins do. But there are restrictions on the use of associations that may lead to the application of left outer joins. For example, a "double" join (i.e., joining to table/view A and then joining to table/view B from fields in A) is not possible with associations in one view definition. Another restriction on the use of associations led to the choice to connect view v_username to the underlying view via a left outer join. Left outer joins and associations can be applied simultaneously, as long as the code for the left outer joins is placed immediately after the select statement for the underlying view, thus making these views part of the dataset to which the other views are associated.

- The association association[0..*] to vibpobjrel would normally lead to a cardinality warning, as a single Business Entity can be connected to multiple business partners, but for different roles. The [1:role = 'ZR0014'] part of code _RE_Partner[1:role = 'ZR0014'].partner prevents this from happening by connecting the Business Entity to only one partner role.

- For the first time, we see the use of a session variable, i.e., $session.system_date. You will learn more about session variables in the "Using Session Variables and Environment Annotations" section of this chapter.

- Also, there is a new annotation called @Consumption. hidden: true. With this annotation we say that the field is too technical for users to be confronted with. It will appear in data previews and such, but not in query outputs (or in this case a list of attributes).

- Through the annotation @Semantics.text: true, the field vibdbe.xwetext will not appear in the list of attributes, but will be the source of the Text option of Business Entity.

- At the end of the projection area, the associations _ CompanyCode, _RE_StdOrt, and _RE_Partner are passed on to provide master data for the attributes Company Code, Regional location, and Station Manager.

We have 12 fields potentially usable as attributes minus 2 that are hidden minus 1 defined as text, leaving 9 attributes. Let's see if this checks out. For a complex view like this, it would be wise to test it separately before connecting it to a cube view. This can be done by building a minimalistic, quick-and-dirty cube view followed by an equally minimalistic, quick-and-dirty query view. Here is the code for the first cube:

```
@EndUserText.label: 'ZC_ZZ_Cube'
@AbapCatalog.sqlViewName: 'ZXZZCUBE'
@VDM.viewType: #COMPOSITE
@Analytics.dataCategory: #CUBE
define view ZC_ZZ_Cube as select from vibdbe
  association[0..1] to ZA_RE_Swenr as _Swenr
    on $projection.bukrs = _Swenr.CompanyCode
      and $projection.swenr = _Swenr.REBusinessEntity
```

```
{
key vibdbe.bukrs,
    @ObjectModel.foreignKey.association: '_Swenr'
key vibdbe.swenr,
    _Swenr.sstdort,
    @DefaultAggregation: #SUM
    1 as counter,
    _Swenr,
    _Swenr._RE_StdOrt
}
```

Here is the code for the query:

```
@EndUserText.label: 'ZQ_ZZ_Query'
@AbapCatalog.sqlViewName: 'ZQZZQUERY'
@VDM.viewType: #CONSUMPTION
@Analytics.query: true
define view ZQ_ZZ_Query as select from ZC_ZZ_Cube
{
    bukrs,
    swenr,
    sstdort,
    counter
}
```

The query output area shown in Figure 6-1 demonstrates that Company Code, Business Entity, and Regional location all have text, and that Business Entity has 1, 2, 3, 4, 5, ... 9 attributes. Well done!

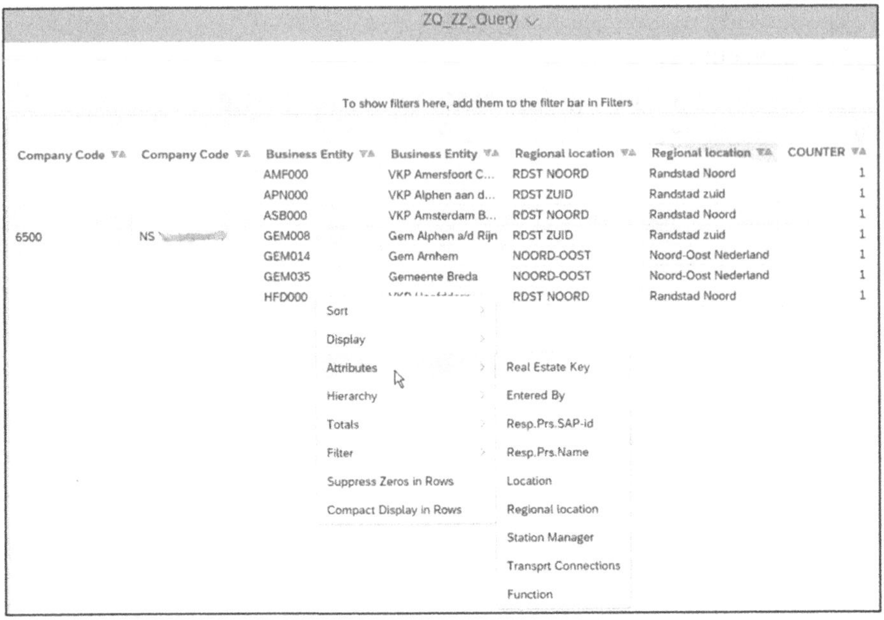

Figure 6-1. *Custom attribute view demoed with a minimalistic test query*

Complex Logic

Real-life business requirements can necessitate logic much more complex than anything covered up to now. That is when the tough get going. Many such examples involve *transpositions*, sometimes from columns to rows, but mostly from rows to columns. These two types of transpositions will be covered in this section, with an example. For the category "complex logic other", I developed an exercise, also based on a case from practice.

Before we start with complex logic, let me give you an important pointer. From the standard SQL examples, I got the impression that it is possible to define a new field and then immediately use it. Unfortunately, that is not possible within the same CDS view. The code shown next will not work, as I defined a new field called StorLoc_EWM_IM in a view and immediately used it in the definition of StorLocCompl. I can use the field

194

StorLoc_EWM_IM, but only in the next CDS view built on top of this one. This is the reason that complex logic often leads to many layers of CDS views.

```
...
case
  when werks_t320 != '' then 'EWM'
  else                       'IM'
end as StorLoc_EWM_IM,
case
  when StorLoc_EWM_IM = 'EWM' and bdmng  = enmng then 'X'
  when StorLoc_EWM_IM = 'EWM' and bdmng != enmng then ''
  else
  spe_gen_elikz
end as StorLocCompl,
...
```

From the knowledge obtained in Chapter 1 that HANA is a columnar database, let me also give you a few pointers of a semiphilosophical nature. A CDS view is not an ABAP program. You are not looping through a data package. A CDS view has no "row awareness." It does not know in which row it is, what the previous row was, and what the next row will be. It does not know anything. It is a view. If it could think, it would only think: "I have columns, I have columns, I have...."

Transposition from Columns to Rows

To illustrate the way in which a transposition from columns to rows operates, I can make use of an SAP-delivered view, i.e., Itemization of COSP_BAK (Kkag_Cosp_Bak_Item_View). The table CO Object: Cost Totals for External Postings (COSP_BAK) has a somewhat old-fashioned structure, as it has the amounts for all 16 fiscal periods in separate columns. Figure 6-2 shows the required transformation for one of the key figures in the table.

GJAHR	WTG001	WTG002	...	WTG016
2021	67.00	68.00	...	24.00

GJAHR	PERIO	WTGBTR
2021	001	67.00
2021	002	68.00
...	...	...
2021	016	24.00

Figure 6-2. *Transposition from columns to rows*

This is the standard SAP code that does the job. For brevity, I removed some repetitive parts here:

```
@AbapCatalog.sqlViewName: 'KKAG_COSPBAK_ITM'
@EndUserText.label: 'Itemization of COSP_BAK'
...
define view Kkag_Cosp_Bak_Item_View as
select
  mandt, objnr, gjahr, wrttp, lednr, versn, kstar, hrkft,
  vrgng, vbund, pargb, beknz, twaer, meinh, beltp, '001' as
  perio, wkg001 as wkgbtr, wkf001 as wkfbtr, wog001 as wogbtr,
  wtg001 as wtgbtr, meg001 as megbtr from cosp_bak
  where wkg001 != 0 or wkf001 != 0 or wog001 != 0 or wtg001 !=
  0 or meg001 != 0
union all select
  mandt, objnr, gjahr, wrttp, lednr, versn, kstar, hrkft,
  vrgng, vbund, pargb, beknz, twaer, meinh, beltp, '002' as
  perio, wkg002 as wkgbtr, wkf002 as wkfbtr, wog002 as wogbtr,
  wtg002 as wtgbtr, meg002 as megbtr from cosp_bak
  where wkg002 != 0 or wkf002 != 0 or wog002 != 0 or wtg002 !=
  0 or meg002 != 0
...
union all select
  mandt, objnr, gjahr, wrttp, lednr, versn, kstar, hrkft,
  vrgng, vbund, pargb, beknz, twaer, meinh, beltp, '016' as
  perio, wkg016 as wkgbtr, wkf016 as wkfbtr, wog016 as wogbtr,
```

```
wtg016 as wtgbtr, meg016 as megbtr from cosp_bak
where wkg016 != 0 or wkf016 != 0 or wog016 != 0 or
wtg016 != 0 or meg016 != 0
```

The core of this solution is formed by the 15 union all statements to connect the 16 columns for fiscal periods. The key figures are renamed from, e.g., wtg001 to wtgbtr. The field Fiscal Period (perio) is manually filled. This type of solution can be used in all cases in which a transposition from columns to rows is required.

Transposition from Rows to Columns

The need for a transposition from rows to columns occurs often, much more so than the other way around. I will therefore present one example in this section rather extensively and two more in the "Author-Delivered Content" section.

The example I will present in this section has to do with the Return List case covered in Chapter 5. For this case, I simplified the requirements and data model a bit compared with the actual project requirements. One of the requirements sacrificed in the simplification was the user status of Maintenance Order. I will discuss the solution for this requirement here, as it is a good example of a transposition from rows to columns.

Gathering all the necessary basic data is not that hard, even though four tables are involved. The code for the basic view is as follows:

```
/* Freek Keijzer, myBrand, 02.06.2020
Basic data for User Status of Order.
Source tables:
AUFK  - " Order master data "
JEST  - " Individual Object Status "
T003O - " Order Types "
TJ30T - " Texts for User Status"
Data restricted to t003o.stsma = 'Z0000004' = 'Maximo interface'.
```

```
-----------------------------------------------------------*/
@EndUserText.label: 'LOG: Data for UserStatus Order'
@AbapCatalog.sqlViewName: 'ZBLOGAUFKJEST'

@AbapCatalog.compiler.compareFilter: true
@AbapCatalog.preserveKey: true
@AccessControl.authorizationCheck: #CHECK

define view ZB_LOG_AUFK_JEST as select from aufk
  inner join jest
    on jest.objnr = aufk.objnr
  inner join t003o
    on t003o.auart = aufk.auart
  inner join tj30t
    on tj30t.stsma = t003o.stsma and
       tj30t.estat = jest.stat    and
       tj30t.spras = 'N'
{
    aufk.aufnr,                 //Order Number (aufk.aufnr)
    aufk.auart,                 //Order Type (aufk.auart)
    jest.stat,                  //Object status (jest.stat/
                                    tj30t.estat)
    jest.inact,                 //Indicator: Status Is Inactive
                                    (jest.inact)
    t003o.stsma,                //Status Profile (t003o/tj30t.
                                    stsma)
    tj30t.txt04,                //Status CHAR-4 (tj30t.txt04)
    tj30t.txt30                 //Status CHAR-30 (tj30t.txt30)
}
where t003o.stsma = 'Z0000004'
```

Figure 6-3 shows the output of this view. We see multiple user statuses for each order in various formats: as an internal key (stat), as a short string (txt04), and as a long string (txt30). The last two come from a language-dependent table, but we restricted the join with this table to language N. Not all statuses are active, and also not all statuses are interesting for the business.

aufnr	auart	stat	inact	stsma	txt04	txt30
AP00000049	ZMX1	E0008		Z0000004	ANNU	Taak geannuleerd
AP00000049	ZMX1	E0001	X	Z0000004	WOM	Wacht op materiaal
AP00000049	ZMX1	E0007	X	Z0000004	WGK	Wacht op goedkeuring
AP00000049	ZMX1	E0006	X	Z0000004	NGVU	Niet gereed voor uitvoering
AP00000049	ZMX1	E0010	X	Z0000004	TKRT	Voorraadtekort
AP00000050	ZMX1	E0001		Z0000004	WOM	Wacht op materiaal
AP00000050	ZMX1	E0006		Z0000004	NGVU	Niet gereed voor uitvoering
AP00000050	ZMX1	E0010		Z0000004	TKRT	Voorraadtekort
AP00000051	ZMX1	E0001		Z0000004	WOM	Wacht op materiaal
AP00000051	ZMX1	E0010		Z0000004	TKRT	Voorraadtekort
AP00000051	ZMX1	E0006		Z0000004	NGVU	Niet gereed voor uitvoering
AP00000052	ZMX1	E0002	X	Z0000004	GGK	Goedgekeurd
AP00000052	ZMX1	E0006		Z0000004	NGVU	Niet gereed voor uitvoering
AP00000052	ZMX1	E0007		Z0000004	WGK	Wacht op goedkeuring
AP00000053	ZMX1	E0006		Z0000004	NGVU	Niet gereed voor uitvoering
AP00000053	ZMX1	E0002	X	Z0000004	GGK	Goedgekeurd
AP00000053	ZMX1	E0007		Z0000004	WGK	Wacht op goedkeuring
AP00000054	ZMX1	E0005		Z0000004	SLUI	Taak sluiten
AP00000054	ZMX1	E0010	X	Z0000004	TKRT	Voorraadtekort
AP00000054	ZMX1	E0006	X	Z0000004	NGVU	Niet gereed voor uitvoering
AP00000054	ZMX1	E0007	X	Z0000004	WGK	Wacht op goedkeuring
AP00000054	ZMX1	E0002	X	Z0000004	GGK	Goedgekeurd
AP00000055	ZMX1	E0002		Z0000004	GGK	Goedgekeurd

Figure 6-3. *Output of views for the user status of Maintenance Order: basic data*

Figure 6-4 shows the business requirement for this data. For each order, the TXT04 version of the statuses are to be gathered in a single field separated by a space. Status data is displayed in this format by many standard SAP transactions and apps, but this format is not stored anywhere in the database. All transactions and apps determine this format on the fly during the transaction runtime. Let's get back to our main topic: this is a classic case of transposition from rows to columns.

AUFNR	TXT04
AP00000050	WOM
AP00000050	NVGU

AUFNR	AufnrUserStat
AP00000050	WOM NVGU

Figure 6-4. *Transposition from rows to columns for the user status (TXT04 → AufnrUserStat) of Maintenance Order (Aufnr)*

Flipping the dataset from columns to rows is done in two steps. Step 1 is going from multiple rows/single column to multiple rows/multiple columns with restricted field definitions using the case statement. Step 2 is going from multiple rows/multiple columns to a single row/multiple columns with an aggregation using the group by statement. We also need to do this only for active and relevant statuses. For the latter, the business provided a list. First here is the code for step 1:

```
/* Freek Keijzer, myBrand, 02.06.2020
"Flip" dataset from rows to columns.
In the next step, this will be aggregated to 1 line per order.
------------------------------------------------------------*/
@EndUserText.label: 'LOG: Data for User Status of Order'
@AbapCatalog.sqlViewName: 'ZPLOGAUFKJEST'

@AbapCatalog.compiler.compareFilter: true
@AbapCatalog.preserveKey: true
@AccessControl.authorizationCheck: #CHECK

define view ZP_LOG_AUFK_JEST as select from ZB_LOG_AUFK_JEST
{
    aufnr,
    inact,
    txt04,
    case when inact = '' and txt04 = 'WOM'  then 'WOM'  else ''
    end as sta01,
```

```
      case when inact = '' and txt04 = 'GGK'  then 'GGK'  else ''
      end as sta02,
      case when inact = '' and txt04 = 'UITV' then 'UITV' else ''
      end as sta03,
      case when inact = '' and txt04 = 'GERE' then 'GERE' else ''
      end as sta04,
      case when inact = '' and txt04 = 'SLUI' then 'SLUI' else ''
      end as sta05,
      case when inact = '' and txt04 = 'NGVU' then 'NGVU' else ''
      end as sta06,
      case when inact = '' and txt04 = 'WGK'  then 'WGK'  else ''
      end as sta07,
      case when inact = '' and txt04 = 'ANNU' then 'ANNU' else ''
      end as sta08
}
```

Figure 6-5 illustrates what this code does. Active and relevant statuses are repeated in a separate column in preparation for the aggregation.

aufnr	inact	txt04	sta01	sta02	sta03	sta04	sta05	sta06	sta07	sta08
AP00000049		ANNU								ANNU
AP00000049	X	WOM								
AP00000049	X	WGK								
AP00000049	X	NGVU								
AP00000049	X	TKRT								
AP00000050		WOM	WOM							
AP00000050		NGVU						NGVU		
AP00000050		TKRT								
AP00000051		WOM	WOM							
AP00000051		TKRT								
AP00000051		NGVU						NGVU		
AP00000052	X	GGK								
AP00000052		NGVU						NGVU		
AP00000052		WGK							WGK	
AP00000053		NGVU						NGVU		
AP00000053	X	GGK								
AP00000053		WGK							WGK	
AP00000054		SLUI					SLUI			
AP00000054	X	TKRT								
AP00000054	X	NGVU								
AP00000054	X	WGK								
AP00000054	X	GGK								
AP00000055		GGK		GGK						

Figure 6-5. *Output of views for the user status of Maintenance Order: step 1 of "flipping" the dataset*

The code for step 2 is the basic aggregation of the new columns to one row per Maintenance Order, as shown here:

```
/* Freek Keijzer, myBrand, 02.06.2020
Aggregation of dataset to 1 line per Order.
----------------------------------------------------------*/
@EndUserText.label: 'LOG: Data for User Status of Order, aggr.'
@AbapCatalog.sqlViewName: 'ZPLOGAUFKJESTAG'
...
define view ZP_LOG_AUFK_JEST_AG as select from ZP_LOG_AUFK_JEST
{
key aufnr,
    max(sta01)  as sta01,
    max(sta02)  as sta02,
    max(sta03)  as sta03,
    max(sta04)  as sta04,
    max(sta05)  as sta05,
    max(sta06)  as sta06,
    max(sta07)  as sta07,
    max(sta08)  as sta08
}
group by aufnr
```

Figure 6-6 shows the result of this step. We now have one row per Maintenance Order with the different statuses in separate columns. In other words, the transposition from rows to columns has been completed.

aufnr	sta01	sta02	sta03	sta04	sta05	sta06	sta07	sta08
AP00000049								ANNU
AP00000050	WOM					NGVU		
AP00000051	WOM					NGVU		
AP00000052						NGVU	WGK	
AP00000053						NGVU	WGK	
AP00000054					SLUI			
AP00000055		GGK						

Figure 6-6. *Output of views for the user status of Maintenance Order: step 2 of "flipping" the dataset*

The remaining transformation to fulfill the requirement is a string transformation: bring the status codes together in one "box" separated by a space. This is also done in two steps. In the first step, a space is added in front of a code string if necessary.

```
/* Freek Keijzer, myBrand, 02.06.2020
Preparation for composition of string.
--------------------------------------------------------*/
@EndUserText.label: 'LOG: Data for User Status of Order, strng'
@AbapCatalog.sqlViewName: 'ZPLOGAUFKJESTSTR'
...
define view ZP_LOG_AUFK_JEST_STR as select from ZP_LOG_AUFK_
JEST_AG
{
    aufnr,
    case
      when sta01 = '' then ''
      else                sta01
    end as str01,
    case
      when sta02 = ''                        then ''
      when sta01 = '' and sta02 != '' then sta02
      else                          concat_with_space ('',sta02,1)
    end as str02,
    ...
```

```
    end as str03,
    ... ...
    end as str08
}
```

In the second step, all separate strings are concatenated into a new field value. Because this view is the final one, this is also the place to document the layered structure of CDS views.

```
/* Freek Keijzer, myBrand, 02.06.2020
Final view for User Status of Order.
In this view the string is composed.
Layered structure of CDS-views:
  ZP_LOG_AUFNR_UserStat        - View for User Status of Order
  |- ZP_LOG_AUFK_JEST_Str      - Preparation for composition of
                                 string
    |- ZP_LOG_AUFK_JEST_Ag     - Aggregation of dataset to 1
                                 line per order
      |- ZP_LOG_AUFK_JEST      - "Flip" dataset from rows to
                                 columns
        |- ZB_LOG_AUFK_JEST - View with basic data
            |- aufk             - Table "Order master data"
            |- jest             - Table "Individual Object Status"
            |- t003o            - Table "Order Types"
            |- tj30t            - Table "Texts for User Status"
-----------------------------------------------------------*/
@EndUserText.label: 'LOG: User Status of Order'
@AbapCatalog.sqlViewName: 'ZPLOGAUFNRUSRSTT'
...
define view ZP_LOG_AUFNR_UserStat as select from ZP_LOG_AUFK_
JEST_Str
{
    aufnr,
```

```
concat(str01,concat(str02,concat(str03,concat(str04,concat(
str05,concat(str06,
  concat(str07,str08))))))) as AufnrUserStat
}
```

Figure 6-7 shows the end result of all the work in this section.

aufnr	AufnrUserStat
AP00000049	ANNU
AP00000050	WOM NGVU
AP00000051	WOM NGVU
AP00000052	NGVU WGK
AP00000053	NGVU WGK
AP00000054	SLUI
AP00000055	GGK

Figure 6-7. *Output of views for the user status of Maintenance Order: end result*

Homework!

I am writing this book sort of like a teacher, am I not? I am going to make it worse by giving you...homework! The transposition examples shown earlier in this section are already quite complex, but there are plenty of other examples of complex logic that have been developed to fulfill the business requirements. But instead of presenting them, I prefer to let you undergo the creative process by working on one particular example yourself as an exercise.

The exercise can be carried out in any S/4HANA system, even in an "empty" development client. It is based on data in calendar tables, which should always be filled. The challenge is to create logic for a period belonging to the last full week in a month, as explained in Figure 6-8, and from now on abbreviated to PLFWIM. The end result should be a list of dates and PLFWIMs like this:

```
Date              PLFWIM

...               ...
25.01.2020        04.2020
26.01.2020        04.2020
27.01.2020        08.2020
28.01.2020        08.2020

...               ...
```

December 2019

1	2	3	4	5	6	7	8	9	10	11	12	13	14	15	16	17	18	19	20	21	22	23	24	25	26	27	28	29	30	31

Week 49.2019 · Week 50.2019 · Week 51.2019 · Week 52.2019

Period 52.2019

January 2020

1	2	3	4	5	6	7	8	9	10	11	12	13	14	15	16	17	18	19	20	21	22	23	24	25	26	27	28	29	30	31

Week 01.2020 · Week 02.202 · Week 03.202 · Week 04.202 · Week 05.2020

Period 04.2020

February 2020

1	2	3	4	5	6	7	8	9	10	11	12	13	14	15	16	17	18	19	20	21	22	23	24	25	26	27	28	29

Week 06.2020 · Week 07.2020 · Week 08.2020 · Week 09.2020

Period 08.2020 · Period 13.2020

Figure 6-8. *Definition of PLFWIM (bottom row for each month)*

All you need is an IDE, the standard SAP CDS view `I_CalendarDate`, and the analytical and creative parts of your brain. And perseverance. And coffee.

This definition, somewhat strange as it may seem, was an actual business requirement that led to a productively used solution. There are bound to be many widely different solutions, but mine is available on GitHub. Do not peek. First try it yourself.

Using Parameters

Parameters can be introduced on any level in a stack of CDS views and propagated all the way up to the query view. We will see two examples of these types of parameters in the "Author-Delivered Content" section.

In one of these, the flattened hierarchy of the GL Account example, a parameter is defined in the basic view.

```
define view ZB_FI_RACCT_HIER_PAR
  with parameters
    p_versn : versn_011
as select from ska1
  left outer join fagl_011zc as _leaf
    on _leaf.versn = :p_versn   and
       _leaf.ktopl = 'NS00'     and
       _leaf.vonkt <= ska1.saknr and
       _leaf.biskt >= ska1.saknr
```

It is propagated all the way to the attribute view.

```
define view ZA_FI_RACCT_HIER_PAR
  with parameters
    p_versn : versn_011
as select distinct from ZP_FI_RACCT_HIER_PAR(p_versn: :p_versn)
```

After this, it can be combined with fact data, applying the parameter in this way:

```
define view Z… as select from Z… as _ap
  association[0..1] to ZA_FI_RACCT_HIER_PAR as _gl_hier3
    on _gl_hier3.ktopl = _ap.ktopl and
       _gl_hier3.saknr = _ap.racct
{
...
    _gl_hier3(p_versn:'NS05').ergsl_lev01 as ergsl3_lev01,
    _gl_hier3(p_versn:'NS05').ergsl_lev02 as ergsl3_lev02,
    _gl_hier3(p_versn:'NS05').ergsl_lev03 as ergsl3_lev03,
    _gl_hier3(p_versn:'NS05').ergsl_lev04 as ergsl3_lev04,
...
}
```

The purpose of this parametrization is to be able to connect more than one version of the flattened hierarchy on GL Account to the same fact data with only one version of the coding.

However, the most common use of parameters is in key figure definitions. From a flexibility point of view, it is to be preferred to introduce these as late as possible in the query view itself. In this way, the parameter will not reduce the overall usability of the cube view. A simple example of the use of a parameter in a key figure definition is shown here. The cube view has Actual and Plan Amounts as the field ksl. In the union, the source indicator was defined as ACDOCA and ACDOCP, respectively. We want to show only one single plan category. For this, a parameter is used.

```
define view ZQ_ZZ_Query
  with parameters
    @EndUserText.label: 'Plan Category'
    @AnalyticsDetails.query.variableSequence : 102
    p_Category : category
as select from ZC_ZZ_Cube
{
...

    @AnalyticsDetails.query.decimals: 0
    @EndUserText.label: 'Actuals'
    case
      when Source = 'ACDOCA' then ksl
      else 0
    end as AmountAct,              //Actual Amount (acdoca.ksl)
    @AnalyticsDetails.query.decimals: 0
    @EndUserText.label: 'Plan'
```

```
case
  when (Source = 'ACDOCP' and category = :p_Category) then ksl
  else 0
end as AmountPlan,                    //Planned Amount (acdocp.ksl)
...
```

An input parameter is a single value and mandatory. The annotation
@AnalyticsDetails.query.variableSequence works across filters via
the annotation @Consumption.filter and parameters to sort them in the
desired order on the selection screen.

Using Session Variables and Environment Annotations

In CDS views, you can make use of some valuable session variables.[1]

```
$session.user                   //log-in SAP user-id,
                                  e.g. 'KEIJZERF'
$session.client                 //log-in system client, e.g. '200'
$session.system_language        //log-in language, e.g. 'N'
$session.system_date            //current date, e.g. '20210121'
```

The most common usage of the system date variable is for time-
dependent master data. Here's an example:

```
define view ZB_FI_PROFCTR as select from cepc
  left outer join csks
    on csks.kokrs  = cepc.kokrs and
       csks.prctr  = cepc.prctr and
       csks.datbi >= $session.system_date and
       csks.datab <= $session.system_date
```

---

[1]SAP Help Portal on "Session Variables": https://help.sap.com/doc/
abapdocu_751_index_htm/7.51/en-us/abencds_f1_session_variable.htm

But the system date variable can also be used for hard-coded filtering or as a default value in a user-input filter. Here's an example of the former, Fiscal Year, equal to the current year:

```
...
$session.system_date as system_date    //in view A
...

...
where gjahr = left(system_date, 4)     //in view B,
                                          on top of A
...
```

What we found particularly useful is applying the `$session.user` session variable as a built-in authorization. For this, we set markers in the cube view for various types of users.

```
define view ZC_... as select from ZP_...
  ...
{
...
//--Definitions based on logged-in user
    case when usrid = $session.user then 'X' else '' end as usrid
                                      //Employee?
    case when vernr_usrid = $session.user then 'X' else ''
    end as vernr_usrid_x,
                                      //Project Responsible?
    case when lm_usrid    = $session.user then 'X' else ''
    end as lm_usrid_x,
                                      //Line Manager?
...
}
```

In the different query versions, we used these markers as hard-coded filters.

```
define view ZQ_... as select from ZC_...
{
    ...
}
where usrid_x = 'X'    //--Data only shown for Employee
```

Quite similar to session variables is the use of environment annotations[2] in parameters. Environment annotations correspond to well-known and often used fields in ABAP programming: #CLIENT (sy-mandt), #SYSTEM_DATE (sy-datum), #SYSTEM_TIME (sy-uzeit), #SYSTEM_LANGUAGE (sy-langu), and #USER (sy-uname). Here the ABAP programming fields are the German-based abbreviations between parentheses.

Here is an example of the use of an environment annotation:

```
define view ZQ_ZZ_Query
  with parameters
    @Environment.systemField : #system_date
    @EndUserText.label: 'Key date'
    p_key_date: dats,
  as select from ZC_ZZ_Cube
```

This will lead to an input box for a date field in the selection screen with the current date as the default option, which can be overwritten.

---

[2]SAP Help Portal on "Environment Annotations": https://help.sap.com/doc/
 f9edb0c2e59e426da97a81719be1d11c/1511%20000/en-US/fd139a3987f84d2082d
 9fd38980dd2c1.html

Compatibility Views

When SAP introduced "simple finance" and "simple logistics," it simultaneously introduced the concept of "compatibility views," also known as *replacement objects*. This topic was presented as follows: if due to database changes a table does not store data anymore, a view is created with the identical name that can be used in software (SAP software as well as custom). The software will thus continue to run without problems in spite of the database changes.

An example where this is carried out in this way is the table for Cost Totals in the Controlling module. This used to be a transparent table containing data named COSP. Now the data is stored in the table COSP_BAK, and COSP became a CDS view built on top of COSP_BAK. This is the way I expected the concept of compatibility views to work.

However, in practice we often encounter a variant of the concept that works quite differently. A fellow developer tried to use data from the Real Estate table called Asset Value Fields (ANLC)—still a transparent table in S/4HANA—in a CDS view but noticed that part of the data was oddly missing. Further investigation pointed out that ANLC cannot be used anymore, but instead a compatibility view named FAAV_ANLC with the description Kompatibilitaets-View fuer Tabelle ANLC (this is the English description, so do not shoot the messenger) is to be used. This view is the SQL view belonging to a CDS view with the same description and with the name FAA_ANLC. Figure 6-9 gives some background on SQL and CDS views.

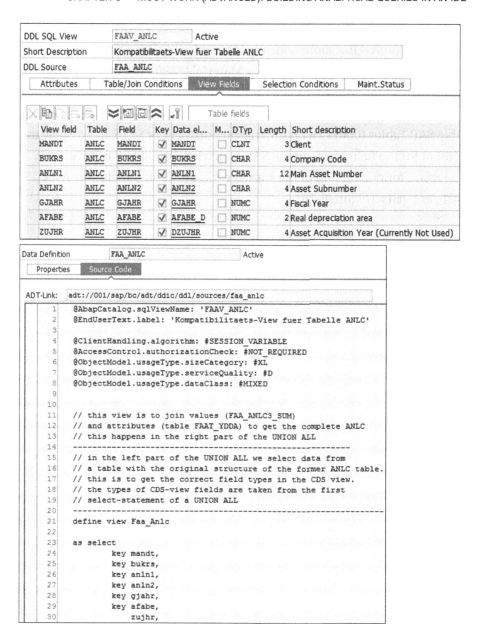

Figure 6-9. *Compatibility view example: SQL view (top) and CDS view (bottom)*

After replacing the table with the view, everything worked just fine. We later encountered the same issue for MM tables like Material Valuation (MBEW) and Storage Location Data for Material (MARD); the tables are still there, but they are not giving the proper data.

A full list of tables to worry about can be produced as follows: open the table SAP Tables (DD02L) with the transaction SE11 or SE16 and display the content for the field Name of the SAP table view (VIEWREF) as not empty. The result for our version of the software has 287 tables, including ANLC, MARD, and MBEW (Figure 6-10).

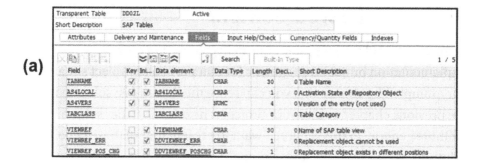

(a)

(b)

(c)

Figure 6-10. *Method to obtain a list of tables for which a compatibility view needs to be used: (a) transaction SE11 for table DD02L; (b) selection on field VIEWREF not empty; (c) part of the output*

Author-Delivered Content

Some embedded analytics solutions delivered as part of an implementation project very specific for that particular project situation. For example, the chance that you can reuse the Return List solution from the previous chapter as is in your project is next to nil. Other solutions are far more generic. In this section, I want to present four of these generic solutions as "author-delivered content." There's no coding in the text of this section. I mean, this is already a 200-plus-pages book—give yourself (and me) a break! All the code is available on GitHub.

Material Classification Characteristics

I have encountered "material classification characteristics" in about 80 percent of all SAP BW implementations I was involved in, and I expect the same to happen in (future) S/4HANA Embedded Analytics implementations. A classification characteristic can be seen as an object somewhere between a customizing object and a data object. It is used as a master data definition, in which sense it acts as customizing, but it is not transported and needs to be entered in each system separately, in which sense it acts as data. Classifications can be used for numerous key characteristics, but material classifications are most commonly used.

In the basic view, data needs to be gathered from four tables in total: General Material Data (MARA), Link between Internal Number and Object (INOB), Characteristic Values (AUSP), and Characteristic (CABN). Note that for other classifications the first source table is different, but the other three are identical. Warning: it may seem like the field Internal characteristic (ausp/cabn.atinn) is a useful field to identify the characteristic, but it is not. As classifications are entered in each system within the DTAP landscape separately, the value of atinn, being a counter, is likely to be different in each system. If all went well during the implementation of classifications (e.g., no typing errors), then the value of Characteristic Name (`cabn.atnam`) will be the same throughout the system landscape, and therefore this field can be used to identify the classification characteristic.

From a date modeling point of view, this is again a classic example of a transposition from rows to columns (Figure 6-11).

MATNR	ATNAM	ATWRT
62001409	NORM	DIN338
62001409	NS_NORM	24-451
83087288	NORM	DIN5526B
83087288	NS_NORM	30-701
YB078890	NORM	CAT II 1000 V ...
YB078890	TYPE	3521976

MATNR	C1_NORM	C1_NS_NORM	C1_TYPE
62001409	DIN338	24-451	
83087288	DIN5526B	30-701	
YB078890	CAT II 1000 V ...		3521976

Figure 6-11. *Transformation from rows to columns for material classification characteristics*

In the code available on GitHub, three material classifications characteristics—NORM, NS_NORM, and TYPE—are transformed into the attribute fields of Material. Next, these fields are added to a custom attribute view and associated with again a minimalistic cube view for testing purposes. Figure 6-12 shows the output of the query.

Material ▽▲	Material ▽▲	Material Group	Norm	NS Norm	Type
62001409	HIGH-SPEED STEEL TWIST-DRILL BIT DIAMETE	SLIJT	DIN338	24-451	#
83087288	SMOOTH BOLT 18*90 WITH SPLIT PIN HOLE AN	SLIJT	DIN5526B	30-701	#
YB078890	Test leads TL175 TwistGuard	SLIJT	CAT II 1000 V, CAT III 1000 V,	#	3521976
YA843427	WINDOW 1001x501,5x7	SLIJT	EN1634 & EN12600	#	#
YA020844	Plate	SLIJT	EN10029-KLASSEA	#	#
KA220462	CRANKSHAFT BETWEEN GEARBOXES	WISSEL	DIN 124532/00	#	1234TEST
FA552147	Retaining ring for bore	SLIJT	DIN472	#	J52

Figure 6-12. Material classification characteristics (Norm, NS Norm, and Type) added to a custom attribute view for Material

Flattened Hierarchies

SAP has a tradition of delivering excellent hierarchies with associated functions for many characteristics. When SAP purchased Business Objects, one of the key issues in merging the BI software from both companies was the fact that SAP's hierarchical functions were more advanced than those of Business Objects. But this being said, there are some clear disadvantages in using the SAP hierarchies in the "standard" way, which is shown in Figure 6-13 for the characteristic GL Account. As an example, the hierarchical levels leading to GL Account 422000 are as follows: the top level is NS00, level 1 is 2, level 2 is 21, level 3 is 210, and finally level 4 is 422. This all looks nice, but if a second dimension is added on the right side of the hierarchy, the display becomes quite messy as values of this second dimension are repeated on all levels of the hierarchy.

Account Number ≜	Account Number ▼≜	Realisatie in (EUR) ▼≜
⌄ 0NS00	GBR	.217
⌄ 02	Resultaatsbijdrage	.217
⟩ 020	Bedrijfsopbrengsten	.446
⌄ 021	Bedrijfslasten	.663
⌄ 0210	Kosten personeel	.223
⟩ 00421	Lonen en salarissen	.573
⌄ 00422	Sociale lasten	.843
422000	Werkgeversbijdr WW	.136
422001	Werkgeversbijdr WIA	.614
422002	Werkg.bijdr ziekte	.858
422003	Werkg.bijdr pensioen	.037
422999	Ov werkgsbijdr	.801
⟩ 00423	Inhuur personeel	.421
⟩ 00424	Overige personeelsko	.386
⟩ 0211	Afschrijvingskosten	.740
⟩ 0212	Verbruik grond- en h	.311
⟩ 0213	Geactiveerde product	.662
⟩ 0214	Kosten uitbesteed we	.283
⟩ 0217	Overige bedrijfslast	.767

Figure 6-13. *Standard way of displaying the hierarchy on GL Account*

For some analytical purposes, users prefer a flattened hierarchy. This means that the various levels of the hierarchy are available as a separate dimension, thus providing a completely different navigational behavior and other flexibility than with the standard display of a hierarchy. As an example, Figure 6-14 shows the same data as Figure 6-13, but now for a flat hierarchy, with level 1 used as a filter and only levels 2 and 4 displayed.

GBR.niv.2 ▲	GBR.niv.2 ▼▲	GBR.niv.4 ▲	GBR.niv.4 ▼▲	Realisatie in (EUR) ▼▲
20	Bedrijfsopbrengsten	0811	Netto omzet	.901
		0821	Overige bedrijfsopbrengsten	.544
		0421	Lonen en salarissen	.573
		0422	Sociale lasten	.843
		0423	Inhuur personeel	.421
		0424	Overige personeelskosten	.386
		0431	Afschrijvingskosten en bijz waardevermind IVA	.390
		0432	Afschrijvingskosten en bijz waardevermind MVA	.227
		0433	Afschrijvingskosten en bijz waardevermind GBR	.124
		0442	Energie/techn.verbruiken	.311
		0451	Geactiveerde productie eigen bedrijf	.662
21	Bedrijfslasten	0461	Kosten uitbesteedwerk en andere externe kst	.216
		0462	Schoonmaakkosten	.015
		0463	Onderhoudswerkzaamheden	.718
		0464	Automatiseringskosten	.335
		0471	Huisvesting-/algemene beheerskosten	.228
		0472	Huur/lease bedrijfsmiddelen	.719
		0473	Reclame/promotie/publ.kst	.775
		0474	Advieskosten	.743
		0475	Overige andere bedrijfslasten (excl int.uren)	.889
		0476	Overige andere bedrijfslasten-interne uren	.585

Figure 6-14. *Example of the use of a "flat hierarchy" on GL Account*

Building a flat hierarchy with CDS views is not that simple because of the way the data is stored in tables. Data is required from the following tables: G/L Account Master (Chart of Accounts) (SKA1), Fin. Statement Structure: Assignment FS Items - G/L Account (FAGL_011ZC), and Fin. Statement Structure: Items in Fin. Statement Structure (FAGL_011PC). If you want text with the different keys (and why wouldn't you?), you also need the table Fin. Statement Structure: Text for Fin. Statement Items (FAGL_011QT). Figure 6-15 shows the relevant data for GL Account 422000. You will be glad to know that ergsl is the Financial Statement Item value, and Stufe is the German word for "level." The hierarchy is stored as a series of parent-child relations. What the code does is "climb up the ladder" from GL Account to a certain hierarchy level and display the value of this level as a separate dimension.

(a)

	VERSN	ERGSL	KTOPL	VONKT	BISKT
	NS00	0422	NS00	0000422000	0000422000
	NS00	0422	NS00	0000422001	0000422001
	NS00	0422	NS00	0000422002	0000422002
	NS00	0422	NS00	0000422003	0000422003
	NS00	0422	NS00	0000422999	0000422999

Table: FAGL_011ZC
Displayed Fields: 5 of   5   Fixed Columns:

(b)

	VERSN	ID	TYPE	ERGSL	PARENT	CHILD	NEXTN	STUFE
	NS00	000001	R	NS00	000000	000002	000000	01
	NS00	000297	P	2	000001	000298	000491	02
	NS00	000318	P	21	000297	000319	000487	03
	NS00	000319	P	210	000318	000320	000370	04
	NS00	000332	P	0422	000319	000333	000338	05

Table: FAGL_011PC
Displayed Fields: 8 of   8   Fixed Columns:

(c)

	VERSN	SPRAS	ERGSL	TXTYP	ZEILE	TXT45
	NS00	N	0422	K	1	Sociale lasten
	NS00	N	2	K	1	Resultaatsbijdrage
	NS00	N	21	K	1	Bedrijfslasten
	NS00	N	210	K	1	Kosten personeel

Table: FAGL_011QT
Displayed Fields: 6 of   6   Fixed Columns:

Figure 6-15. *Data in source tables for the "flat hierarchy" on GL Account*

In the current project, we have built flat hierarchies for GL Account, for multiple versions of the hierarchy, and for Profit Center, Internal Order, and WBS Element. But if you can build one, you can build them all.

Inventory Levels and Movements

I have analyzed a lot of standard SAP CDS views with varying appreciation, but I became most enthusiastic when I analyzed the standard CDS content in the Inventory domain. Some talented and creative SAP developers were on the job there! Also, the simplification brought by Simple Logistics and the processing power of the HANA database triumphantly came together here. The data modeling problem for inventory levels is that these are not stored as such in the database, only in the inventory movements leading up to the levels. This used to result in complex data warehouse solutions with things like "snapshots" or "moving pointers." All this does not appear to be necessary anymore. The standard content includes views that go through all the records in the table Material Documents (MATDOC) to calculate the inventory levels of all materials on a specific date in the past during query runtime. This is a great chance for the HANA database to prove its power, because 10 years after go-live it needs to go through 10 years of data, even when we are interested only in last month's inventory levels.

The SAP-delivered CDS views in the Inventory domain belong to application component MM-IM-VDM-SGM. Figure 6-16 shows the analytical queries in this application component. Analyzing these queries leads to a number of observations.

- The query Goods Movement Analysis (C_GoodsMovementQuery) is the only one on the Material Document Item level. It includes movements, but not levels.

- The query Material stock for period by type (C_MaterialStockTimeSeries) is extremely cool, as it provides the flexibility to display times series for inventory levels for all period types one can think of: years, months, weeks, days, and so on. However, it includes only levels, not movements.

- The bottom two queries in the list include values next to quantities, but the two most interesting queries, the ones just mentioned, do not.

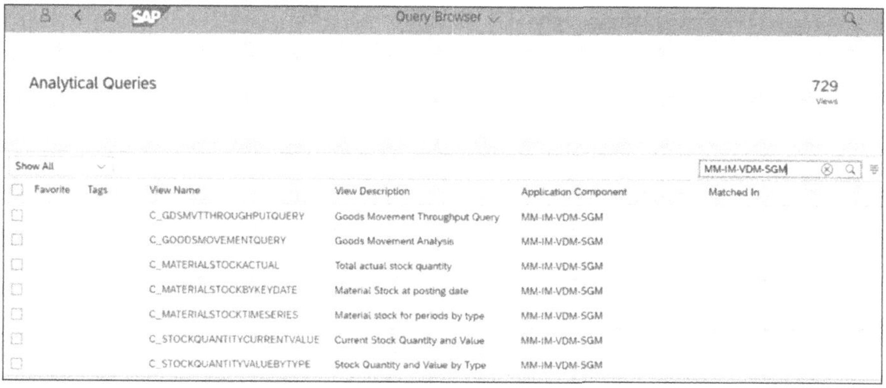

Figure 6-16. *SAP standard analytical queries in the Inventory domain*

Figure 6-17 gives a graphical overview of the full layered structure of the standard CDS content in the Inventory domain. The graph shows that levels and movements are not combined anywhere. To determine KPIs like Inventory Turnover, it is a requirement that levels and movements are combined in the same query. It is also a requirement for such higher-level KPIs to be able to express the quantities in a common unit across all materials. Values in a shared currency are suitable for this purpose.

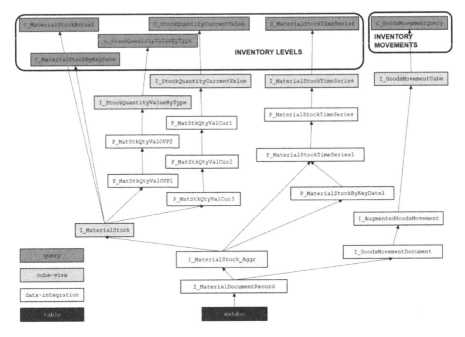

Figure 6-17. *Graphical display of SAP-delivered CDS views in the Inventory domain. Lower-left corner: explanation of the use of colors*

In conclusion, SAP developers created many clever functions, but they are spread all over the content instead of concentrated within one or two branches of the content. This is exactly what I am offering as author-delivered content:

- A version of "Goods Movement Analysis" with levels next to the already present movements and values next to quantities

- A version of "Material stock for period by type" with movements next to the already present levels and values next to quantities

In my view, this is excellent stuff, which is 70 percent SAP and 30 percent me.

But how will this solution perform after a few years? In the current project, we expect a growth of the MATDOC table with half a million records per year. SAP's estimate is that we do not need to worry for another 10 years or so. By then, SAP will have developed a quantum-leap database that can process one zillion records in one nanosecond.

Financial Actuals, Plan, and Commitments

The data integration between Actuals and Plan-data is straightforward, because the involved source tables, ACDOCA and ACDOCP, are structured almost identically as in Simple Finance. Commitment amounts and quantities from procurement, however, are stored in an old CO table, called Commitments Management: Line Items (COOI), which is structured very differently. The data integration of the Commitments data with Actuals and Plan-data therefore requires more effort. Figure 6-18 shows a graphical representation of the data model for Commitments, as used in the example.

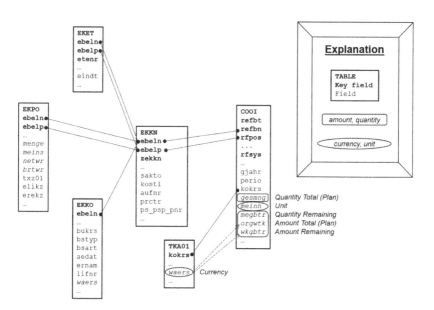

Figure 6-18. *Data model for the Commitments part of the Financial Actuals-Plan-Commitments comparison*

The quantities and amounts are shown in the table Commitments Management: Line Items (COOI), which can be linked via Purchasing Document/Item with the table Account Assignment in Purchasing Document (EKKN). This contains the account assignment fields under their old CO names: G/L Account (ekkn.sakto), Cost Center (ekkn.kostl), Order (ekkn.aufnr), Profit Center (ekkn.prctr), and WBS Element (numeric, ekkn.ps_psp_pnr). Additional data is retrieved from other procurement tables (EKKO, EKPO, EKET). This illustrates that data is coming from everywhere. This implies challenges in integrating this widely differently structured data. The author-delivered content for the Actuals-Plan-Commitments comparison shows how these challenges can be overcome.

Making the Data Less Real-Time

Can you believe that? We finally have real-time data, and users start complaining that the data is "too real-time"? Ungrateful bunch. But after a brief period of disappointment, subservient as we are, we start thinking about how to fulfill even this requirement.

The complainers are probably used to working with data stored overnight in a data warehouse and "frozen" for use on the next day. As a result, they tend to get nervous when the query output changes every time they press F5. We cannot provide data storage with embedded analytics, but in many cases we can provide the "freezing" function. For this, we need to find fields for all transaction data sets brought together that are or can be transformed into a creation date. Sometimes this is an easy task, and sometimes it is not. For financial queries, like the Financial Actuals, Plan, and Commitments example of the previous section, we were confronted with the "too real-time data" complaint. In this example, the key figures are coming from the tables ACDOCA, ACDOCP, and COOI. Each of these tables has a field that can be transformed into a Creation Date field. See the following code for details:

```
define view ZP_FI_ACDOCAPCOOI_UN as
select from ZB_FIGL_ACDOCA as _ac
  ...
{
    'ACDOCA' as Source,
    //Source = 'ACDOCA', 'ACDOCP' or 'COOI'
    ....
    tstmp_to_dats(_ac.timestamp,abap_system_timezone( $session.
    client,'NULL' ),
      $session.client,'NULL' ) as zcpudt,
                  //Creation Date derived from acdoca.timestamp
    ...
}
union all
select from ZB_FIGL_ACDOCP
{
    'ACDOCP' as Source,
    //Source = 'ACDOCA', 'ACDOCP' or 'COOI'
    ...
    left(reqtsn,8) as zcpudt,
    //Creation Date derived from acdocp.reqtsn
...
}
union all
select from ZB_PUR_COOI
{
    'COOI' as Source,
    //Source = 'ACDOCA', 'ACDOCP' or 'COOI'
    ...
```

```
    bldat_cooi as zcpudt,
    //Creation Date = Document Date (cooi.bldat)
...
}
```

In a query view, a consumption filter of type Interval can then be defined on the Creation Date field.

```
//--Creation Date determined in various ways
    @Consumption.filter: {selectionType: #INTERVAL,
multipleSelections: false,
      mandatory: false }
    zcpudt,
//Creation Date (acdoca.timestamp/acdocp.reqtsn/cooi.bldat)
```

The query user can enter dates from 01.01.1900 until the current date minus one for the old-school data warehouse experience. Initially, we delivered the query with these dates filled in as default values for the interval, but this caused upheaval on the real-time data side of the user community.

Multilingual Descriptions of Field Names

We started this chapter with a way to provide multilingual descriptions of field *values*: the custom multilingual text view. For real multilingual operation, we also need to provide multilingual descriptions of field *names*.

This is not an issue for fields that inherit their descriptions from a multilingual data element, as such fields will automatically have multilingual descriptions. But it is an issue in cases in which the description was overwritten with the @EndUserText.label annotation. In such cases, two things can happen if a user logs in with a language differing from the language in which the CDS view was developed: either no description is displayed or the description in the development language—the only one available—is displayed. The latter option is of course the best the system can do, and that is what happens in the selection screen and in the output of an analytical query. For the fields with overwritten description, a translation needs to be carried out. I will demonstrate this using the custom attribute view example from the beginning of this chapter and translate it from English (EN) to Dutch (NL). Figure 6-19 displays the issue to be solved by the translation.

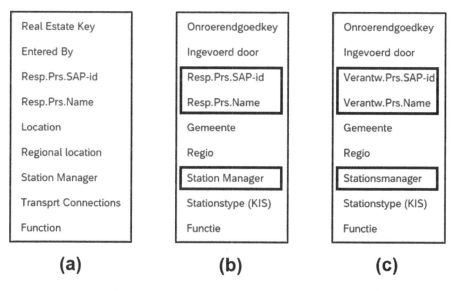

(a)   **(b)**   **(c)**

Figure 6-19. *Mulitilingual descriptions of field names: (a) EN field names with EN as logged-in language; (2) untranslated field names with NL as logged-in language; (3) translated field names with NL as logged-in language*

For the translation, we can apply the generic transaction Translation Editor (SE63). Figure 6-20 shows that we need to choose Short Texts and then the Object Type CDS Views (DDLS).

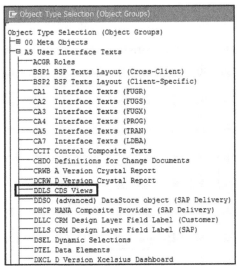

Figure 6-20. *Transaction Translation Editor (SE63): starting up for CDS views*

The screen in which the translation needs to be carried out lists the objects with the translation issue: the description of the query itself and the three overwritten field labels (Figure 6-21). It also shows three buttons with somewhat confusing descriptions when hovering over them. Do not worry, because you need only the left one: Create Proposal Immediately (System Standard with Status S). But the translation does not start with these buttons, but with double-clicking one of the descriptions to be translated. A new input box appears in which the translation of the description can be entered. Then click the Create Proposal button. Repeat this until everything is nice and green and click Save.

```
DDLS (ZZ) enUS -> nlNL: ZA_RE_SWENR

▲ ▼   🗑 ↶ 📑 🔧 🗹   🔗 🔁 ⅠⅠ 🗟   🎞 🔍 🗹   🗂

(No comment exists for object)

[00001  DDDDLSRC02BT]                    0-🔳 🗖 🗹 🏳       (60)
RE: Business Entity attributes                🖑 Create Proposal Immediately (System Standard with Status S)
RE: Complex attributen|

[00002  DDDDLSRC03NT FIELDLABEL]    ▓▓▓ 0-🔳 🖵 🗹 🏳       (250)
Resp.Prs.SAP-id

[00003  DDDDLSRC03NT FIELDLABEL]    ▓▓▓ 0-🔳 🖵 🗹 🏳       (250)
Resp.Prs.Name

[00004  DDDDLSRC03NT FIELDLABEL]    ▓▓▓ 0-🔳 🖵 🗹 🏳       (250)
Station Manager
```

```
DDLS (ZZ) enUS -> nlNL: ZA_RE_SWENR

▲ ▼   🗑 ↶ 📑 🔧 🗹   🔗 🔁 ⅠⅠ 🗟   🎞 🔍 🗹   🗂

(No comment exists for object)

[00001  DDDDLSRC02BT]               ▓▓▓ 1-🔳 🖵 🗹 🏳  ⊚S ⊚S  (60)
RE: Business Entity attributes
RE: Complex attributen
RE: Complex attributen

[00002  DDDDLSRC03NT FIELDLABEL]    ▓▓▓ 1-🔳 🖵 🗹 🏳  ⊚S ⊚S  (250)
Resp.Prs.SAP-id
Verantw.Prs.SAP-id
Verantw.Prs.SAP-id

[00003  DDDDLSRC03NT FIELDLABEL]    ▓▓▓ 1-🔳 🖵 🗹 🏳  ⊚S ⊚S  (250)
Rasp.Prs.Name
Verantw.Prs.Name
Verantw.Prs.Name

[00004  DDDDLSRC03NT FIELDLABEL]    ▓▓▓ 1-🔳 🖵 🗹 🏳  ⊚S ⊚S  (250)
Station Manager
Stationsmanager
Stationsmanager
```

Figure 6-21. *Transaction Translation Editor (SE63): entering the translations*

Figure 6-19c showed the result of these actions.

"Jump To" Functionality

As mentioned in the previous chapter, "Renaming fields to English-based names used in SAP standard views has the additional advantage that options to use the Jump To functionality from analytical queries will become available." Now the time has come to demonstrate this advantage. In the Return List case from the previous chapter, we renamed six fields to names used by standard SAP apps. This action alone can generate a long list of standard apps when the Jump To button is clicked, i.e., all apps for which one of the field names is a semantic object under the header "Target Mapping(s)" in the Fiori Apps Library (Chapter 2). Note that only apps are shown for which the user is authorized.

To control the content of the Jump To list, we can add a semantic object, e.g., Maintenance Order, to the URL of the query. Figure 6-22 shows the details of how to do this. The query is identified by XQUERY= followed by 2C concatenated with the technical SQL view name of the query. The semantic object is to be inserted immediately after this as &XSEMANTIC_ OBJECTS=MaintenanceOrder. The figure also shows the resulting list of target destinations when the Jump To button is clicked.

Figure 6-22. *Expanding the URL with a semantic object: (a) how to do it; (b) result*

A more interesting way to use the Jump To functionality is by right-clicking a row in the query output area. The next two figures show how this works. The Jump To menu options via the right-click menu are the same as via the Jump To button (Figure 6-23). When used, the target destination app, in this case Display Maintenance Order, is opened in a separate browser tab. The difference with the use of the Jump To button lies in the context that is taken from the source query to the target app. In this case, the app is automatically opened for the order from which the jump takes place (Figure 6-24).

		MM: Return List ⌄				

To show filters here, add them to the filter bar in Filters

Order ▲	Order ▽▲	Quantity ▽▲	Returned ▽▲	Remaining ▽▲	Received ▽▲	Numb.of Deliv. ▽▲
AP00001715	BS10_08938_OB_STLOC_R05_V840	1 PC	1 PC	0 PC	0 PC	1
AP00001716	BS10_08938_SB_STLOC_R05_V840	1 PC	1 PC	0 PC	0 PC	1
AP00001717	BS10_08947_SB_STLOC_R01_S100			0 PC	0 PC	0
AP00001718	BS10_08995_OB_STLOC_R02_EXTL	Sort ＞		1 PC	0 PC	0
AP00001719	BS10_09638_GGK_WGK_VBT	Display ＞		0 PC	0 PC	1
AP00001727	BS10_11846_AFTER_STAGE_3_UITV	Attributes ＞		0 PC	0 PC	1
AP00001729	BS10_11847_OB_VRACHT_TKRT			0 PC	0 PC	1
AP00001731	BS10_11936_OB_MATNO_CHANG...	Hierarchy ＞		0 PC	0 PC	1
AP00001736	BS10_12215_OB_STLOC_EMPTY_...	Totals ＞		0 PC	0 PC	1
AP00001737	BS10_12215_OB_STLOC_EMPTY_...			0 PC	0 PC	1
AP00001738	BS10_14466_1_WGK_NA_IN_PROC	Filter ＞		0 PC	0 PC	2
AP00001739	BS10_14466_2_NA_IN_PROC_DEL	Suppress Zeros in Rows		6 PC	0 PC	1
AP00001740	BS10_14466_3B_VUIL_DEL_IN_PR...	Compact Display in Rows		6 PC	0 PC	1
AP00001741	BS10_14466_3_VUIL_DEL			6 PC	0 PC	0
AP00001742	BS10_14466_4_NA_IN_PROC_DO...	Jump To ＞	Actual Settlement			2
AP00001745	BS10_14533_2_MHD_OB_RES_VUIL	1 PC	0 PC	Change Maintenance Order		0
AP00001746	BS10_14533_3_MHD_DOWN_UNS...	1 PC	1 PC			1
AP00001747	BS10_14562_HIGHEST_LVL_ASSET	3 PC	3 PC	Create Maintenance Order		1
AP00001750	BS10_15221_WH_IN_PROC_DOWN	1 PC	1 PC	Display Maintenance Order ☌		1
AP00001751	BS10_15283_2_WGK_VUIL_DEL	6 PC	0 PC	Display Maintenance Order (Object Page)		0
AP00001752	BS10_15283_GERE_RETOUR_CORR	7 PC	5 PC	Display Material Availability (IWBK)		2
AP00001760	SC101_CHANGE_FIELDS	1 PC	0 PC			0
AP00001764	SC201_STAT_HAPPY_ALL	1 PC	1 PC	Display PM orders		1
AP00001769	ST001_HAPPY_FLOW	3 PC	3 PC	Find Maintenance Order and Operation		1
AP00001770	ST002_FIRST_WOM_THEN_HAPPY	3 PC	3 PC			1
AP00001774	ST006_GGK_VRIJ_WGK_HAPPY	3 PC	3 PC	List of Goods Movements for Order		1
AP00001775	ST007_GGK_WGK_HAPPY	3 PC	3 PC	Maintenance Planning Overview		1
AP00001777	ST009_WOM_WGK_HAPPY	3 PC	3 PC			1
AP00001778	ST011_SAD_GERE_ANNU	3 PC	3 PC	Manage Maintenance Order List		1
AP00001783	ST016_GGK_WGK_DATE_CHG	3 PC	3 PC	0 PC	0 PC	1

Figure 6-23. *Jump-to functionality from a row in the query output area: menu options*

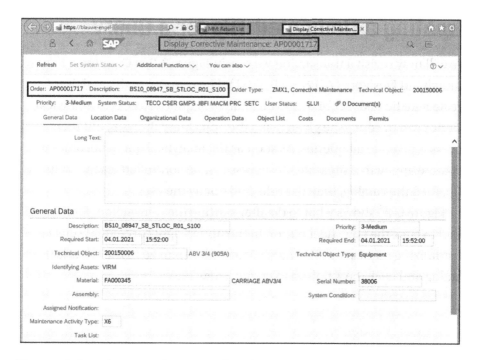

Figure 6-24. *Jump-to functionality from a row in the query output area: target destination opened with context*

Jumping to standard apps is a convenient way to provide access to a level of detail you do not want to have in the query itself. Examples include the following: providing indirect access to all user statuses or system statuses of an object instead of a selected subset, to all classification characteristics of a material or other object, or, in the example shown in Figure 6-24 to the details of a maintenance order including the long text.

The Jump To functionality can also be deployed from one analytical query to another, but this requires the development of specific semantic objects in the Fiori Launchpad Designer.

Creating a Dedicated Tile for a Query

We will now revisit a transaction we saw in Figure 2-2 in Chapter 2: Fiori Launchpad Designer (/UI2/FLPD_CUST). The purpose of this visit is to create a dedicated tile for a custom analytical query. Access to analytical queries can of course be given using the app Query Browser, but then access is given to all queries. As soon as the analytical query becomes a separate app with a separate tile, access can be controlled via the route app, then the catalog, then the role, and finally the user.

Figure 6-25 shows what to do after starting the transaction. First we need to click the cogwheel button in the upper-right corner and select a customizing request for the changes to made. Then go to the technical catalog and click the + button to create a new tile.

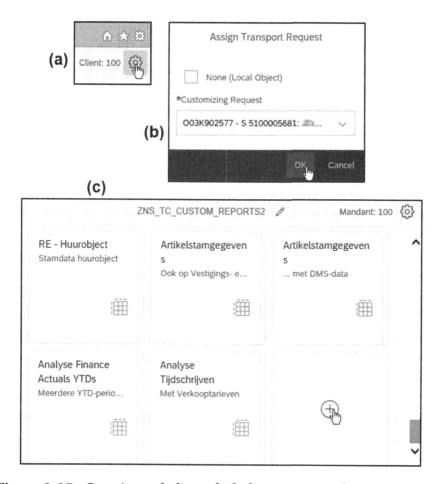

Figure 6-25. *Creating a dedicated tile for a query with transaction Fiori Launchpad Designer (/UI2/FLPD_CUST): (a) button Settings in the upper-right corner; (b) customizing the request; and (c) in the technical catalog clicking the + button to create new tile*

The next step is to fill in the details for the tile (Figure 6-26). The entries for Semantic Object and Action are always the same. The Parameters box is filled with 2C, concatenated with the technical SQL view name of the query plus the code for the Jump To target, if required. In the current project, we chose the same icon for all custom analytical queries to make them easily recognizable for users, but feel free to be more creative. Finally, there are three entry boxes for descriptions: Title and Subtitle will appear at the top, and Information will appear at the bottom of the tile. The last step is of course to click Save. CDS views and the like are cross-client objects, but tiles are client-dependent, so you may need to use the transaction Client Copy by Transport Request (SCC1) to transport from one client to another in the development system.

Figure 6-26. *Creating a dedicated tile for a query with transaction Fiori Launchpad Designer (/UI2/FLPD_CUST): entering details for the tile*

As soon as the tile is created in a technical catalog, it can be found by using the app finder and added to the home page or to another group. The resulting tile will often show the abbreviated description in the tile itself, but full-length descriptions will appear when hovering over the tile (Figure 6-27).

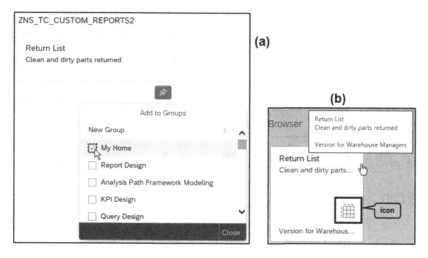

Figure 6-27. *Creating a dedicated tile for a query with transaction Fiori Launchpad Designer (/UI2/FLPD_CUST): (a) adding the new tile via the app finder to the home page; (b) final result*

Data Authorization

Giving limited access to a dedicated tile for a query via specific roles is a form of "access authorization." Another important part of any authorization concept is "data authorization." With this we mean that users are allowed to only create/change/display things within certain values of objects, usually organizational objects like Company Code. The general recommendation for data authorization in a BI environment is to keep it simple! BI is display only, so no one can break anything. It is technically possible to implement data authorization on the lower nodes of the Profit Center hierarchy, and if you hate your IT support organization, you should probably do that. If not, keep it simple.

In the current project, we implemented data authorization on the Company Code level for the financial cube views only. That is pretty simple. The coding is also pretty simple. In Figure 5-1, we saw the folder structure in Eclipse for the development of CDS views. We now need to build an object in the folder Access Controls. Say we want to build a data authorization on the cube view ZC_FIGL_ActPlanComp from the previous chapter. Then the code of the access control ZR_FIGL_ActPlanComp would be something like this:

```
@EndUserText.label: 'Data-authorization on CoCode'
@MappingRole: true
define role ZR_FIGL_ActPlanComp
{
    grant select on ZC_FIGL_ActPlanComp
      where (CompanyCode) = aspect pfcg_auth(f_ska1_buk, bukrs,
      actvt='03');
}
```

The rest of the work is up to the authorization staff. If only all things in life were this simple.

Query Performance

The HANA database is an animal. Raaaah! But everything has its limitations. If you run a query on more than 10 million records of data, it is almost certain you will have a notable response time. If query performance becomes unacceptably poor, there are "functional" measures one can take to limit the volume of the dataset, e.g., making more fields available in the selection screen to give users the opportunity to influence the response time or making more filters mandatory to force users to at least think about limiting the dataset before running the query. But often, there are also technical improvements possible in the design of the stack of CDS views leading to the analytical query.

But before solving an issue, one first needs to identify it. Analysis and optimization of query performance are complex topics deserving a book of their own. Nevertheless, I will discuss them briefly in the next two sections.

Performance Analysis

It would be great if S/4HANA Embedded Analytics had a luxurious performance statistics tool like BW Statistics. Unfortunately, this is not the case, at least not yet. The best alternative is the transaction SQL Monitor (SQLM).[3]

Quite useful, however, is the good-old back-end transaction System Trace (ST01). The trace is to be started immediately before and stopped immediately after running of the query. The query can be run with transaction Query Monitor (RSRT), but also from Fiori. Figure 6-28 shows what to expect of this approach. The trace display shows many records. Usually, the record with the SQL view name of the cube CDS view in the Object Name column has the longest runtime. Selecting this column and clicking Display Execution Plan brings you to the next screen, where you can select Explain with Variables and analyze the SQL statement and the execution plan. The first and second screens in Figure 6-28 do not belong together, as the execution plan of the cube view of the first screen was more than 20 screen-pages long. It's a lot of data, but if you take your time, you can derive some useful information.

---

[3]SAP Note 2602326, "Usage statistics for CDS views": https://launchpad. support.sap.com/#/notes/0002602326

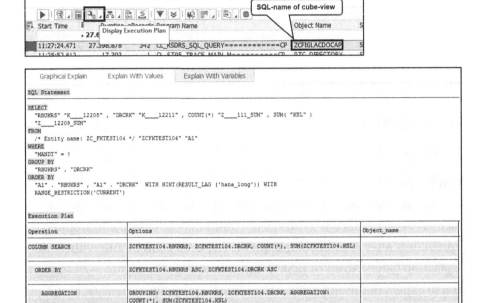

Figure 6-28. *Performance analysis with the transaction System Trace (ST01)*

A less old-school approach is the native HANA method of analyzing query performance using HANA PlanViz Execution. For this, database access to HANA is required. Figure 6-29 gives an example of the types of graphs one can expect with this tool.

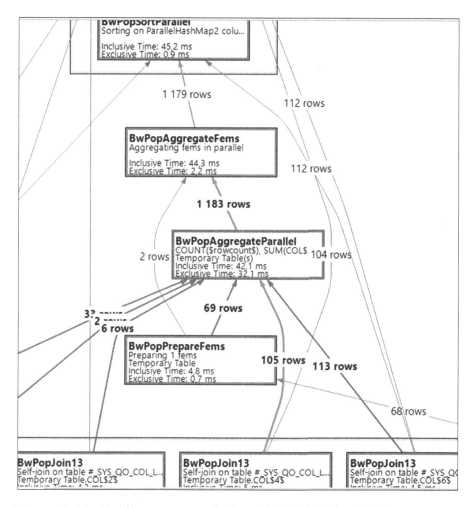

Figure 6-29. *Performance analysis with HANA PlanViz Execution. Picture by courtesy of Sergio Santos, SAP*

Performance Optimization

Analyzing performance is one thing; improving it is another. We had some initial performance issues with the financial queries, for which we sought cooperation with SAP. This is the set of performance-improving measures we came up with.

- Technically, left outer joins and associations are almost
  the same, but performance-wise associations are to be
  preferred. When analyzed with ST01, the trace display
  shows that associations are not part of the big "cube
  query" but launch separate queries, thus improving
  overall query runtime.

- We're using secondary indexes on tables. This may
  sound old-school, but it is still valid.

- On two occasions, SAP pointed out methods to instruct
  the OLAP machine to work in a certain way. The first
  recommendation was the dbHint annotation shown
  here. And that is how I pass it on to you readers. Feel
  free to try it. It can make things better, but it can also
  make things worse. If it makes things worse, take it out.

  ```
  @AbapCatalog.dbHints: [{dbSystem: #HDB, hint:
  'use_olap_plan'}]
  ```

- The second method to steer the OLAP machine in a
  certain direction is the use of performance annotations,
  or as I tend to call them "T-shirt size annotations."
  Their purpose is to give the OLAP machine a heads-
  up on what to expect in a data volume. Ideally, these
  annotations are used in all CDS views of the stack.
  See Figure 6-30 for an explanatory table and a coding
  example.

- SAP recommends "trimming down unused columns
  in views." I understand the recommendation, but as a
  BI consultant striving for the optimal reuse of objects, I
  find this recommendation hard to follow. Our approach
  was to have one big cube view for each reporting

domain that included all key figures and characteristics required for all queries and to "trim down" the number of fields on the query level. This is quite different from the "trim down from top to bottom" approach SAP recommends, something I see more as a programmer's approach. This is an approach that would also lead to potentially a separate stack of CDS views for each query, ergo more CDS views and more complexity, especially for the support organization. What we now try to do is find a balance between performance optimization and reusability. For example, we had one cube view for financial Actuals + Plan-data, which we also used for queries on Actuals data only. Based on the "trim down" recommendation, we now have separate cube views for Actuals, Actuals+Plan, and Actuals+Plan+Commitments.

- The big winner was replacing the `union` statement with `union all` (great catch, Danny!).

service Quality	Usage	size Category	Expected dataClass	Number of tables	Functions	Aggregation	Data Classes	Buffering	Testing	SELECT fld FROM view WHERE key LIMIT 1	SELECT * FROM view WHERE key LIMIT 1
A	may be consumed within business logic for high volume transactions or background processing	S, M, L, XL or XXL	transactional, master, customizing, org, meta, but not mixed	≤ 3	no	no	all identical	buffered when all underlying tables buffered	Automatic generic	< 1ms	< 2ms
B	may be consumed within business logic for transactions or background processing			≤ 5	only if applied to result set (conversions)					< 2ms	< 5ms
C	may be consumed from the UI in transactions for single object retrieval, may not be used within application logic.		mixed	≤ 15	no aggregation of a huge number of table rows					< 10ms	< 20ms
D	may be consumed for analytical reporting	XXL	mixed	< 100					Manual		define realistic test case on realistic test data and define KPIs (default < 500ms)
X	is built to push down application code to HANA										As class D or improved performance and throughput compared to implementation without code push-down

```
@ObjectModel: {
        usageType:{
                 sizeCategory: #XXL,
                 serviceQuality: #D,
                 dataClass:#TRANSACTIONAL
        }
}
```

Figure 6-30. *Performance annotations: explanatory table and coding example. Picture by courtesy of Sergio Santos, SAP*

Transporting CDS Views

Why should transporting embedded analytics objects through the DTAP landscape be any different from transporting ERP objects, you may wonder? Well, you are right, technically it should not be. But in practice, it is. That has to do with the high level of interdependency of analytics objects.

Tools like the Change Request Manager (ChaRM) of SAP Solution Manager can do a good job in a situation where many consultants and developers work on the same objects having an occasional interdependency. If consultant A puts a customizing object in transport X and consultant B puts a new version of the same object in transport Y, then ChaRM makes sure that transport Y does not overtake transport X. It works like a charm (pun intended).

The situation for analytics is quite different: there's usually a small number of developers working on a large number of objects with a high level of interdependency. A large portion of these dependencies are not in the line of view of a tool like ChaRM. For example, CDS view P is part of transport X. CDS view Q is built on top of CDS view P and put into transport Y. Transport Y overtakes transport X. ChaRM gives no warning as no shared objects are involved. But CDS view Q cannot be activated in the target system due to an absence of CDS view P, and transport Y gives the highly feared RC8 error message during import.

My personal advice is to get back to the basics. The order of transport release in D = the import order in T = the import order in A = the import order in P. It should be common sense. This means that the pace at which transports go through the DTAP landscape is determined by the slowest transport of the lot. That is where the agile and DevOps topics of the next chapter come in.

Analysis for Office

In Chapter 1, I briefly introduced Analysis for Office (AfO) as part of SAP's portfolio of BI tools. I will mention it once more in this chapter, as it is an excellent "second front end" for analytical queries next to Fiori.

I call it a "second front end" on purpose and not a second tool, as no additional development effort is required for AfO to be able to consume an analytical query. The only thing that needs to be done is set the marker for Use in Key User Apps under Properties and then API State. In Figure 6-31 you see me carry this out for the Return List query we have grown so accustomed to.

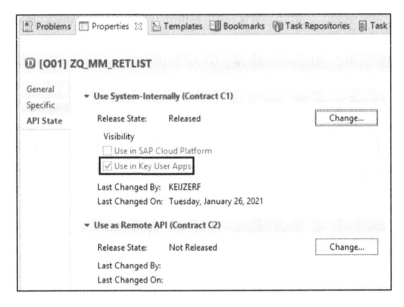

Figure 6-31. *Analysis for Office: making it required for an analytical query to be consumed by AfO*

Analysis for Office can now connect to the system and consume the query. The same selection screen appears as in Fiori, but it's now in an Excel-environment (Figure 6-32). In a next step, the query output is presented, also in an Excel environment (Figure 6-33).

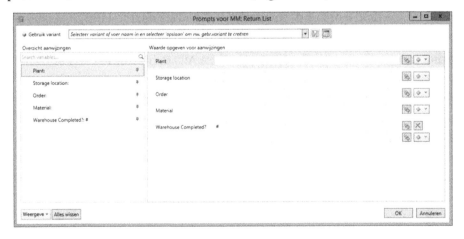

Figure 6-32. *Analysis for Office: selection screen*

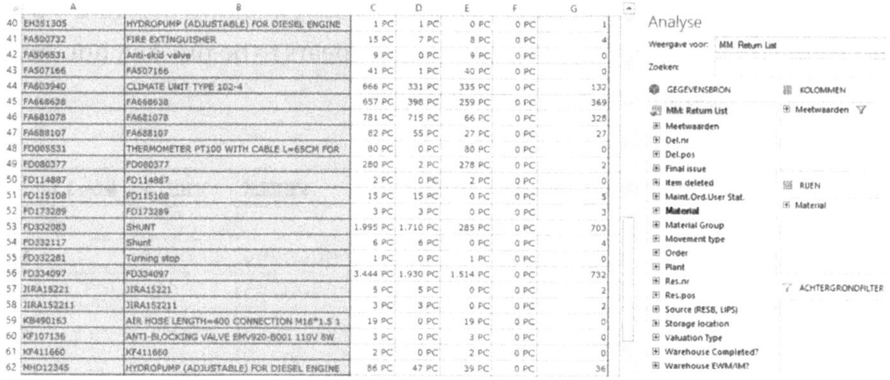

Figure 6-33. *Analysis for Office: query output*

It has definite advantages to make AfO available for the user community as an alternative front end. First, it means users have a choice in how they want to consume the analytical queries. Having a choice is always good. Second, Excel lovers will appreciate it up to a level in which they will carry you around on their shoulders. Finally, AfO is more mature than Fiori-based embedded analytics. To give an example, defining Jump To functionality with the Report-To-Report Interface transaction (RSBBS) is more refined than what we described earlier in this chapter.

Topics Not Covered by This Book...for a Reason

There are a couple of topics I will not cover in this book, but in my view that's for a good reason.

Let me start with exception aggregation, which I'll first illustrate with an example before continuing. In the previous chapter, we discussed a cardinality issue in which the sum of quantity bdmng became 22 when it should have been 12. See Figure 6-34a to refresh your memory. What can be achieved with an exception aggregation on bdmng is shown in Figure 6-34b and Figure 6-34c. The cardinality issue still appears to be present, but the sum of bdmng is somehow magically correct.

(a)

RSNUM	RSPOS	BDMNG	MEINS	VBELN	VBELP	#Deliv.
0000003510	0002	3.000	PC			
0000003744	0008	4.000	PC	0180000294	000010	1
0000003745	0002	5.000	PC	0180000295	000010	1
0000003745	0002	5.000	PC	0180000296	000010	1
0000003745	0002	5.000	PC	0180000297	000010	1
		22.000				**4**

(b)

RSNUM	RSPOS	BDMNG	MEINS	VBELN	VBELP	#Deliv.
0000003510	0002	3.000	PC			
0000003744	0008	4.000	PC	0180000294	000010	1
0000003745	0002	5.000	PC	0180000295	000010	1
0000003745	0002	5.000	PC	0180000296	000010	1
0000003745	0002	5.000	PC	0180000297	000010	1
		12.000				**4**

(c)

RSNUM	RSPOS	BDMNG	MEINS	#Deliv.
0000003510	0002	3.000	PC	
0000003744	0008	4.000	PC	1
0000003745	0002	5.000	PC	3
		12.000		**4**

Figure 6-34. *Example of exception aggregation (same example as in Chapter 5): (a) without exception aggregation; (b) with exception aggregation on key figure bdmng; (c) OLAP behavior of exception aggregation on key figure*

The exception aggregation is a clever trick by the OLAP machine, but it's often not well-understood by users. Your first response to Figure 6-34b may very well be "This is just wrong." Another reason not to use it is the fact that exception aggregations are known to be severe performance breakers for CDS views. Feel free to use it anyway, but do not say I did not warn you.

Other topics not covered are table functions[4] and virtual elements.[5] Why? Simply because we did not need them up to now, so we don't have any experiences in the field. Maybe we are exceptionally creative with standard ABAP CDS, who knows?

Long text is also not covered. A *long text* is…well…long text consisting of multiple lines, stored in generic tables for all long text across the system and made available in transactions via the function module READ_TEXT. Figure 6-24 shows a Long Text box for Maintenance Order. Long text has a tradition of being a problem for SAP BI tools, and S/4HANA Embedded Analytics is no exception. We received multiple requirements for long text from the business, and therefore we explored solutions with table functions and virtual elements, but without success. We did, however, succeed in finding acceptable workarounds in all cases. One of the workarounds has already been shown, i.e., jumping to a standard app that already displays the long text. Another workaround we are currently implementing is copying a selected set of long text to a custom table, each line in a different field, which makes the text accessible for standard ABAP CDS. A mechanism is in place to keep the text as real-time as possible, but it will always be near real-time. It's not a pretty solution, but it's a solid one with a good performance.

BW queries are the last topic not covered. In the last few chapters, we built a query as if it were "just another CDS view" but with special annotations. If you take a good look at Figure 2-13, you can see that the query for the standard Trial Balance app we explored so intensively in Chapter 2 is built differently, i.e., as a BW query. BW queries can also be developed in Eclipse, but in another perspective, i.e., the BW Modeling

---

[4]SAP Help Portal on ABAP CDS Table Functions: https://help.sap.com/viewer/f2e545608079437ab165c105649b89db/7.5.7/en-US/e5529f75afbc43e7803b30346a56f963.html

[5]SAP Help Portal on Virtual Elements in CDS: https://help.sap.com/viewer/cc0c305d2fab47bd808adcad3ca7ee9d/7.51.7/en-US/a7fc007921d44263b09ccc092392b05f.html

perspective shown in Figure 5-1a. Dmitry Kuznetsov makes a strong case for the use of a BW query as the top layer of the stack of CDS views by default.[6] The main reason is additional functionalities, like reusable structures and more advanced variables. I tried this approach, but found that for me the pros were outweighed by the cons. The technology behind BW queries is less well integrated with the Fiori technology, which makes it for instance more complex to turn the query into a dedicated tile. Nonetheless, it is an option, so you should make your own judgment. But for me, I embrace the new and let go of the old.

Retrospective

"Embrace the new and let go of the old" is also a good way to start this retrospective. If you start working in the column-based SQL world that SAP S/4HANA Embedded Analytics constitutes and you are coming from a traditional SAP BI and/or an ABAP programming background, then you need to reset your brain. SQL has no "row awareness." You need to think about columns only. Sometimes you need many layers of CDS views for a solution you could have built in a single ABAP program. Accept it, and move on. Namaste.

I have not been subtle regarding my opinion of the tooling in a S/4HANA SaaS environment. Having only left outer joins in your toolbox and having to rely on SAP to prepare the required unions, inner joins, and aggregations for you in its VDM is quite frustrating. When confronted with real-life business requirements, the SaaS tooling does not bring you far.

But the on-premise tooling for ABAP CDS development is a completely different ball game. So far, we managed to successfully fulfill all the operational reporting requirements with ABAP CDS. This does not mean

---

[6]Dmitry Kuznetsov, "First Steps in SAP S/4HANA Embedded Analytics," Espresso Tutorials, 2020

that all users embrace the end result of the tooling from the start. Moving to S/4HANA usually also means replacing back-end access for users with Fiori access, not only for reporting. Users often have a hard time adapting to working in a browser, especially if their situation does not exhibit the benefits of a browser-based user interface for other devices than desktop PCs. Offering Analysis for Office as a second front end for analytical queries definitely helps in the user acceptance of the new situation.

As a developer, you never want to say "no, that is not possible," and so far I never had to with ABAP CDS. Solutions are sometimes complex, sometimes dirty, nearly always quite different from a corresponding solution in a traditional SAP situation (ABAP programming, BW), and often appealing to creativity, but solutions can always be found. Well, with one exception: there is more than one default value in a filter (SAP, why?). But in short, this is good stuff!

CHAPTER 7

Extensibility, OData, and Beyond

Chapter 1 consisted of miscellaneous intro topics to prepare you for the five chapters on embedded analytics content becoming more hardcore with each chapter. This final chapter consists of miscellaneous outro topics: topics sideways related to embedded analytics and best discussed after the earlier chapters with all the meaty content.

Building S/4HANA Embedded Analytics objects, either with tiles or in an IDE, is a specific form of S/4HANA extensibility. The first section of this chapter covers S/4HANA extensibility in general and presents alternatives for embedded analytics based on CDS views in case other types of functionality are required. A CDS view can easily be turned into an OData service. The second section covers OData services and other forms of APIs, as well as their role in SAP's integration strategy. The third section is more practical in nature, as it describes how to turn a CDS view into an OData service. The next two sections discuss two hot topics in the IT world, Agile Development and DevOps, but in the context of analytics. Finally, having read this book, you probably have only one question left: which type of person is suitable to do this type of work? This question is addressed in the closing section of the book.

© Freek Keijzer 2021
F. Keijzer, *SAP S/4HANA Embedded Analytics*, https://doi.org/10.1007/978-1-4842-7017-2_7

S/4HANA Extensibility

Reading through Chapters 3 and 4, you probably noticed some frustration on my side. Trying to fulfill real-life analytical business requirements with the limited toolbox of the SaaS version of S/4HANA brings little joy. The limited toolbox discussed in these chapters are examples of "in-app extensibility." Having said this, I think it is time to take a broader look at SAP ERP extensibility in general.

Before S/4HANA, there were two methods to add custom functionality to SAP ERP: modifications and custom enhancements. Modifications are changes made in the SAP-delivered source code, whereas custom enhancements are additional ABAP coding in places where this is allowed, such as exits and BADIs. Modifications have so many downsides that they are rarely seen in practice. In SaaS-version S/4HANA, modifications and custom enhancements are no longer possible. SAP manages the software of S/4HANA Cloud, and a clear isolation of SAP-delivered code is required.

Figure 7-1 illustrates the difference between the "old" way to add custom functionality to SAP ERP, custom enhancements, and the new way, which is by using extensions. The only options to add custom functionality are in-app extensibility and side-by-side extensibility. These options are the only possible methods for SaaS version S/4, but also the *recommended* methods for on-premise S/4. The big advantage of following the extensibility principles for S/4HANA Cloud as well as for S/4HANA on-premise is that upgrade issues should not occur, and if they do, they should be solved by SAP. SAP guarantees that ERP processes are not disrupted by database and software changes if the extensibility principles are followed. From an analytics point of view, SAP takes responsibility for its virtual data model (VDM), which is based on whitelisted CDS views. Any changes in the underlying database should be compensated in the VDM.

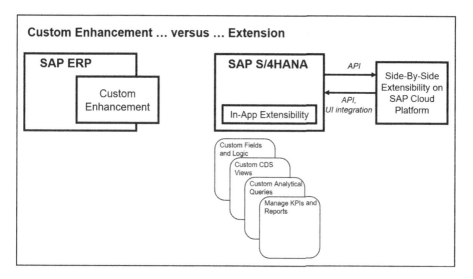

Figure 7-1. *SAP ERP extensibility: custom enhancement versus extension*

In-app extensibility is formed by a range of tiles, some of which we saw in previous chapters. Figure 7-2 displays the Extensibility group of tiles, but apps like Custom Analytical Queries and Manage KPIs and Reports can also be seen as a form of in-app extensibility. The exact tiles shown in this group will depend heavily on the SaaS version versus the on-premise and software versions.

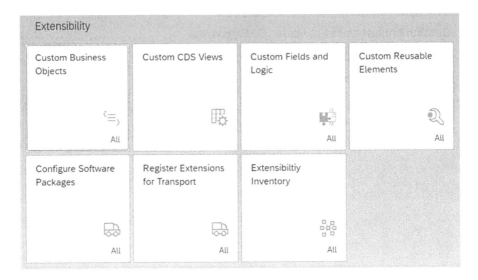

Figure 7-2. *Tiles within the Extensibilty group*

If in-app extensibility does not suffice, then side-by-side extensibility needs to be explored.[1] With this method, the process in S/4 takes a step outside to a separate platform where the extension is developed. The process returns to S/4 afterward, taking the changes from the extension with it. Side-by-side extensibility applied to analytics comes down to data being exported out of S/4 to a separate platform where a custom report is created. The recommended environment for all custom-specific extensions is the SAP Cloud Platform (SCP).

Side-by-side extensibility can have various forms. SAP's original idea was to make the same technology available via the WebIDE on SCP that is used for its own apps: SAPUI5. The skills required to develop in SAPUI5 are a mixture of JavaScript and XML, which are skills abundantly available among the web designer community but quite rare within the SAP community. The SAPUI5 offering was not catching on as hoped, and

---

[1]*Extending SAP S/4HANA. Side-By-Side Extensions with the SAP S/4HANA Cloud SDK*, Herzig et al., SAP Press, 2018

customers often decided to apply a low-code solution. To take advantage of the abundant ABAP programming expertise within the SAP community, SAP introduced a RESTful ABAP toolset to be used on SCP. Last but not least, developers can use their own favorite tools on SCP. This option borrows its name from restaurants without an alcohol license: bring your own. Figure 7-3 presents a decision tree for which tools to use under which circumstances.

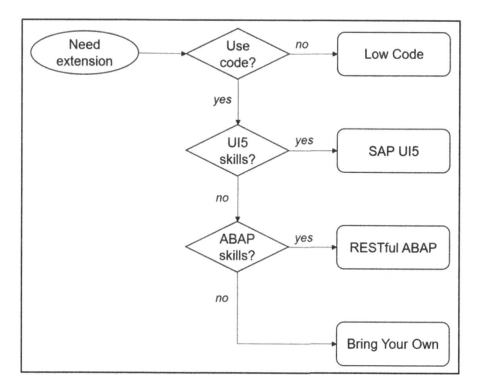

Figure 7-3. *Decision tree for which technology to use for side-by-side extensibility*

Let's go through the options for side-by-side extensibility. The first option is low-code. Two software packages are front-runners in building low-code solutions on top of SAP ERP: Mendix and OutSystems. Figure 7-4 is part of a commercial slide created by myBrand, the company I currently work for, to promote the application of OutSystems. Low-code software provides building blocks and even complete apps out of the box to create solutions. All this is done with no code or almost no code and thus is considered low-code.

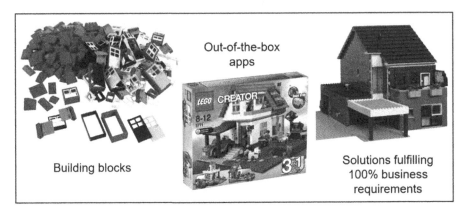

Figure 7-4. *Low-code software providing building blocks and out-of-the-box apps to create complete solutions*

Allow me to discuss the second and third options together and by referencing a TechEd 2019 presentation I attended with the following title: Feel Left Behind? Develop SAP Fiori and SAPUI5 with SAP Web IDE for ABAPers.[2] In this presentation, developers with a web design background are called *digital natives*, and developers with an ABAP background are called *digital immigrants.* The purpose of the presentation was to reassure the digital immigrants that there still is a future for them in the SAP developer community, as long as they are willing to work on the Cloud Platform in the WebIDE and to learn JavaScript, HTML5, and more. But as I experienced personally, UI5 has a rather steep learning curve. To lower the threshold, SAP made building blocks available, such as UI5 Web Components, SAP Fiori Elements, and predefined SAP Fiori page types.

---

[2]"Feel Left Behind? Develop SAP Fiori and SAPUI5 with SAP Web IDE for ABAPers," UX101, SAP Teched Barcelona, 2019

To lower the threshold for the digital immigrants even more, SAP made it possible to do part of the developments in the familiar ABAP programming language: the ABAP RESTful application programming model.

A remarkable demonstration of the fourth option, the bring-your-own option, takes place in the openSAP course "Create and Deliver Cloud-Native SAP S/4HANA Extensions."[3] In this course, SAP employees are having the time of their lives building extensions to S/4HANA on the SCP, but while using the Java programming language, working in the non-SAP IDE IntelliJ IDEA, and having them supported by all sorts of open source tools like Maven, GitHub, Docker, Hystrix, Jenkins, Kibana, and what have you. "Bring your own" indeed.

The decision tree of Figure 7-3 appears to be very skills-based, and indeed, the available skills are important and can even lead the decision. But there are of course more considerations when choosing one option or the other. Can requirements be met by, for instance, low-code, or are the requirements too specific? How do the options compare when looking at the required effort to build and maintain the solution?

APIs and OData Services

If you take another look at Figure 7-1, you will notice the term API. An *application programming interface* (API) is a "computing interface defining interactions between software intermediaries." APIs are at the core of SAP's integration strategy. SAP is moving toward this future as there are more APIs in each new software version, but for many transactions this is not readily available yet. In Figure 7-1, there is an API going out of S/4HANA and an API going back in. The latter is often replaced by user interface integration. This means that the custom extension remains on SCP, but the

---

[3]OpenSAP course, "Create and Deliver Cloud-Native SAP S/4HANA Extensions": https://open.sap.com/courses/s4h13

user does not notice as the custom function is presented by the same user interface, e.g., Fiori Launchpad, as if it were part of S/4HANA all along.

In the same way that the SAP Fiori Apps Reference Library is the one-stop shop for standard SAP apps, the SAP API Business Hub is the one-stop shop for standard SAP APIs.[4] Figure 7-5 shows the initial page. APIs are available for both S/4HANA Cloud and S/4HANA on-premise, but also for all satellite cloud systems and for SCP. There are more APIs available for S/4HANA Cloud than for S/4HANA on-premise, which reflects the fact that APIs are more important in a cloud implementation, because custom enhancements are not technically possible.

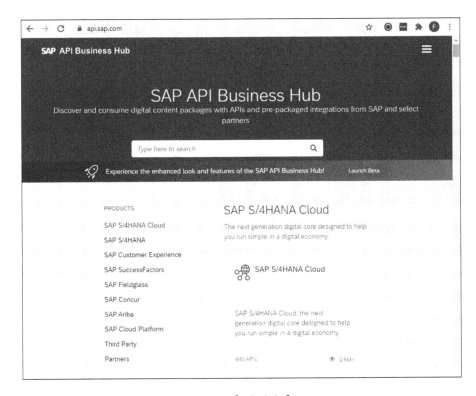

Figure 7-5. *SAP API Business Hub: initial page*

---

[4]SAP API Business Hub: https://api.sap.com/

APIs can generally be divided into categories based on the protocol used. The REpresentational State Transfer (REST) protocol is used for synchronous requests with response. The Simple Object Access Protocol (SOAP) is preferred for asynchronous messaging. The Open Data (OData) protocol is a subcategory of REST-based APIs.[5] The API Business Hub offers two types of standard APIs, OData and SOAP, in an approximately 50-50 division (Figure 7-6).

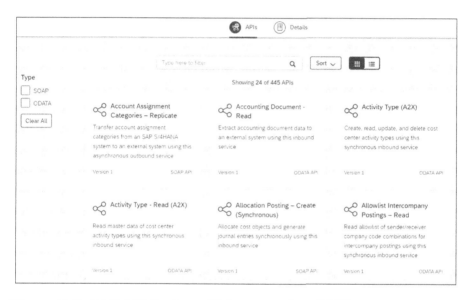

Figure 7-6. *SAP API Business Hub: examples of APIs*

We already encountered OData APIs in previous chapters. If in Figure 4-20 we would have selected the option OData API instead of Analytical, we would have created an object for external use instead of internal use. Also, in the IDE chapters, we encountered the annotation @OData.publish: true numerous times. OData is the integration method best suited for use in combination with CDS views.

---

[5]OData website: https://www.odata.org/

But what does an OData service look like? Figure 7-7 shows an example for the OData service PurchaseOrderItems from SAP's demo system ES5. ES5 is gateway demo system continuously emitting OData services.[6] I'm not quite sure if *emitting* is the proper word, but you catch my drift. The output looks like an XML-file with some metadata. In principle, if someone wants your data, all you need to do is send the URL of the OData service. Well, and open the ports, arrange the system user authorizations...those sorts of things.


```
▼<entry>
  ▼<id>
    https://sapes5.sapdevcenter.com/sap/opu/odata/sap/EPM_REF_APPS_PO_APV_SRV/PurchaseOrderItems(POId='300000002',POItemPos='10')
   </id>
  ▼<title type="text">
    PurchaseOrderItems(POId='300000002',POItemPos='10')
   </title>
   <updated>2019-03-27T21:30:14Z</updated>
   <category term="EPM_REF_APPS_PO_APV_SRV.PurchaseOrderItem" scheme="http://schemas.microsoft.com/ado/2007/08/dataservices/scheme"/>
   <link href="PurchaseOrderItems(POId='300000002',POItemPos='10')" rel="self" title="PurchaseOrderItem"/>
  ▼<content type="application/xml">
    ▼<m:properties xmlns:m="http://schemas.microsoft.com/ado/2007/08/dataservices/metadata" xmlns:d="http://schemas.microsoft.com/ado/2007/08/dataservices">
       <d:POId>300000002</d:POId>
       <d:POItemPos>10</d:POItemPos>
       <d:Product>10" Portable DVD player</d:Product>
       <d:Price>449.99</d:Price>
       <d:PriceCurrency>USD</d:PriceCurrency>
       <d:GrossAmount>1606.46</d:GrossAmount>
       <d:GrossAmountCurrency>USD</d:GrossAmountCurrency>
       <d:Quantity>3</d:Quantity>
       <d:QuantityUnit>EA</d:QuantityUnit>
       <d:DeliveryDate>2019-02-09T23:00:00.0000000</d:DeliveryDate>
     </m:properties>
   </content>
</entry>
```


Figure 7-7. *OData service: example of output*

A set of two blogs describes a joint development by Hồng Ngọc Vũ and myself, in which OData services play a key part in the system integration.[7,8] Figure 7-8 shows the system landscape. OData was used between the ES5 system and SCP. An OData adapter was built on SCP to convert the data to a virtual table as a starting point for a native HANA model. Inside SCP,

[6]"New SAP Gateway Demo System available," Andre Fischer, December 2017: `https://blogs.sap.com/2017/12/05/new-sap-gateway-demo-system-available/`

[7]"SAP end-to-end scenario from S/4HANA Cloud via HANA Modeling in SCP to SAC," Freek Keijzer, April 2019. `https://blogs.sap.com/2019/05/15/sap-end-to-end-scenario-from-s4hana-cloud-via-hana-modeling-in-scp-to-sac/`

[8]"Data Visualization app on SAP Cloud Platform versus graphical report in SAP Analytics Cloud," Hồng Ngọc Vũ & Freek Keijzer, May 2019. `https://blogs.sap.com/2019/05/15/data-visualization-app-on-sap-cloud-platform-versus-graphical-report-in-sap-analytics-cloud/`

OData was used between the native HANA model and a UI5 application. Two scenarios were demonstrated—from ES5 to SCP to SAC and from ES5 to SCP to UI5 app on SCP—that are completely virtual, so real-time data is shown, with no intermediate data storage. How cool is that?

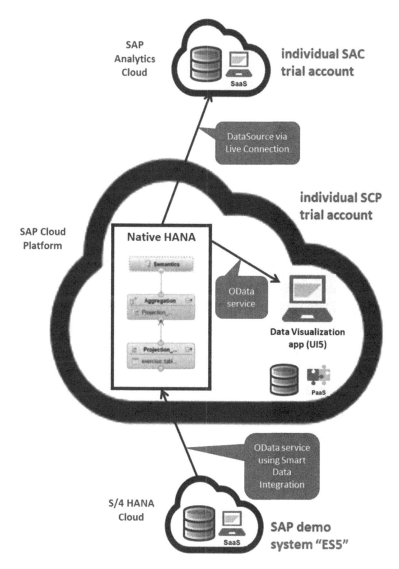

Figure 7-8. *System landscape with OData integration*

How to Turn a CDS View into an OData Service

When I started writing this final chapter, I had the strong intention to make it free of any hands-on exercises. But I am afraid I cannot help it: I am a hands-on person. By now you will have realized how useful it can be to be able to turn a CDS view into a working OData service. Indeed, it's very useful. So, let's get to work.

For SaaS version S/4, the world of tiles, we first need to use the tile Custom CDS View to mark a CDS view as an OData API instead of Analytical. The service name is the name of the custom CDS view followed by _CDS. Follow-up actions include creating a Custom Communication Scenario tile and a Communication Arrangement tile. But in a cloud project with a smaller project team, there is probably only one person doing these tasks, and by the fact that you are reading this book I boldly draw the conclusion that you are not that person.

For on-premise S/4, I will give more detail. Here, creating an OData service from a CDS view is easy: just add annotation @OData.publish: true. But this OData service will not be active and will not work. To make it work, additional steps need to be carried out. Once the OData annotation is added, the IDE will display a warning as shown in Figure 7-9: "Service ... is not active." To activate the service, we need to go to back-end transaction Activate and Maintain Services (/IWFND/MAINT_SERVICE) and click Add Service. What no one is telling you is that on the next screen you need to fill in **LOCAL** for System Alias before you can find your OData service. Once you find it, click Add Selected Services.

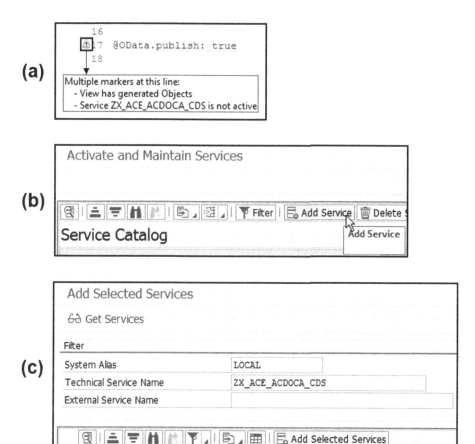

Figure 7-9. *Activating the OData service in on-premise S/4HANA: (a) warning message in the IDE; (b) Activate and Maintain Services; (c) Add Selected Services*

Back on the main screen, you can now find and select the OData service. There are two more things you need to do here. In the bottom-left area called ICF Nodes, click ICF Nodes and then select Activate. In the bottom-right area called System Aliases, select Customizing, then Edit, then Transport, and then Include in Request. Everything needs to be green before you continue (Figure 7-10).

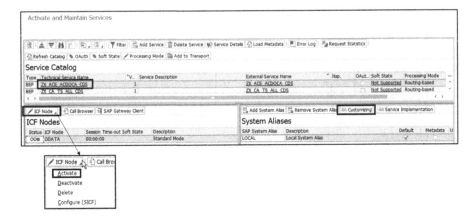

Figure 7-10. *Activating the OData service in on-premise S/4HANA: activate ICF node; include system alias in change request*

To test the freshly activated service on the back end, go to ICF Nodes and select SAP Gateway Client. Click Entity Sets, and then select Execute. If data appears as shown in Figure 7-11, your work has not been in vain.

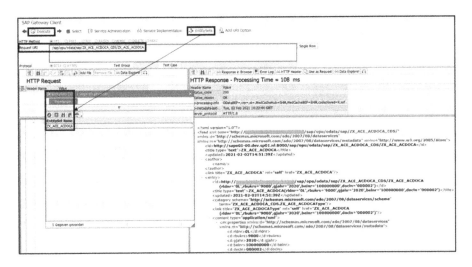

Figure 7-11. *Testing the OData service in the back end*

The proof is in the pudding, which means seeing the same output in a browser. For this you need to combine the URL of the system with the request URI shown in Figure 7-11. Figure 7-12 shows the result of a successful front-end test.

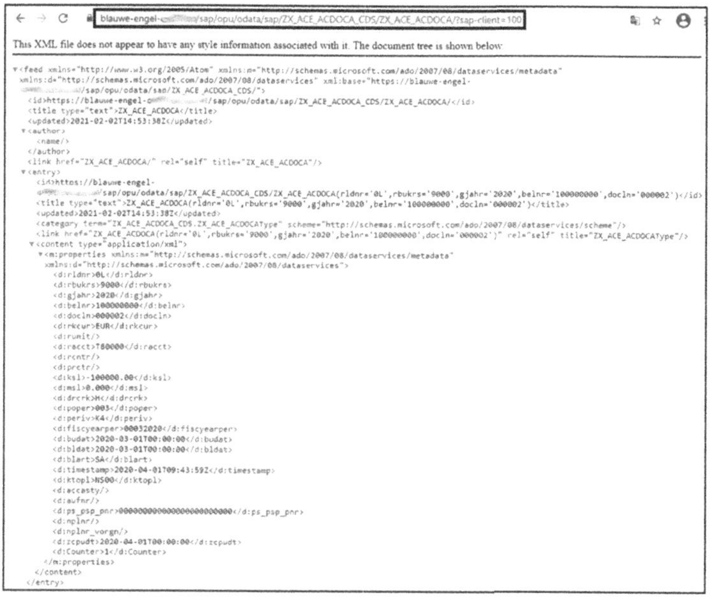

Figure 7-12. *Testing the OData service in a browser*

If all went well, you will have collected a bunch of objects in two types of transports: a client-independent workbench request and a client-dependent customizing request. Do not forget to copy the customizing request if you want to use the OData service in another client of the development system. Figure 7-13 shows the objects you should have collected. If objects are missing in your transport, you need to do some more fiddling. It is not an exact science.

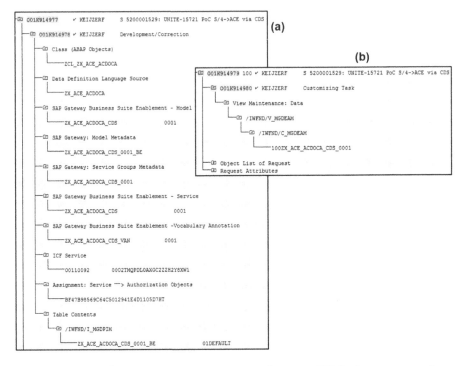

Figure 7-13. *Objects in SAP transports for one CDS view generating one OData service: (a) workbench request; (b) customizing request*

Agile Development and Business Intelligence

Business intelligence is a somewhat peculiar area in the ICT world. It is highly technical and "databasey," but it also requires deep user interaction to deliver good results. In the latter aspect, BI resembles user-interface applications for data input, albeit on the output side of the ICT landscape. For the data-input applications, agile project methodologies are successful and have become the standard. But does this mean that agile methodologies are also successful for BI projects? In this section, I will share some thoughts and experiences on this topic.

One thing I do know from 20 years of experience with BI projects is that the waterfall approach does not work for BI! Let me first explain what the waterfall approach is. First, a representative of the user organization puts a lot of time and effort into a functional design, which is a comprehensive document describing in detail the expectation of what the software should be able to do after completion. Second, a developer goes through this functional design and drafts a technical design, an equally comprehensive document describing what is to be developed in detail. Then another developer goes to an isolated island for half a year to build everything in one go, at the end delivering it for testing. Meanwhile, the environment changes, technology changes, requirements change, and everyone is disappointed by the result. This is a bit of a black-and-white story put this way, but in my experience is quite true. To be honest, I have been sabotaging the waterfall approach almost from the start by saying things like: "I wouldn't put too much detail in your document. Why don't we sit side by side and you can explain to me what you need." Usually this is a relief for the other person as well, because few people find pleasure in writing lengthy documents.

If you are interested in the details of the Agile Manifesto, then the interweb is your friend,[9] but what I would like to do is focus on its four principles and how valid these are in the context of BI projects.

- *Individuals and Interactions over processes and tools*:
  This means having less formal meetings and progress
  reports and having more project team members
  working together in the same location. This is probably
  a good idea for most ICT projects, but especially so
  for BI projects. The most productive hours in my work
  as a BI specialist were spent sitting side by side with a
  business user.

---

[9]Manifesto for Agile Software Development: https://agilemanifesto.org/

- *Working software over comprehensive documentation*:
  The whole idea behind Agile Development is to keep
  the developer going and focused. With regard to
  documentation, this means less paperwork before and
  during development and more effective documentation
  after completion. Inline documentation in the code
  itself is much more effective than separate documents
  stored somewhere on a file server. Let's be honest: a
  couple of years after completion, another developer
  needs to do some modifications, the initial developer
  is on another continent, and the PDF that was
  carefully drafted is nowhere to be found. What the new
  developer will do is look at the code. How fortunate
  would it be if the documentation were right there?

- *Customer collaboration over contract negotiation*:
  Some companies prefer a fixed-price approach toward
  ICT projects as this seems to provide more certainty
  regarding costs for the development. In reality, a
  contract is written with all sorts of assumptions and
  boundary conditions included that cannot be met by
  the business side of the project, so the most important
  assumption is that the requirements delivered by the
  business are right the first time. Fixed-price projects
  are often characterized by a hard relationship between
  customer and service provider, while having the
  tendency to exceed projected costs anyway.

- *Responding to change over following a plan*: This may be the most important reason why the waterfall approach fails so dramatically in BI projects: it is humanly impossible to correctly specify a new management report without seeing some sort of example of what it could look like. Seeing a first version of a management report usually leads to an aha moment by the business users, after which the inspiration starts flowing and the business is perfectly capable of defining the remaining steps toward a finished product.

The real strength in taking an agile approach to BI development in my view lies in prototyping, or doing it wrong the first time. Do not attempt to fulfill 100 percent of requirements in the first try, but aim at the easiest 80 percent of requirements, and deliver this ASAP as a prototype in a test environment to be assessed by the businesspeople involved in the project. Such a prototype helps business users to define their requirements, because as stated earlier they usually need some sort of example to do this. Even a crappy prototype can help tremendously in this process: "That is not at all what I want...this is what I want!"

An agile approach can give managers the feeling that all the structure has been abandoned: no more fixed scope, no more fixed project plan, no more fixed anything. This leads to a strong desire to have some alternative structure to grab on to. This is provided by the Scrum framework. A software development project is split up into short cycles called *sprints* with flexible scope and planning over the project as a whole, but there are fixed scope and fixed planning within one sprint. Ideally, all people involved in the project such as developers, testers, and business representatives work together in the same location organized as a Scrum team. One of the business representatives, called Product Owner, is empowered to make all the decisions on behalf of the business. The team includes a Scrum master, who is not involved in any of the activities but is there to guide the process.

The framework comes with a list of artifacts, tools, and special language: product/ sprint backlog, sprint planning meeting, definition of done, sprint review and retrospective, and burn-down chart. These are my two favorites:

- *Daily Scrum*: This is a daily session, time-boxed to 15 minutes in total, in which progress is monitored and bottle necks are identified. The meeting can be structured in such a way that all team members briefly communicate what they did since the last meeting, what they plan to do until the next, and which obstacles they are experiencing in making progress. Although not required, team members often share this information while standing up to encourage keeping it short. Discussions are cut off. If follow-up is required, a separate meeting is planned with only the involved team members present. I once worked in a Scrum team in which the Product Owner was located in Dublin, my key user was in Belfast, most developers were in Nieuwegein in the Netherlands, and I was in Almelo in the Netherlands. Even in this far from ideal situation, the daily meeting, although online and not standing up, helped enormously in bringing this project forward.

- *Scrum board*: This is a board with usually four
  sections from left to right: To Do, Doing, Done, and
  Impediments. Tasks are assigned to team members
  and moved from left to right. The board can be physical
  with sticky notes on a wall (Figure 7-14) or part of a
  software program like JIRA. This whole visual approach
  gives a perfect overview of progress and issues and
  harmonizes with how the human brain works. I
  personally suspect that moving pieces of paper from
  left to right in some way stimulates the production of
  endorphins in the brain, thus causing people to work
  way harder than they should. It is a conspiracy.

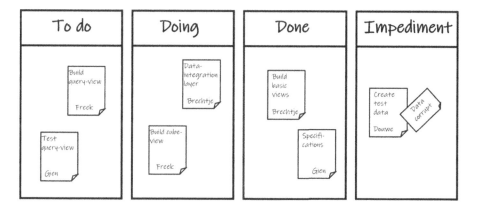

Figure 7-14. A Scrum board

The most valuable part of the agile approach in my view is the concept
of prototyping, which is also part of the Scrum framework in the form of
the minimum viable product. Don't aim for full functionality in one go, but
do it in cycles.

Nearly all projects I have worked on over the past years apply the Scrum methodology, but never to the letter. I don't think it is an official term, but we call this Scrummish. Product Owners usually are not fully empowered, the full team is not present at the same location, the daily stand-up is not as daily as it should be, and in general there is a lot to be desired. But even when the Scrum methodology is not implemented to the full 100 percent, it brings a lot of benefits. As for my experience, the more Scrum, the better.

DevOps and Business Intelligence

Greenfield implementations are the best. The productive system is empty. There is nothing there to break by importing a change request. These are ideal circumstances for a "development cowboy" like me. But a system does not stay greenfield forever. For instance, the project I am currently involved in goes live in waves. After the go-live of wave 1, the productive system is not empty anymore, and the support organization starts protecting what is there against developers like me working on wave 2. From that point in time onward, there is a conflict of interest between development and operations, as illustrated in Figure 7-15. This conflict of interest is usually less for BI objects, as BI objects will only break other BI objects and not other types of ERP objects. The dependency goes one-way. For example, if someone removes a custom Z-field from table ACDOCA, then all of a sudden *all* analytical queries in the financial domain become inactive. But it's never the other way around.

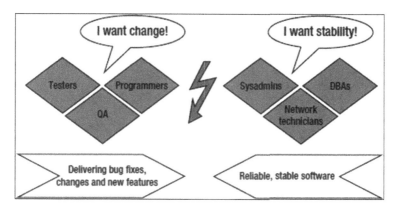

Figure 7-15. *DevOps strives to improve collaboration between development and operations.[10] Examples of development roles on the left side, and (technical) operations roles on the right side (source: Hüttermann, Michael, DevOps for Developers: Integrate Development and Operations, the Agile Way, Figure 2-2 ©Apress, 2012)*

DevOps is a way to solve the conflict of interest by putting the dev people and ops people together in one team. The term DevOps was introduced by Belgian national Patrick Debois in 2009. Bringing dev and ops people together is a good idea. It will give developers more focus on building solutions that can be supported. Also, knowledge transfer from dev to ops will be much better in a DevOps setting. I do, however, foresee some difficulties in combining dev and ops tasks in one person. In my experience, outstanding development consultants and support consultants have quite different personalities.

Some characteristics of DevOps match particularly well with the BI type of work. Short development cycles will promote a continuous flow of transports, thus avoiding transport issues as described in the previous chapter. Also, a high frequency of delivery of product versions matches well with Agile Development and with BI objects. If a first version of an

---

[10]*DevOps for Developers*, Michael Hüttermann, Apress, 2012

analytical query is made available in the productive system, a large group of users can use it and give input on improving the second version. And, no, this is not testing in production, as the first version already was good and useful.

Ideal Skill Set for an Embedded Analytics Expert

For six chapters now, you have seen what the SAP S/4HANA Embedded Analytics work involves. And now you want to hire a person to become an expert at this work. Or train one. Or become one yourself. But what is the ideal skill set for such a person? I have been asked exactly this question a number of times already. Let me try to answer the question using the MoSCoW prioritization technique.

- *Must have*: There really is only one thing you absolutely must have to do this type of work, and that is a willingness to be somewhat of a pioneer. The tooling is quite good, especially when working in an IDE, but you will encounter issues for which the solution cannot be found online. Do not get irritated by functions that do not work, but use the functions that do. And be creative.

- *Should have*: Having a general SAP business intelligence background will help a great deal for two reasons: (1) experienced SAP BI specialists have good knowledge of the SAP database; (2) the BI specialist will already have a focus on layered architecture and reusability of objects. Another type of expertise giving a person a head-start is SQL coding or native HANA development. Such developers will already have the column-oriented mindset required to build high-quality solutions based on CDS views. A combination of both types of expertise would be ideal, but also hard to find.

- *Could have*: Some types of expertise are required on a less frequent basis, the most important one being Fiori expertise. Activities such as creating a tile for an analytical query or activating an OData service are usually seen as tasks for the Fiori consultant, but it increases efficiency if the embedded analytics consultant can do such tasks as well. Especially in a SaaS environment, it will be useful to have some knowledge of the "side-by-side extensibility" alternatives for embedded analytics, e.g., low-code or UI5.

- *Will not have*: Personally, I would not hire anyone who does not drink beer. But that is probably because I am a brewer. Is that even legal, excluding someone for such a reason? OK, just forget about this bullet point!

Epilogue

You have reached the end of reading this book. Earlier, I reached the end of writing it. To be exact, today it is February 7, 2021. The Netherlands is in lockdown. We have a curfew from 9 p.m. until 5 a.m. This book kept me busy during most of the COVID-19 crisis. What to do now?

Dear reader, I would like to thank you for your attention. It has been a pleasure writing for you. If you have any questions or remarks, feel free to reach out.

Index

D

Printed in the United States
by Baker & Taylor Publisher Services